HTML5 Multimedia Development Cookbook

Recipes for practical, real-world HTML5
multimedia-driven development

Dale Cruse

Lee Jordan

[PACKT]
PUBLISHING

BIRMINGHAM - MUMBAI

HTML5 Multimedia Development Cookbook

First published: May 2011

Production Reference: 1160511

Published by Packt Publishing Ltd.
32 Lincoln Road
Olton
Birmingham, B27 6PA, UK.

ISBN 978-1-849691-04-8

www.packtpub.com

Cover Image by Jacqueline Stetson (jstetson@gmail.com)

Credits

Authors

Dale Cruse

Lee Jordan

Reviewers

Shi Chuan

Christopher Scott Hernandez

Laurentiu Nicolae

Acquisition Editor

Steven Wilding

Development Editor

Kartikey Pandey

Technical Editor

Arun Nadar

Project Coordinator

Leena Purkait

Proofreader

Clyde Jenkins

Indexer

Monica Ajmera Mehta

Rekha Nair

Production Coordinators

Shantanu Zagade

Melwyn D'sa

Cover Work

Shantanu Zagade

Foreword

Maybe you've heard the story—or probably urban legend—about the university that didn't lay any grass or pour any concrete when it first opened, leaving the campus grounds as solid dirt. Then, as students began to traverse the campus from one class to the next, campus planners mapped the common paths they took, and then landscaped and paved concrete trails based on these paths.

HTML5 shares the same moral as that story: Utility based on convention. An extraordinary update to the web's markup language, the HTML5 specification incorporates many of the conventions we've all been using in our markup and formalizes them as an official recommendation.

Dale Cruse's HTML5 Multimedia Development Cookbook comes at the perfect time when many of us are transitioning to this new specification. Browser vendors, thankfully, are following suit by adopting HTML5 components at an impressive pace.

But the real secret sauce of Dale's work is the fact that this book—the one you're holding now—is a cookbook in every respect (and from a guy who doubles as a wine savant, no less). Its pages are filled with recipes for creating successful, real-world implementations of HTML5 websites. You'll find thorough, detailed chapters covering forms, video, audio, and much more. There's even a chapter that'll help you style your HTML5 using CSS3, and a chapter explaining how to ensure your HTML5 content is accessible to those using assistive technologies. Every chapter includes exceptional examples from across the web, carefully dissected.

Dale is a master chef when it comes to web standards and forward-thinking, and backwards-compatible markup. I've had the pleasure of working with him in the past on a project of mine, and it was just as clear then as it is now that he knows his stuff. Whether it's the remarkable or the commonplace, the innovative or the practical, Dale Cruse's HTML5 Multimedia Development Cookbook will have you preparing, sautéing, and serving incredible HTML5 websites in no time. Bon appétit.

Cameron Moll
Founder of AuthenticJobs.com
Author of *Mobile Web Design* and Co-author of *CSS Mastery: Advanced Web Standards Solutions*

About the Authors

Dale Cruse, a Boston-area web developer, has been publishing websites for high-profile clients ranging from the U.S. Army to Bloomingdale's since 1995. He has been a guest lecturer at the Art Institute of New England and is currently pursuing speaking opportunities. Contact him at `http://dalejcruse.com`.

He is also the author of the Champagne blog *Drinks Are On Me* at `http://drinksareonme.net`.

A number of people contributed to the success of this book, and it would take more space than I have to thank each one individually.

Thank you to the entire Packt Publishing team for working so diligently to help me develop such a high quality product of which we can all be proud of.

For my friend of roughly 20 years, Michelle Yaiser: Thank you for believing in me through thick and thin.

Web developer Paul Ramos and I complete each other's sentences. Thank you for being there, brother.

Roxane Velozo is the Robin to my Batman. Thanks for being the best professional sidekick a superhero could ever have.

For Jeffrey Zeldman, Cameron Moll, and Dan Cederholm: I could never hope for a better trio of professional role models. Thank you, gentlemen.

Lee Jordan is a designer and new media developer. She brings a strong design background and concern for the visual and emotional impact of media to web-based projects. Experienced in multiple CMS platforms including Expression Engine, Plone, WordPress, PostNuke, and Google's Blogger, she has maintained, explored, and used most of them on a day-to-day basis. She spends her spare time as the leader of a local scout troop, taking long hikes with her family in the beautiful North Georgia woods, trying to taste test every variety of chocolate that exists, and playing with code and pixels. Design topics or whatever she can think of at the time are posted on her blog at `http://leejordan.net.`

Lee has written three previous books with Packt Publishing: *Project Management for dotProject*, *WordPress Themes 2.8*, and *Blogger: Beyond the Basics*.

I couldn't do this without the support of my family, but it is one special person's time to shine—Jason—keep trying and don't give up. Sometimes all we need is practice and the will to keep moving forward.

About the Reviewers

Shi Chuan is an open web developer, member of HTML5 Boilerplate, and the lead of Mobile Boilerplate. Shi has over four years of experience in web development. Half indie and half commercial, he worked with both MNCs and small local startups.

Shi Chuan has spent a large portion of his career working in digital adverting. He worked for Ogilvy Singapore, and helped the launch with many brand site, and micro-site, for clients like Yahoo, Nokia, Levi's, IBM, and many other global companies around the world. What he also enjoys is to work with smaller clients that allow him greater freedom to experiment with real cool and kick-ass stuff.

As a member of HTML5 Boilerplate, he has developed a stronger sense of community and web evangelism. He is excited about the future of the technology and is doing the best he can to embrace fashion's free culture and to help shape a better web. He has a semi-regular blog at: `http://www.blog.highub.com`.

Christopher Scott Hernandez has been working on the web since his freshman year in high school, when he designed and developed a product catalog for his father's upholstery business. Born and raised in beautiful Austin, Texas, he now lives in sunny Philadelphia and works as a web developer for an international e-commerce agency. When he's not pushing pixels or developing websites, Chris enjoys spending time with his brilliant wife Josie and their canine trio: Darwin, Truman, and Toby. He also maintains a blog and portfolio at `http://christopher-scott.com`.

Laurentiu Nicolae is a Web developer, with over 5 years of experience. He has been working as a freelancer for different clients from Europe and the United States, and now he is working for BootsnAll. He is specialized in developing websites, being a "native writer" in web languages, like PHP, HTML, XHTML, CSS, and JavaScript. He lives in Bucharest, Romania with his wife, Georgiana, and their son Matei.

www.PacktPub.com

Support files, eBooks, discount offers and more

You might want to visit www.PacktPub.com for support files and downloads related to your book.

Did you know that Packt offers eBook versions of every book published, with PDF and ePub files available? You can upgrade to the eBook version at www.PacktPub.com and, as a print book customer, you are entitled to a discount on the eBook copy. Get in touch with us at service@packtpub.com for more details.

At www.PacktPub.com, you can also read a collection of free technical articles, sign up for a range of free newsletters, and receive exclusive discounts and offers on Packt books and eBooks.

http://PacktLib.PacktPub.com

Do you need instant solutions to your IT questions? PacktLib is Packt's online digital book library. Here, you can access, read, and search across Packt's entire library of books.

Why subscribe?

- ▶ Fully searchable across every book published by Packt
- ▶ Copy and paste, print, and bookmark content
- ▶ On demand and accessible via web browser

Free access for Packt account holders

If you have an account with Packt at www.PacktPub.com, you can use this to access PacktLib today and view nine entirely free books. Simply use your login credentials for immediate access.

Table of Contents

Preface

HTML5 Multimedia Development Cookbook will show you exactly how to use the latest front-end web technologies like a pro. You'll learn how HTML5 is a quantum leap difference from all previous versions and why it matters. Whether you're a seasoned pro or a total newbie, this book gives you the roadmap to what's next.

Starting with an overview of what's new in HTML5, we quickly move on to practical examples. From there, we continue our exploration, all the way to the most cutting-edge experiments. There's much to know about the new HTML5 specification. This book examines spec excerpts and relates them to examples currently in use. Woven with a rich tapestry of theory, practicality, code samples, screenshots, business wisdom, and links to additional resources, this book will have eager developers coming back to it again and again. HTML5 Multimedia Development Cookbook is the essential guide to the latest front-end web development technologies.

What this book covers

In *Chapter 1, Structuring for Rich Media Applications*, we'll begin by examining HTML5's state of readiness by analyzing browser support. Then we'll lay the groundwork for how to use HTML5's new elements successfully.

Chapter 2, Supporting the Content, makes us rethink the approach the developers used to create generic containers to house various types of content.

Chapter 3, Styling with CSS, demonstrates how to use CSS3 to support HTML5. We'll also look at styling in modern vs. legacy browsers and what to expect.

Chapter 4, Creating Accessible Experiences, is not a typical regurgitation of Section 508. Instead, we'll employ some of the freshest technologies to support our online experiences.

Chapter 5, Learning to Love Forms, we'll closely examine the new HTML5 input types. Also included is an analysis of which browsers support each new type.

Chapter 6, Developing Rich Media Applications Using Canvas, is the most forward-thinking chapter of the entire book. The discussion will center on how to develop for this new type of interactivity and includes some surprising browser support statistics.

Chapter 7, Interactivity using JavaScript, is jam packed with recipes to extend the new HTML5 audio and video elements. Roll up your sleeves for this one!

Chapter 8, Embracing Audio and Video, we dig into the core HTML audio and video experiences. We will construct our own player while still supporting accessibility.

Chapter 9, Data Storage, takes a detailed look at a unique aspect of HTML5 and how to wield it. Recipes include working with JSON, SQL, and GeoLocation.

What you need for this book

Requirements for this book are slim: All you really need is a computer with an Internet connection, a web browser, and a code editor. Patience and a sense of humor don't hurt either.

Who this book is for

HTML5 has become the most-searched-for new job keyword. Whether you are in the market for a new job or just looking to take that next step in your current organization, knowing how to wield this new technology will give you the edge.

Conventions

In this book, you will find a number of styles of text that distinguish between different kinds of information. Here are some examples of these styles, and an explanation of their meaning.

Code words in text are shown as follows: "The new <header> is where we often store things like logos, company slogans, and other types of branding usually associated with mastheads."

A block of code is set as follows:

```
<div id="search-form">
  <form role="search" method="get" id="searchform"
    action="http://devinsheaven.com/" >
    <div>
      <label for="s">Search for:</label>
      <input type="text" value="" name="s" id="s" />
      <input type="submit" id="searchsubmit" value="Search" />
    </div>
  </form>
</div>
```

When we wish to draw your attention to a particular part of a code block, the relevant lines or items are set in bold:

```
<body>
  <header>
    <hgroup>
      <h1>Roxane is my name.</h1>
      <h2>Developing websites is my game.</h2>
    </hgroup>
  </header>
  <nav role="navigation">
    <ul>
      <li><a href="#About">About</a></li>
      <li><a href="#Work">Work</a></li>
    </ul>
  </nav>
</body>
```

New terms and **important words** are shown in bold. Words that you see on the screen, in menus or dialog boxes for example, appear in the text like this: "Choose **Tools | Embed This Video** from the Vimeo main menu."

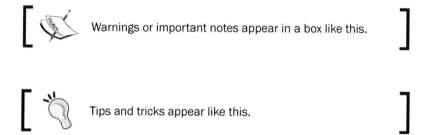

> Warnings or important notes appear in a box like this.

> Tips and tricks appear like this.

Reader feedback

Feedback from our readers is always welcome. Let us know what you think about this book—what you liked or may have disliked. Reader feedback is important for us to develop titles that you really get the most out of.

To send us general feedback, simply send an e-mail to feedback@packtpub.com, and mention the book title via the subject of your message.

If there is a book that you need and would like to see us publish, please send us a note in the **SUGGEST A TITLE** form on www.packtpub.com or e-mail suggest@packtpub.com.

If there is a topic that you have expertise in and you are interested in either writing or contributing to a book, see our author guide on www.packtpub.com/authors.

Customer support

Now that you are the proud owner of a Packt book, we have a number of things to help you to get the most from your purchase.

Downloading the example code

You can download the example code files for all Packt books you have purchased from your account at `http://www.PacktPub.com`. If you purchased this book elsewhere, you can visit `http://www.PacktPub.com/support` and register to have the files e-mailed directly to you.

Errata

Although we have taken every care to ensure the accuracy of our content, mistakes do happen. If you find a mistake in one of our books—maybe a mistake in the text or the code—we would be grateful if you would report this to us. By doing so, you can save other readers from frustration and help us improve subsequent versions of this book. If you find any errata, please report them by visiting `http://www.packtpub.com/support`, selecting your book, clicking on the **errata submission form** link, and entering the details of your errata. Once your errata are verified, your submission will be accepted and the errata will be uploaded on our website, or added to any list of existing errata, under the Errata section of that title. Any existing errata can be viewed by selecting your title from `http://www.packtpub.com/support`.

Piracy

Piracy of copyright material on the Internet is an ongoing problem across all media. At Packt, we take the protection of our copyright and licenses very seriously. If you come across any illegal copies of our works, in any form, on the Internet, please provide us with the location address or website name immediately so that we can pursue a remedy.

Please contact us at `copyright@packtpub.com` with a link to the suspected pirated material.

We appreciate your help in protecting our authors, and our ability to bring you valuable content.

Questions

You can contact us at `questions@packtpub.com` if you are having a problem with any aspect of the book, and we will do our best to address it.

1
Structuring for Rich Media Applications

In this chapter, we will cover:

- ▸ Setting up an HTML5 test area
- ▸ Using the `header` tag for logos and site titles
- ▸ Creating a table of contents using the `nav` tag
- ▸ Using `section` tags to structure areas of a page
- ▸ Aligning graphics using the `aside` tag
- ▸ Display multiple sidebars using the `aside` tag
- ▸ Implementing the `footer` tag
- ▸ Applying the `outline` algorithm
- ▸ Creating a stylish promo page in HTML5

Introduction

"Who dares, wins." – unknown

Don't listen to the naysayers: Many aspects of HTML5 (no space) are here, ready for us to use. Despite what some people might think, there's no far-flung date at which time you can start using this collection of new technologies. The truth is, the next generation of web markup isn't a distant dream on the horizon—it is here now, ready to explore and use.

No website can exist without at least some simple HyperText Markup Language. This open technology is that important. If you've been using HTML to create and publish websites and applications for years, you might feel as though you've mastered the language by now. You already know the benefits of semantic markup, separation of content, presentation and behavior, and are well versed in accessibility concerns. Things might be feeling a bit dull and boring. You're ready for a new challenge.

Or perhaps you're a young developer building your first website and need to know the ins and outs of using the latest and greatest technologies and have an eye to the future of web development.

Either way, your path is clear: Building on your existing HTML and related technology coding abilities, this book will push your skills to the next level and quickly have you creating amazing things HTML was never capable of before.

If you're feeling complacent, read on. The truth is there has never been a more exciting time to be a web developer. Richer interfaces, the ubiquity of the Internet, and the rise of mobile devices are just the kind of new challenges for which you're looking.

Fortunately, HTML5, a liberal helping of Cascading Style Sheets, and a dash of JavaScript, rise to meet those new challenges. The latest innovations in web development make this a new golden age for online publishers. After what was a lull for many of us, we are now quickly discovering that developing for the web is fun again! After all, HTML5 represents evolution—not revolution.

Over the course of several successful high-profile client projects, I've used a custom JavaScript methodology to deploy aspects of HTML5 and still support older browsers, including Microsoft Internet Explorer 6.

In the recipes contained within, you'll learn this powerful methodology and how to use many of the still developing HTML5 standards and features in a real-world, live production environment.

When we develop with HTML5, we take the basic principle of semantic naming (naming things what they are instead of naming things how they appear) to a whole new level. This is the key factor that makes HTML5 different from all of its predecessors. Throughout the course of this book you will find yourself rethinking and optimizing many of your code-naming conventions.

Though the HTML5 proposed recommendation from the Web Hypertext Application Technology Working Group (WHATWG) is not slated for full implementation until 2022, thanks to forward-thinking browser manufacturers, there is no reason you cannot start using it now and reap the benefits of better semantic naming, enhanced accessibility, and much, much more.

So let's get cooking!

In this chapter, we will show you how to set up your development environment including using the appropriate DOCTYPE and which browsers to utilize, and how to use specific new tags including:

- ► `<header>` – a group of introductory or navigational aids
- ► `<nav>` – for navigation lists
- ► `<section>` – to differentiate between areas of a page
- ► `<aside>` – to align specific elements
- ► `<footer>` – the bottommost information on a page or in a section

Finally, we will put all those elements together to create a stylish professional promo page all with HTML5.

Setting up an HTML5 test area

If we're going to build new and exciting projects using HTML5, we need to set ourselves up for success. After all, we want to ensure that what we build will display and behave in a predictable way for ourselves and our clients. Let's build a test suite with a code editor and at least one web browser.

Getting ready

There are a few things we need to get started. At minimum, we all need a code editor and a browser in which to view our work. Seasoned professionals know we really need an array of browsers that reflect what our audience uses. We want to see things the way they do. We *need* to see things the way they do.

How to do it...

Many web developers say they're capable of writing code using nothing but plain text software like Notepad for Microsoft Windows or TextEdit for Mac OSX. That's great, but despite the bragging, we don't know a single web developer who actually works this way day in, day out.

Instead, most use some sort of development application like Adobe Dreamweaver (available for Windows and Mac) or Aptana Studio (available for Windows and Mac and Linux) or Coda (my personal preference, which is Mac only) or TextMate (also Mac only).

Let's start by downloading at least one of these applications:

- ▶ Adobe Dreamweaver: `http://adobe.com/products/dreamweaver`
- ▶ Aptana Studio: `http://aptana.com`
- ▶ Coda: `http://panic.com/coda`
- ▶ TextMate: `http://macromates.com`

Application icons for the most common web editors are shown here:

Adobe Dreamweaver   Aptana Studio   Coda   TextMate

How it works...

In order for the code we create to render properly, we're going to need a web browser—probably more than one. Not all browsers are created equal. As we will see, some browsers need a little extra help to display some HTML5 tags. Here are the browsers we'll use at a minimum.

If you use OSX on a Mac, Apple Safari is already installed. If you're a Microsoft Windows user, Internet Explorer is already installed.

If you use a modern mobile device like an iPhone or Android for development, it already has at least one browser installed too.

Since we'll do our actual coding on the desktop, let's get started by downloading a few browsers from the following locations. Note: Microsoft Internet Explorer is PC only.

- ▶ Apple Safari: `http://apple.com/safari`
- ▶ Google Chrome: `http://google.com/chrome`
- ▶ Mozilla Firefox: `http://getfirefox.com`
- ▶ Microsoft Internet Explorer: `http://windows.microsoft.com/en-US/windows/products/internet-explorer`

Application icons for the most common desktop web browsers are shown here:

Apple Safari   Google Chrome   Microsoft Internet Explorer   Mozilla Firefox

There's more...

Why do we need more than one browser? Two reasons:

- These applications have different rendering engines and interpret our code in slightly different ways. That means no matter how valid or well intentioned our code is, sometimes browser behavior is unpredictable. We have to plan for that and be flexible.

- We can't always predict which browser our audience will have installed and on which device so we need to be one step ahead of them as developers to best serve their needs as well as our own.

WebKit rendering engine

Luckily, Safari and Chrome use the same WebKit rendering engine. Mobile Safari for iPhone and iPad, as well as the web browser for Android mobile devices, all use a version of the WebKit rendering engine also.

Gecko rendering engine

Firefox and its mobile version both use the Gecko rendering engine.

Trident rendering engine

I just wanna tell you how I'm feeling. Gotta make you understand: Microsoft has changed and updated its Internet Explorer rendering engine named Trident several times over the years, making our lives as developers quite difficult. We often feel like we're aiming at a moving target. With Internet Explorer 10 on the horizon, it appears that won't change any time soon.

See also

Camino (Mac only) and Opera (for Microsoft Windows, Apple OSX, Linux, and mobile devices) both produce excellent alternative browsers that support many of HTML5's features. Consider adding these browsers to your test suite as well.

▸ Camino: `http://caminobrowser.org`

▸ Opera: `http://opera.com`

Application icons for the Camino and Opera web browsers are shown here:

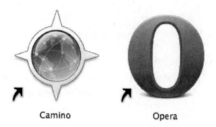

Camino   Opera

Now that we have a development environment and more than one browser, let's create some code!

Progressive Enhancement

We're going to build our page using the concept of progressive enhancement, which means starting with plain old HTML for markup, then layering CSS for presentation and lastly adding a touch of JavaScript for behavior. One of the best analogies we've heard is that basic HTML is like black and white TV. Adding CSS is like adding color and adding JavaScript is kind of like adding high definition.

Using the header tag for logos and site titles

"The `<header>` *element represents a group of introductory or navigational aids. A* `<header>` *element is intended to usually contain the section's heading (an* `<h1>`- `<h6>` *element or an* `<hgroup>` *element), but this is not required. The* `<header>` *element can also be used to wrap a section's table of contents, a search form, or any relevant logos." - WHATWG's HTML5 Draft Standard -* `http://whatwg.org/html5`

Getting ready

The first thing you'll notice about HTML5 is the DOCTYPE. If you're a veteran of web development, you'll be glad to know we no longer have to use such long, convoluted DOCTYPEs as:

```
<!DOCTYPE html PUBLIC "-//W3C//DTD XHTML 1.0 Strict//EN" "http://www.
w3.org/TR/xhtml1/DTD/xhtml1-strict.dtd">
```

or:

```
<!DOCTYPE html PUBLIC "-//W3C//DTD XHTML 1.0 Transitional//EN" "http://
www.w3.org/TR/xhtml1/DTD/xhtml1-transitional.dtd">
```

or:

```
<!DOCTYPE html PUBLIC "-//W3C//DTD XHTML 1.0 Frameset//EN" "http://
www.w3.org/TR/xhtml1/DTD/xhtml1-frameset.dtd">
```

HTML5 eliminates the need for Strict, Transitional, and Frameset DOCTYPEs. Actually, it eliminates the need for DOCTYPES altogether. Without one, older versions of Internet Explorer slip into Quirks mode and no one wants that. Instead, we can use the simple:

```
<!DOCTYPE html>
```

Finally, one DOCTYPE to rule them all.

Let's start with a basic bare bones page structure with which we should all be familiar:

```
<!DOCTYPE html>
<html lang="en">
<head>
  <meta charset="UTF-8">
  <title></title>
  <!--[if lt IE 9]><script
    src="http://html5shiv.googlecode.com/svn/trunk/html5.js">
    </script>[endif]-->
  <meta name="viewport" content="width=device-width,
    initial-scale=1.0">
</head>
<body>
</body>
</html>
```

Quotes were necessary to create valid XHTML, but because HTML5 is not coupled to XML, those are optional in the HTML5 specification. However, the author would recommend quoting attributes whenever possible.

Keen eyes will also note the `<meta name="viewport" content="width=device-width, initial-scale=1.0">`. That isn't going to do much for us just yet, but will be vital when previewing your work on mobile devices.

Closing our tags is optional as well. Though it's a good practice, you should weigh whether it's worth the development time and added page weight.

You'll also notice a conditional comment checking to see if the user is using Internet Explorer. If so, we tell the browser to execute Remy Sharp's "HTML5 Shiv" script, which simply tells IE to behave: `<article>`, `<aside>`, `<audio>`, `<canvas>`, `<command>`, `<datalist>`, `<details>`, `<embed>`, `<figcaption>`, `<figure>`, `<footer>`, `<header>`, `<hgroup>`, `<keygen>`, `<mark>`, `<meter>`, `<nav>`, `<output>`, `<progress>`, `<rp>`, `<ruby>`, `<section>`, `<source>`, `<summary>`, `<time>`, `<video>`, `<wbr>`.

Darn that Internet Explorer. It lacks discipline.

How to do it...

We're going to create a single-page professional web portfolio for a young developer named Roxane. Let's say that Roxane is a talented web developer with a lot of skill, just like you. She deserves a professional single-page portfolio site worthy of her talent and so do you. Feel free to substitute your information for hers in the following examples.

Let's start by using the first new `<header>` tag to define the topmost area of our overall page.

While we're at it, we're going to incorporate the new `<hgroup>` tag to contain the headers in our new `<header>` tag.

```
<!DOCTYPE html>
<html lang="en">
<head>
  <meta charset="UTF-8">
  <title>Roxane</title>
  <!--[if lt IE 9]><script
    src="http://html5shiv.googlecode.com/svn/trunk/html5.js">
    </script>[endif]-->
  <meta name="viewport" content="width=device-width,
    initial-scale=1.0">
</head>
<body>
  <header>
    <hgroup>
      <h1>Roxane is my name.</h1>
```

```
      <h2>Developing websites is my game.</h2>
    </hgroup>
  </header>
</body>
</html>
```

"The <hgroup> element represents the heading of a section. The element is used to group a set of <h1>-<h6> elements when the heading has multiple levels, such as subheadings, alternative titles, or taglines." - WHATWG's HTML5 Draft Standard - http://whatwg.org/html5

How it works...

The new <header> is where we often store things like logos, company slogans, and other types of branding usually associated with mastheads. It is often the first block-level element on an HTML5 page and is commonly used for headings like <h1>, <h2>, and so on. The result is a more semantically rich code base from which to build.

There's more...

Before HTML5, all <div>s were given equal weight by the browser software as well as by leading search engines like Google, Yahoo!, and Bing. But we know the intent of <div id="header"> just isn't as obvious as the new <header>. Instead, the HTML5 specification prefers to name things what they actually *are*. Now, HTML5 recognizes that not all <div>s are created equal by replacing some with more semantic terms like the new <header> and <nav> and <footer> for more data richness.

Use <header> elsewhere

Interestingly, the masthead isn't the only place you can use the new <header> tag. In HTML5, it's also perfectly acceptable to use the new <header> tag inside just about any block-level element.

Content, not position

The new <header> tag does most often appear at the top of a web page, but it doesn't always have to appear there. Remember that semantically, the new <header> tag is defined by its contents, not its position.

Semantic naming

Semantic naming also makes our jobs as web developers much easier. The intent of something like the new `<footer>` tag is much more obvious labeled like the ambiguous `<div id="belowleft">` for example.

The Key to Semantic Naming

Name things what they are – not how they appear.

See also

We will continue to reference the WHATWG's HTML5 Draft Standard at `http://whatwg.org/specs/web-apps/current-work/multipage`, as it is an essential guide to the HTML5 evolution.

Creating a table of contents using the nav tag

"The `<nav>` element represents a navigation section where only sections that consist of primary navigation blocks are appropriate for the `<nav>` element." - WHATWG's HTML5 Draft Standard - `http://whatwg.org/html5`

Like the new `<header>` tag replacing outmoded naming conventions like `<div id="header">`, we can also replace `<div id="nav">` with the simple new `<nav>`. Makes much more sense, doesn't it? We think so too.

Getting ready

We're going to add the primary navigation bar like we so often see on web pages. This enables users to easily maneuver from page to page or, in this case, within the same page. Roxane wants to showcase her biographical information, work samples, and ways to contact her, so we'll use those as our anchors.

How to do it...

Let's create our navigation bar using the two most typical elements:

1. An unordered list
2. Accompanying hypertext links

```
<!DOCTYPE html>
<html lang="en">
```

```
<head>
  <meta charset="UTF-8">
  <title>Roxane</title>
  <!--[if lt IE 9]><script
    src="http://html5shiv.googlecode.com/svn/trunk/html5.js">
    </script>[endif]-->
  <meta name="viewport" content="width=device-width,
    initial-scale=1.0">
</head>
<body>
  <header>
    <hgroup>
      <h1>Roxane is my name.</h1>
      <h2>Developing websites is my game.</h2>
    </hgroup>
  </header>
  <nav>
    <ul>
      <li><a href="#About">About</a></li>
      <li><a href="#Work">Work</a></li>
      <li><a href="#Contact">Contact</a></li>
    </ul>
  </nav>
</body>
</html>
```

How it works...

Previously, we would have used something like `<div id="nav">` to store our navigation list in it. But with HTML5, the new `<nav>` tag is all that's necessary.

When we apply CSS, we'll float those list items and make them appear more like a traditional web navigation bar.

There's more...

The beauty of naming things more semantically is that now portions of our pages do exactly what we think they should do—a `<header>` contains heading information, `<nav>` contains navigation aids, and so on. Eschew obfuscation.

Use <nav> elsewhere

Like <header>, <nav> can appear in more than one place on a page.

More semantic = more gooder

Remember also that more semantic naming can usually lead to shorter, leaner code. After all, <nav> is certainly shorter than the common <div id="nav">. And it makes more sense to both humans and machines. That means less for us to write, which saves us time. That also means less code for the browser to interpret and display, which saves download and render time. It also gives meaning and structure to the content, similar to the way an outline provides meaning and structure to a research paper. Everybody wins.

Still evolving

Originally, the new <nav> element was only for "primary" navigation blocks. However, Ian Hickson, the driving force behind HTML5, updated the specification to be "major" navigation blocks instead.

See also

Since it's a still-evolving standard, you're encouraged to contribute to the evolution of HTML5 and help shape the language. Join the WHATWG's help@whatwg.org mailing list to make suggestions and ask questions. Instructions for signing up are at: http://whatwg.org/mailing-list#help.

Using section tags to structure areas of a page

"The <section> element represents a generic document content block or an application block. A <section>, in this context, is a thematic grouping of content, typically with a heading. " - WHATWG's HTML5 Draft Standard - http://whatwg.org/html5

Getting ready

Let's add the new <section> tags for each of the primary areas of Roxane's single-page portfolio site. These <section>s will then be used as containers, each with a heading and generic content that will contain her biographical information, work examples, and contact methods.

How to do it...

The use of the new `<section>` tag can be tricky. There are a number of things it isn't, but only certain things that it is.

```html
<!DOCTYPE html>
<html lang="en">
<head>
  <meta charset="UTF-8">
  <title>Roxane</title>
  <!--[if lt IE 9]><script
    src="http://html5shiv.googlecode.com/svn/trunk/html5.js">
    </script>[endif]-->
  <meta name="viewport" content="width=device-width,
    initial-scale=1.0">
</head>
<body>
  <header>
    <hgroup>
      <h1>Roxane is my name.</h1>
      <h2>Developing websites is my game.</h2>
    </hgroup>
  </header>
  <nav>
    <ul>
      <li><a href="#About">About</a></li>
      <li><a href="#Work">Work</a></li>
      <li><a href="#Contact">Contact</a></li>
    </ul>
  </nav>
  <section id="About">
    <h3>About</h3>
    <p>I'm a front-end developer who's really passionate about
      making ideas into simply dashing websites.</p>
    <p>I love practical, clean design, web standards give me joyful
      chills, and good usability tickles the butterflies
      in my stomach.</p>
  </section>
  <section id="Work">
    <h3>Work</h3>
    <p>sample 1</p>
    <p>sample 2</p>
    <p>sample 3</p>
  </section>
  <section id="Contact">
```

```
        <h3>Contact</h3>
        <p>email</p>
        <p>phone</p>
        <p>address</p>
    </section>
  </body>
</html>
```

How it works...

We've used the new `<section>` tag not as a generic replacement for the `<div>`, but instead in the semantically correct way as a related grouping that usually contains a heading.

There's more...

If the content grouping isn't related, it probably shouldn't be a `<section>`. Consider a `<div>` instead.

Section doesn't equal div

Remember: If it doesn't have a `<header>`, it probably doesn't need a `<section>`. Use `<section>` to group content, but `<div>` when grouping items purely for stylistic reasons.

Section guidelines

Still aren't sure if `<section>` is the right tag to use? Remember these guidelines:

> ▶ Are you using it solely for styling or scripting? That's a `<div>`.
>
> ▶ If any other tag is more appropriate, use it instead.
>
> ▶ Use it only if there's a heading at the start of the content.

Still evolving

HTML5 is a constantly evolving set of standards. The latest bit of guidance from the WHATWG suggests:

> *"Authors are encouraged to use the `<article>` element instead of the `<section>` element when it would make sense to syndicate the contents of the element."*

Publishing an about page? That's probably going to be a good `<section>` candidate.

See also

The new `<section>` tag can also support the cite attribute for citations.

Aligning graphics using the aside tag

"The `<aside>` element represents a section of a page that consists of content that is tangentially related to the content around the `<aside>` element, and which could be considered separate from that content." - WHATWG's HTML5 Draft Standard - `http://whatwg.org/html5`

Getting ready

Let's use the new `<aside>` tag in a common way: to create a sidebar of thumbnail images listing what Roxane has been busy reading recently.

How to do it...

In the past we floated images or lists to the right or left of our text. That still works, but now we can make better use of the improved semantics in HTML5 by using the new `<aside>` tag to accomplish a similar visual effect. Let's use:

- An ordered list
- Thumbnail images
- Book titles

```
<!DOCTYPE html>
<html lang="en">
<head>
  <meta charset="UTF-8">
  <title>Roxane</title>
  <!--[if lt IE 9]><script
    src="http://html5shiv.googlecode.com/svn/trunk/html5.js">
    </script>[endif]-->
  <meta name="viewport" content="width=device-width,
    initial-scale=1.0">
</head>
<body>
  <header>
    <hgroup>
      <h1>Roxane is my name.</h1>
      <h2>Developing websites is my game.</h2>
```

```
      </hgroup>
    </header>
    <nav>
      <ul>
        <li><a href="#About">About</a></li>
        <li><a href="#Work">Work</a></li>
        <li><a href="#Contact">Contact</a></li>
      </ul>
    </nav>
    <section id="About">
      <h3>About</h3>
      <p>I'm a front-end developer who's really passionate about making
        ideas into simply dashing websites.</p>
      <p>I love practical, clean design, web standards give me joyful
        chills, and good usability tickles the butterflies
        in my stomach.</p>
    </section>
    <section id="Work">
      <h3>Work</h3>
      <p>sample 1</p>
      <p>sample 2</p>
      <p>sample 3</p>
    </section>
    <section id="Contact">
      <h3>Contact</h3>
      <p>email</p>
      <p>phone</p>
      <p>address</p>
    </section>
    <aside>
      <h4>What I'm Reading</h4>
      <ul>
        <li><img
          src="http://packtpub.com/sites/default/files/imagecache/
          uc_thumbnail/26880S_MockupCover.jpg"
          alt="Inkscape 0.48 Essentials for Web Designers">
          Inkscape 0.48 Essentials for Web Designers</li>
        <li><img
          src="http://packtpub.com/sites/default/files/imagecache/
          uc_thumbnail/bookimages/0042_MockupCover_0.jpg"
          alt="jQuery 1.4 Reference Guide">
          jQuery 1.4 Reference Guide</li>
        <li><img
          src="http://packtpub.com/sites/default/files/imagecache/
          uc_thumbnail/98810S_MockupCover.jpg"
          alt="Blender 2.5 Lighting and Rendering">
```

```
          Blender 2.5 Lighting and Rendering</li>
      </ul>
    </aside>
  </body>
</html>
```

Note: In this case, quote marks are needed around ALT tags to ensure validity.

How it works...

The `<aside>` tag is effectively used to place items like images and text that are often less important than the primary page content.

There's more...

Semantically, `<aside>` is similar to a sidebar. That doesn't necessarily refer to position – but instead to tangentially related content.

Not all <section>s are alike

Though `<section>` is a generic hunk of related content, think of `<header>`, `<nav>`, `<footer>` and `<aside>` as specialized types of `<section>`.

Tip to remember

Content can live without the `<aside>` tag, but the `<aside>` tag can't live without content.

Aside from <aside>

The `<aside>` tag definition has been broadened to include not just information about an `<article>` to which it may be related, but to also include information related to the site itself, like a blogroll.

See also

Jeremy Keith penned the outstanding "*HTML5 For Web Designers*" which is considered the least you need to know to understand the new group of technologies. Find it at: `http://books.alistapart.com/products/html5-for-web-designers`.

Displaying multiple sidebars using the aside tag

"The <aside> *element represents a section of a page that consists of content that is tangentially related to the content around the* <aside> *element, and which could be considered separate from that content." - WHATWG's HTML5 Draft Standard -* http://whatwg.org/html5

Getting ready

It seems like every blog and many other types of websites have sidebars filled with all sorts of information. Here, we're going to add an additional sidebar to Roxane's single-page portfolio site using the new <aside> tag.

How to do it...

Roxane wants to let people know where else she can be reached, and so do you. Let's use the <aside> tag to create a sidebar and draw attention to her web presence:

```
<!DOCTYPE html>
<html lang="en">
<head>
  <meta charset="UTF-8">
  <title>Roxane</title>
  <!--[if lt IE 9]><script
    src="http://html5shiv.googlecode.com/svn/trunk/html5.js">
    </script>[endif]-->
  <meta name="viewport" content="width=device-width,
    initial-scale=1.0">
</head>
<body>
  <header>
    <hgroup>
      <h1>Roxane is my name.</h1>
      <h2>Developing websites is my game.</h2>
    </hgroup>
  </header>
  <nav>
    <ul>
      <li><a href="#About">About</a></li>
      <li><a href="#Work">Work</a></li>
      <li><a href="#Contact">Contact</a></li>
```

```
      </ul>
  </nav>
  <section id="About">
    <h3>About</h3>
    <p>I'm a front-end developer who's really passionate about making
      ideas into simply dashing websites.</p>
    <p>I love practical, clean design, web standards give me joyful
      chills, and good usability tickles the butterflies
      in my stomach.</p>
  </section>
  <section id="Work">
    <h3>Work</h3>
    <p>sample 1</p>
    <p>sample 2</p>
    <p>sample 3</p>
  </section>
  <section id="Contact">
    <h3>Contact</h3>
    <p>email</p>
    <p>phone</p>
    <p>address</p>
  </section>
  <aside>
    <h4>What I'm Reading</h4>
    <ul>
      <li><img
        src="http://packtpub.com/sites/default/files/imagecache/
        uc_thumbnail/2688OS_MockupCover.jpg"
        alt="Inkscape 0.48 Essentials for Web Designers">
        Inkscape 0.48 Essentials for Web Designers</li>
      <li><img
        src="http://packtpub.com/sites/default/files/imagecache/
        uc_thumbnail/bookimages/0042_MockupCover_0.jpg"
        alt="jQuery 1.4 Reference Guide">
        jQuery 1.4 Reference Guide</li>
      <li><img
      src="http://packtpub.com/sites/default/files/imagecache/
      uc_thumbnail/9881OS_MockupCover.jpg"
      alt="Blender 2.5 Lighting and Rendering">
      Blender 2.5 Lighting and Rendering</li>
    </ul>
  </aside>
  <aside>
    <h4>Elsewhere</h4>
    <p>You can also find me at:</p>
```

```
    <ul>
    <li><a href="http://linkedin.com/in/">LinkedIn</a></li>
     <li><a href="http://twitter.com/">Twitter</a></li>
     <li><a href="http://facebook.com/">Facebook</a></li>
    </ul>
   </aside>
 </body>
 </html>
```

How it works...

Building on the success we had previously with the `<aside>` tag, we've used it again to align information that is subsequent to the main information.

There's more...

Just because a design calls for a sidebar, don't automatically reach for the `<aside>` tag. Carefully consider your content before considering position.

Pull quotes good for <aside>

Pull quotes are common in news articles, and therefore prime candidates to be contained by the `<aside>` tag.

Remember to validate

We need to add quotes around those anchors to make them valid.

See also

Together, Bruce Lawson and Remy Sharp penned the outstanding *Introducing HTML5* reference available at: `http://peachpit.com/store/product. aspx?isbn=0321687299`

Implementing the footer tag

"The `<footer>` element represents a footer for the completed documented or its nearest ancestor sectioning content." - WHATWG's HTML5 Draft Standard - `http://whatwg.org/html5`

Getting ready

We've all used footers on our web pages—typically for things like secondary navigation and more. This contains all the information you typically see at the bottom of a page, like a copyright notice, privacy policy, terms of use, and many more. Like the new `<header>` tag, the new `<footer>` tag can occur in more than one place.

How to do it...

In this case, we're going to use the new `<footer>` tag to place Roxane's copyright information at the bottom of the page.

And that's one to grow on

Remember: Copyright does not mean you have the right to copy it!

```html
<!DOCTYPE html>
<html lang="en">
<head>
  <meta charset="UTF-8">
  <title>Roxane</title>
  <!--[if lt IE 9]><script
    src="http://html5shiv.googlecode.com/svn/trunk/html5.js">
    </script>[endif]-->
  <meta name="viewport" content="width=device-width,
    initial-scale=1.0">
</head>
<body>
  <header>
    <hgroup>
      <h1>Roxane is my name.</h1>
      <h2>Developing websites is my game.</h2>
    </hgroup>
  </header>
  <nav>
    <ul>
      <li><a href="#About">About</a></li>
      <li><a href="#Work">Work</a></li>
      <li><a href="#Contact">Contact</a></li>
    </ul>
  </nav>
  <section id="About">
    <h3>About</h3>
```

```
        <p>I'm a front-end developer who's really passionate about
          making ideas into simply dashing websites.</p>
        <p>I love practical, clean design, web standards give me joyful
          chills, and good usability tickles the butterflies
          in my stomach.</p>
      </section>
      <section id="Work">
        <h3>Work</h3>
        <p>sample 1</p>
        <p>sample 2</p>
        <p>sample 3</p>
      </section>
      <section id="Contact">
        <h3>Contact</h3>
        <p>email</p>
        <p>phone</p>
        <p>address</p>
      </section>
      <aside>
        <h4>What I'm Reading</h4>
        <ul>
          <li><img
            src="http://packtpub.com/sites/default/files/imagecache/
            uc_thumbnail/2688OS_MockupCover.jpg"
            alt="Inkscape 0.48 Essentials for Web Designers">
            Inkscape 0.48 Essentials for Web Designers</li>
          <li><img
            src="http://packtpub.com/sites/default/files/imagecache/
            uc_thumbnail/bookimages/0042_MockupCover_0.jpg"
            alt="jQuery 1.4 Reference Guide">
            jQuery 1.4 Reference Guide</li>
          <li><img
            src="http://packtpub.com/sites/default/files/imagecache/
            uc_thumbnail/9881OS_MockupCover.jpg"
            alt="Blender 2.5 Lighting and Rendering">
            Blender 2.5 Lighting and Rendering</li>
        </ul>
      </aside>
      <aside>
        <h4>Elsewhere</h4>
        <p>You can also find me at:</p>
        <ul>
          <li><a href="http://linkedin.com/in/">LinkedIn</a></li>
          <li><a href="http://twitter.com/">Twitter</a></li>
          <li><a href="http://facebook.com/">Facebook</a></li>
```

```
      </ul>
    </aside>
    <footer>
      <h5>All rights reserved. Copyright Roxane.</h5>
    </footer>
  </body>
</html>
```

How it works...

Though this `<footer>` is located at the bottom of Roxane's single-page portfolio site, it can be used elsewhere on a page, such as at the bottom of a `<section>` tag to contain information like author, publication date, and so on. The result is more flexible than something like the old `<div id="footer">` allowed us. In this and many other instances, HTML5's new tags allow us to place appropriate tags where they make the most sense, based on our content, not our layout.

There's more...

The HTML5 specification suggests author information be included in the new `<footer>` tag no matter if the `<footer>` is part of a `<section>` or `<article>` or even at the bottom of the page.

This happens usually

The vast majority of the time, you'll use the `<header>` tag at the top of your document, the `<footer>` tag at the bottom, and `<aside>` tags for the sides.

Flexible footer content

When the `<footer>` element contains entire sections, they represent appendices, indexes, long colophons, verbose license agreements, and other such content.

More flexible footer content

The new `<footer>` tag can also contain information like author attribution, links to related documents, copyright, and so on.

See also

Mark Pilgrim created a terrific free online HTML5 reference _Dive Into HTML5_ located at: `http://diveintohtml5.org`.

Applying the outline algorithm

Luckily for us, HTML5 now has a method of assembling an outline of our pages in browsers, so search engines as well as accessibility technologies can make better sense of them. We're going to make use of the HTML5 Outliner at: `http://gsnedders.html5.org/outliner`

Getting ready

To use the HTML5 Outliner, we can use HTML stored on our local computer or code visible via a URL. Make sure to save the code we've been creating locally or upload it to a publicly accessible web server for this step.

How to do it...

Let's make sure to save this document either on a local hard drive or remote server. We'll visit `http://gsnedders.html5.org/outliner` to create our outline.

Using our previous code example, we can generate the following code outline:

1.   Roxane is my name.
2.   Untitled Section
3.   About
4.   Work
5.   Contact
6.   What I'm Reading
7.   Elsewhere
8.   All rights reserved. Copyright Roxane.

How it works...

> *"It is defined in terms of a walk over the nodes of a DOM tree, in tree order, with each node being visited when it is entered and when it is exited during the walk."*
> *- WHATWG*

There's more...

It's assumed that content following any heading is related to that heading. Therefore we can use many of the new HTML5 tags like `<section>` to explicitly demonstrate the beginning and ending of related content.

Are you sure?

If the HTML5 Outliner tool displays messages like "Untitled Section" you should rethink how you're using each of your tags and ensure your approach matches the intent of the specification.

An exception

"Untitled Section" messages should be treated as warnings instead of errors. While `<section>` and other new HTML5 tags require a heading tag, it's perfectly valid not to have one for `<nav>` areas.

Remember accessibility

The outline created ensures us that the code we've created is compliant with the W3C's standards for markup, as well as advanced technologies like WAI-ARIA for accessibility requirements.

 Good accessibility design is good web design.

See also

The `http://html5doctor.com` site is a terrific interactive reference written by seven thought leaders including Rich Clark, Bruce Lawson, Jack Osborne, Mike Robinson, Remy Sharp, Tom Leadbetter, and Oli Studholme.

Creating a stylish promo page in HTML5

Our pal Roxane's single-page portfolio site has come together using more than a few of the new HTML5 elements. She's ready to show the world she's a forward-thinking web developer, ready to tackle advanced projects.

Getting ready

We've done the prep work by assembling much of the content for the single-page portfolio site. It isn't very stylish just yet, but when we layer CSS on top of it, this will really come together and be as stylish as our imaginations will allow.

How to do it...

Here's the code we have so far. It's valid against the World Wide Web Consortium's HTML5 and Section 508 accessibility tests. This unstyled code should be easily viewable in any modern web browser whether it's on the desktop or a mobile device.

```
<!DOCTYPE html>
<html lang="en">
<head>
  <meta charset="UTF-8">
  <title>Roxane</title>
  <!--[if lt IE 9]><script
    src="http://html5shiv.googlecode.com/svn/trunk/html5.js">
    </script>[endif]-->
  <meta name="viewport" content="width=device-width,
    initial-scale=1.0">
</head>
<body>
  <header>
    <hgroup>
      <h1>Roxane is my name.</h1>
      <h2>Developing websites is my game.</h2>
    </hgroup>
  </header>
  <nav>
    <ul>
      <li><a href="#About">About</a></li>
      <li><a href="#Work">Work</a></li>
      <li><a href="#Contact">Contact</a></li>
    </ul>
  </nav>
  <section id="About">
    <h3>About</h3>
    <p>I'm a front-end developer who's really passionate about
      making ideas into simply dashing websites.</p>
    <p>I love practical, clean design, web standards give me joyful
      chills, and good usability tickles the butterflies
      in my stomach.</p>
  </section>
```

```
<section id="Work">
  <h3>Work</h3>
  <p>sample 1</p>
  <p>sample 2</p>
  <p>sample 3</p>
</section>
<section id="Contact">
  <h3>Contact</h3>
  <p>email</p>
  <p>phone</p>
  <p>address</p>
</section>
<aside>
  <h4>What I'm Reading</h4>
  <ul>
    <li><img
      src="http://packtpub.com/sites/default/files/imagecache/
      uc_thumbnail/2688OS_MockupCover.jpg"
      alt="Inkscape 0.48 Essentials for Web Designers">
      Inkscape 0.48 Essentials for Web Designers</li>
    <li><img
      src="http://packtpub.com/sites/default/files/imagecache/
      uc_thumbnail/bookimages/0042_MockupCover_0.jpg"
      alt="jQuery 1.4 Reference Guide">
      jQuery 1.4 Reference Guide</li>
    <li><img
      src="http://packtpub.com/sites/default/files/imagecache/
      uc_thumbnail/9881OS_MockupCover.jpg"
      alt="Blender 2.5 Lighting and Rendering">
      Blender 2.5 Lighting and Rendering</li>
  </ul>
</aside>
<aside>
  <h4>Elsewhere</h4>
  <p>You can also find me at:</p>
  <ul>
    <li><a href="http://linkedin.com/in/">LinkedIn</a></li>
    <li><a href="http://twitter.com/">Twitter</a></li>
    <li><a href="http://facebook.com/">Facebook</a></li>
  </ul>
</aside>
<footer>
  <h5>All rights reserved. Copyright Roxane.</h5>
</footer>
</body>
</html>
```

How it works...

A single-page portfolio site makes a lot of sense for a developer or designer, as all the information is quickly available to those in hiring positions, like human resources teams or recruiters.

There's more...

This is exactly the kind of professional single-page portfolio site Roxane needs to demonstrate she's a forward-thinking developer learning to wield the next generation of web standards.

Try sans shiv

As an experiment, turn off the "HTML5 Shiv" JavaScript reference in the code and see how various versions of Internet Explorer treat our new HTML5 tags.

Mobile first

Remember to consider mobile displays when creating this and other websites. There's almost never a good reason to block entire groups of people from seeing your content.

IE evil?

Over the past 15 years or so, we've spent a lot of time and effort bashing Microsoft Internet Explorer for its lack of standards support and buggy interpretation of the box model. The upcoming IE10 brings us closer to a more unified web development world, but we still remain years away from being free of cursing IE.

For lots of single-page portfolio and other website inspiration, visit the `http://onepagelove.com` gallery.

The unstyled single-page portfolio as it displays on most major modern desktop web browsers:

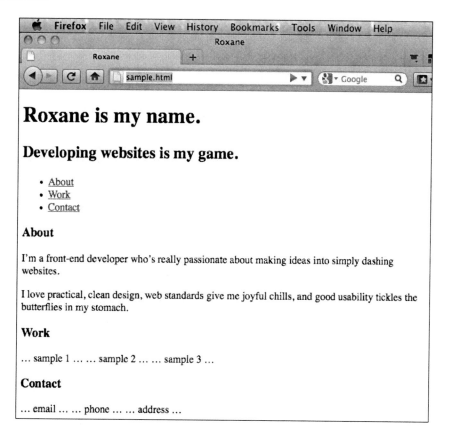

2
Supporting the Content

In this chapter, we will cover:

- ▸ Structuring a blog `article`
- ▸ Highlighting text using the `mark` element
- ▸ Using the `time` element
- ▸ Specifying the `pubdate` of an `article`
- ▸ Displaying comment blocks using the `article` element
- ▸ Adding fonts dynamically with @font-face
- ▸ Adding drop shadow effect to fonts
- ▸ Applying gradient effects to fonts
- ▸ Annotating visual elements using the `figure` tag

Introduction

"On the web, a man should not be judged by the color of his skin but by the content of his content." - Internet meme

One of the most significant differences between HTML5 and all previous versions of HTML is that before we built generic `<div>`s and other such generic containers without much knowledge of what content would go in them. With the advent of HTML5, that comes to an end. To be correct according to the specification semantically, we need to know what the content is so we can wrap it with the most appropriate new element tag. While this may mean we developers have to think differently, a new challenge is exactly why we're here. In this chapter we'll look at some examples of how to do just that using several of HTML5's new elements.

"In case of conflict, consider users over authors over implementers over specifiers over theoretical purity." - Priority of Constituencies

Throughout this chapter, we'll show you how to use the new `<article>` element to mark up both blog posts and comments, add a meaningful publication date to an `<article>`, use the new `<mark>` element to highlight text, and how to note visual elements using the new `<figure>` element. We'll then turn our attention to some new methods of styling text with font replacement techniques, as well as adding drop shadows and gradients to our text.

Structuring a blog article

"The `<article>` element represents a self-contained composition in a document, page, application, or site and that is, in principle, independently distributable or reusable, e.g. in syndication. This could be a forum post, a magazine or newspaper article, a blog entry, a user-submitted comment, an interactive widget or gadget, or any other independent item of content." - WHATWG's HTML5 Draft Standard - `http://whatwg.org/html5`

Getting ready

Blog entries are perfect candidates for the new `<article>` element, which is designed for syndicated content.

For this recipe, let's start by identifying the major elements of a blog `<article>`: There's usually a headline in the form of a heading tag, the blog entry itself consisting of several paragraphs and perhaps one or more images, and some information that usually includes the author's name and other related metadata. Notice this is all self-contained related content.

How to do it...

We're going to continue using the new HTML5 `<header>` and `<footer>` elements. The headline, entry and meta-information should be wrapped in their own unique tags, like `<h2>`, multiple `<p>`s and the new `<footer>`.

Let's start with a foundation very similar to what we used in the last chapter, and add our new `<article>` element twice:

```
<!DOCTYPE html>
<html lang="en">
<head>
  <meta charset="UTF-8">
  <title>Blog Title</title>
  <!--[if lt IE 9]><script
    src="http://html5shiv.googlecode.com/svn/trunk/html5.js">
```

```
      </script>[endif]-->
    <meta name="viewport" content="width=device-width,
      initial-scale=1.0">
  </head>
  <body>
  <article>
    <header>
      <h2>Headline</h2>
    </header>
    <p>First paragraph</p>
    <p>Second paragraph</p>
    <footer>Meta information.</footer>
  </article>
  <article>
    <header>
      <h2>Headline</h2>
    </header>
    <p>First paragraph</p>
    <p>Second paragraph</p>
    <footer>Meta information.</footer>
  </article>
  </body>
  </html>
```

Put your code on a diet?

Ready for a shocker? Want to have your mind blown? The `<html>` and `<head>` and `<body>` tags (as well as their closing tags) are now optional in the HTML5 specification. Sure, you could leave them in there, and your pages will validate just fine, but why should we? If remove them from the previous code, we are left with the spartan:

```
<!DOCTYPE html>
<meta charset="UTF-8">
<title>Blog Title</title>
<!--[if lt IE 9]><script
  src="http://html5shiv.googlecode.com/svn/trunk/html5.js">
    </script>[endif]-->
<meta name="viewport" content="width=device-width,
  initial-scale=1.0">
<article>
  <header>
    <h2>Headline</h2>
  </header>
  <p>First paragraph</p>
  <p>Second paragraph</p>
  <footer>Meta information.</footer>
```

```
    </article>
    <article>
      <header>
        <h2>Headline</h2>
      </header>
      <p>First paragraph</p>
      <p>Second paragraph</p>
      <footer>Meta information.</footer>
    </article>
```

Don't believe me? Run that code through the World Wide Web Consortium's validator at: `http://validator.w3.org`, and you'll see it displays correctly in the browser.

Well, not so fast buster. The problem is that removing those elements breaks our code for screen readers. Uh oh. Strike one. Also, removing the `<body>` tag breaks our new HTML5-enabling JavaScript for Internet Explorer. Strike two. And guess what? You can see it coming, can't you? Yes, removing the `<html>` tag removes the language of the page. There it is: Strike three.

So let's add those elements back in, shall we?

```
    <!DOCTYPE html>
    <html lang="en">
    <head>
      <meta charset="UTF-8">
      <title>Blog Title</title>
      <!--[if lt IE 9]><script
        src="http://html5shiv.googlecode.com/svn/trunk/html5.js">
        </script>[endif]-->
      <meta name="viewport" content="width=device-width,
        initial-scale=1.0">
    </head>
    <body>
      <article>
        <header>
          <h2>Headline</h2>
        </header>
        <p>First paragraph</p>
        <p>Second paragraph</p>
        <footer>Meta information.</footer>
      </article>
      <article>
        <header>
          <h2>Headline</h2>
        </header>
        <p>First paragraph</p>
```

```
      <p>Second paragraph</p>
      <footer>Meta information.</footer>
    </article>
  </body>
</html>
```

There, that's better.

How it works...

Remember, the new `<article>` element is a collection of related information intended for syndication via RSS or another means.

There's more...

Richer, more meaningful semantics is perhaps the most significant goal for HTML5. It's better for machines, better for authors, and most importantly, better for our audiences.

Validation as an aid, not a crutch

As we saw previously, removing the `<html>` and `<head>` and `<body>` tags render a still valid page. So that begs the question of how valid validators are. Unlike the XML world, HTML5 can use incorrect syntax and still render just fine.

The author makes every effort to validate his code whenever possible. It's not necessary to be slavish to the validator, but it's always a good quality control check. And the closer you get to valid code, the better chance browsers will display your work in as consistent a manner as possible.

Eric Meyer's funny

The author loves how CSS guru Eric Meyer thinks about validators:

Where to find validators

You can make good use of code validators at:

- ▶ `http://validator.nu`
- ▶ `http://validator.w3.org`

See also

Kristina Halvorson's book "*Content Strategy For The Web*" (`http://contentstrategy.com`) was an instant classic from the time of its release. In it, Halvorson, CEO of Minneapolis-based company Brain Traffic, clearly defines the process of how to create and deliver useful and usable content for online audiences.

Highlighting text using the mark element

"The `<mark>` *element represents a run of text in one document marked or highlighted for reference purposes, due to its relevance in another context. When used in a quotation or other block of text referred to from the prose, it indicates a highlight that was not originally present but which has been added to bring the reader's attention to a part of the text that might not have been considered important by the original author when the block was originally written, but which is now under previously unexpected scrutiny. When used in the main prose of a document, it indicates a part of the document that has been highlighted due to its likely relevance to the user's current activity." - WHATWG's HTML5 Draft Standard* - `http://whatwg.org/html5`

Getting ready

When viewing search results, you'll often find the term for which you searched highlighted. Instead of relying on a semantically meaningless tag, we can now use the more meaningful `<mark>` element.

How to do it...

In this recipe, you'll see `HTML5doctor.com` has an excellent example of how to use the new `<mark>` element to highlight a search results term. This gives a useful semantic hook not only for styling but also for the machine tracking the results.

```
<!DOCTYPE html>
<html lang="en">
<head>
  <meta charset="UTF-8">
```

```
    <title></title>
    <!--[if lt IE 9]><script
      src="http://html5shiv.googlecode.com/svn/trunk/html5.js">
      </script>[endif]-->
    <meta name="viewport" content="width=device-width,
      initial-scale=1.0">
  </head>
  <body>
    <h1>716,000,000 search results for
      the query "<mark>HTML5</mark>"</h1>
    <section id="search-results">
        <article>
          <h2><a href="http://en.wikipedia.org/wiki/HTML_5">
            <mark>HTML5</mark> - Wikipedia, the free
            encyclopedia</a></h2>
          <p><mark>HTML5</mark> is the next major revision of
            <mark>HTML</mark> ("hypertext markup language"), the core
            markup language of the World Wide Web. The WHATWG started
            work on the ... <a
            href="http://en.wikipedia.org/wiki/HTML_5">
            Read more</a></p>
        </article>
        <article>
          <h2><a href="http://dev.w3.org/html5/spec/Overview.html">
            <mark>HTML5</mark></a></h2>
          <p>A vocabulary and associated APIs for <mark>HTML</mark> and
            XHTML. Editor's Draft 16 August 2009. Latest Published
            Version: http://w3.org/TR/<mark>html5</mark>/; Latest
            Editor's ...           <a
            href="http://dev.w3.org/html5/spec/Overview.html">
            Read more</a></p>
        </article>
    </section>
  </body>
</html>
```

Adding a simple style declaration like:

```
<style type="text/css">
  mark {background-color: yellow; font-weight: bold;}
</style>
```

in the `<head>` section helps us render this highlighted text:

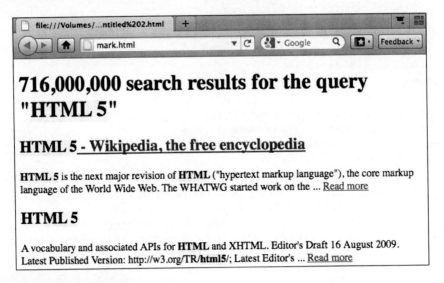

How it works...

The new `<mark>` element simply highlights a word or phrase to draw the reader's attention. To do this, simply specify the `<mark>` to be bold or italicized or highlighted in some way in your corresponding Cascading Style Sheet.

There's more...

Sure, you could mark up and style a search-results page to use the `<b>` or `<i>` or even `<span>` tags to indicate for which term the search took place, but each of those tags only affects the presentation layer. They lack meaning. The new `<mark>` element can accomplish the same visual effect, while also adding that extra meaning to your markup. In fact, the new `<mark>` element is full of win.

<Mark> long and prosper

Another great use of the new `<mark>` element is highlighting a date in a calendar picker, as we often see on any date-based reservation system website like `Priceline.com`.

`Priceline.com` highlights the current date by default when booking your itinerary. Instead of using a semantically meaningless tag to achieve this, the new `<mark>` element could be a perfect candidate to use.

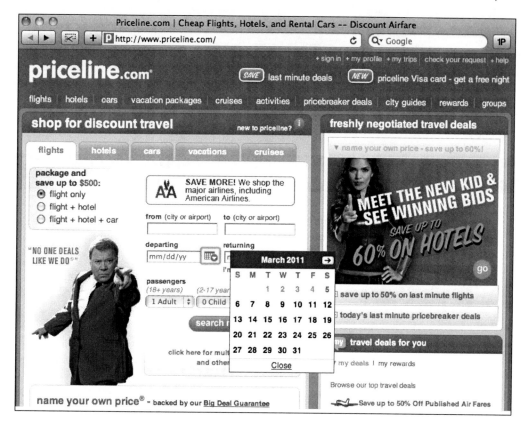

Waiting for browsers

The new `<mark>` element isn't fully supported by any web browser at the time of this writing. Though the extra semantic meaning may not be apparent to machine readers, we can still use the new `<mark>` element as a stylistic "hook" until the day its meaning is fully supported by a variety of browsers.

Is "future proof" a word?

Remember that HTML5's new elements attempt to add extra meaning to our markup. The goal is never to take away meaning or break pages. With this in mind, it becomes much more palatable to layer on new elements like the `<mark>` element that's not fully implemented by browsers yet. Even if its meaning is not fully understood by machines yet, it certainly does not hurt to add it and make our pages as "future proof" as we possibly can.

See also

In 2001, Carrie Bickner prepared the "New York Public Library Online Style Guide" (`http://legacy.www.nypl.org/styleguide`) for branches of the NYPL to use when updating their websites. In this seminal publication, Bickner made the case for web standards by separating content (markup) from presentation (Cascading Style Sheets) from behavior (JavaScript). The publication was extremely forward-thinking for the time and was in use for many years.

Using the time element

"The `<time>` element represents either a time on a 24-hour clock, or a precise date in the proleptic Gregorian calendar, optionally with a time and a time-zone offset." - WHATWG's HTML5 Draft Standard - `http://whatwg.org/html5`

Getting ready

The new `<time>` element is a powerful way to display time or a specific date.

How to do it...

In this recipe we'll display dates and times that will be readable for both humans and machines. Let's look at four examples.

```
<!DOCTYPE html>
<html lang="en">
<head>
  <meta charset="UTF-8">
  <title></title>
  <!--[if lt IE 9]><script
    src=http://html5shiv.googlecode.com/svn/trunk/html5.js>
    </script>[endif]-->
  <meta name="viewport" content="width=device-width,
    initial-scale=1.0">
</head>
<body>
  <article>
    <header>
      <h2>Headline</h2>
      <time datetime="2010-11-29">November 29, 2010</time>
    </header>
    <p>First paragraph</p>
    <p>Second paragraph</p>
```

```
    <footer>Meta information.</footer>
  </article>
  <article>
    <header>
      <h2>Headline</h2>
      <time datetime="2010-11-29">Nov. 29</time>
    </header>
    <p>First paragraph</p>
    <p>Second paragraph</p>
    <footer>Meta information.</footer>
  </article>
  <article>
    <header>
      <h2>Headline</h2>
      <time datetime="2010-11-29">the date this was written</time>
    </header>
    <p>First paragraph</p>
    <p>Second paragraph</p>
    <footer>Meta information.</footer>
  </article>
  <article>
    <header>
      <h2>Headline</h2>
      <time datetime="2010-11-29T11:34">the date and time this was
        written</time>
    </header>
    <p>First paragraph</p>
    <p>Second paragraph</p>
    <footer>Meta information.</footer>
  </article>
</body>
</html>
```

How it works...

We can use the new `<time>` element to indicate specific dates, times, or both.

There's more...

The new `<time>` element specifies an exact moment in time—not a time period.

Odd rules

One interesting aspect of the new `<time>` element is that you can't use a date before the Christian Era. You also can't use a date like "November 2010." Whatever date we specify must be a positive, specific date—not a relative one. The HTML5 Working Group continues to address this seemingly arbitrary restriction.

<time>'s Time will come

Browsers display the new `<time>` element but don't do anything special with it—*yet*.

Always remember SEO

Time. Why are we so obsessed with it? One very valid reason to focus on time and dates on the web is Search Engine Optimization. SEO, once seen as some sort of mysterious voodoo only black hatted wizards understood, is now everyone's responsibility online. You spend time creating good code and expect a writer to create content worth reading. Now go one step further and ensure that your intended audience can actually find the content you have taken the time to create. And the new `<time>` element is just one of the ways search engines draw attention to the most recent content.

See also

The new HTML5 `<time>` element is a possible addition to the Microformats movement. Microformats promise to add additional semantic meaning to our markup. Though not officially a standard, Microformats are slowly gaining acceptance in the web development community. Learn more at `Microformats.org`.

Specifying the pubdate of an article

"The `pubdate` attribute is a boolean attribute. If specified it indicates that the date and time given by the element is the publication date and time of the nearest ancestor `<article>` element, or, if the element has no ancestor `<article>` element, of the document as a whole." - WHATWG's HTML5 Draft Standard - `http://whatwg.org/html5`

Getting ready

The new `pubdate` is an attribute for the new `<time>` element when it exists within the new `<article>` element. It allows us to be even more precise when presenting the date and time of publication.

How to do it...

In this recipe we'll build on the new `<time>` element from the last recipe and add the new optional `pubdate` attribute to display our publication date.

```html
<!DOCTYPE html>
<html lang="en">
<head>
  <meta charset="UTF-8">
  <title></title>
  <!--[if lt IE 9]><script
    src=http://html5shiv.googlecode.com/svn/trunk/html5.js>
    </script>[endif]-->
  <meta name="viewport" content="width=device-width,
    initial-scale=1.0">
</head>
<body>
  <article>
    <header>
      <h2>Headline</h2>
      <p>Published on <time datetime="2010-11-29" pubdate>
        November 29, 2010</time> in the something category.</p>
    </header>
    <p>First paragraph</p>
    <p>Second paragraph</p>
    <footer></footer>
  </article>
  <article>
    <header>
      <h2>Headline</h2>
      <p>Published on <time datetime="2010-11-28" pubdate>
        November 28, 2010</time> in the something category.</p>
    </header>
    <p>First paragraph</p>
    <p>Second paragraph</p>
    <footer></footer>
  </article>
</body>
</html>
```

How it works...

Pubdate is simply a binary variable, or Boolean, attribute to denote when something was published.

There's more...

You can think of `pubdate` as adding extra information to an element (`<time>`) that is already providing extra information. It is like the cherry on a sundae. And who doesn't like cherries on their sundaes?

Still waiting on browsers

We are getting really forward-thinking by including new elements like `<mark>`, `<time>`, and `pubdate`, as none are fully supported by any browser—*yet*.

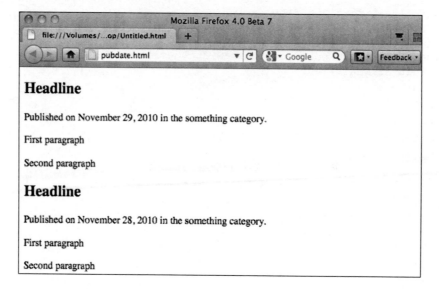

Modern browsers like Firefox display the new `<time>` element and `pubdate` attribute natively without styling.

Extra credit

You can code the new `pubdate` Boolean attribute as `<time datetime="2010-11-29" pubdate="pubdate">` if you want to conform to XML syntax.

Let's end confusion

Even though HTML5 is still quite new, there's already some confusion about the new `pubdate` Boolean attribute. Some think it should generate the date of publication based on your computer clock or a server. That's not its role. Its role is to produce a machine-readable publication date that is useful no matter what text you may put after it.

See also

Tantek Celik has created a very useful site at `http://favelets.com` that features all sorts of "bookmarklets" or in-browser JavaScript commands. Use these to do things like validate HTML5, CSS, and anchors all in the same window. Very helpful!

Displaying comment blocks using the article element

"The `<article>` *element represents a self-contained composition in a document, page, application, or site and that is, in principle, independently distributable or reusable, e.g. in syndication. This could be a forum post, a magazine or newspaper article, a blog entry, a user-submitted comment, an interactive widget or gadget, or any other independent item of content." - WHATWG's HTML5 Draft Standard -* `http://whatwg.org/html5`

Getting ready

We can certainly make the case for marking up blog comments using the new `<article>` element too. In this recipe, we will do exactly that.

How to do it...

Let's use the new `<article>` element to mark up a block of blog comments.

```
<!DOCTYPE html>
<html lang="en">
<head>
  <meta charset="UTF-8">
  <title></title>
  <!--[if lt IE 9]><script
    src=http://html5shiv.googlecode.com/svn/trunk/html5.js>
    </script>[endif]-->
  <meta name="viewport" content="width=device-width,
    initial-scale=1.0">
</head>
<body>
  <article>
    <header>
      <h3>Comment by:
        <a href="http://dalejcruse.com">Dale J Cruse</a></h3>
      <p>On <time datetime="2010-11-29">November 29, 2010</time></p>
```

```
    </header>
    <p>The is the first paragraph of my comment</p>
    <p>The is the second paragraph of my comment</p>
    <footer>
      <p><small>Creative Commons Attribution-ShareAlike
        License</small></p>
    </footer>
  </article>
  <article>
    <header>
      <h3>Comment by:
        <a href="http://dalejcruse.com">Dale J Cruse</a></h3>
      <p>On <time datetime="2010-11-29">November 29, 2010</time></p>
    </header>
    <p>The is the first paragraph of my comment</p>
    <p>The is the second paragraph of my comment</p>
    <footer>
      <p><small>Creative Commons Attribution-ShareAlike
        License</small></p>
    </footer>
  </article>
</body>
</html>
```

How it works...

"Wait a minute," you are thinking. "A blog comment isn't an `<article>`!" you exclaim. Not so fast, buster. If we analyze the components of a blog comment, we'll find the same elements common to other `<article>`s.

There's more...

While we're at it, let's check out that new `<small>` element in the previous `<footer>`s. Previously, `<small>` was a presentational element that denoted physically small text. Not anymore! Now `<small>` has been redefined for use this way:

> *"The `<small>` element represents so called 'small print' such as legal disclaimers and caveats." - WHATWG's HTML5 Draft Standard* - `http://whatwg.org/html5`

Blog comments

Since blog comments and their comment feeds can be intended for syndication, there's even more reason to use the new `<article>` element.

Value comments

Comments. They are found in just about any blog worth its readership. No matter if we're creating our own sites or our own blog content management systems, we deserve to treat the code for comments with every bit as much care and attention as we do the actual blog posts themselves.

Opportunity's yours

`Disqus.com` is the online home of the most widely used blog comments plugin. Publishers can easily incorporate it into their sites without much programming effort. So where does that leave us? Well, no matter whether you use Disqus or any other commenting system, somebody had to develop that code, right? It might as well be you!

See also

Josh Duck has created the clever and useful Periodic Table of HTML5 Elements at: `http://joshduck.com/periodic-table.html`. There, Josh smartly groups categories of similar new elements like Root element, Text-level semantics, Document sections, and more!

Adding fonts dynamically with @font-face

Not so long ago, we designers and developers were limited to only a select few "web safe" fonts for text. If we wanted to display text in a font face that wasn't considered "safe," we made an image out of it. It was dumb, but we had no other choice. Now we do. The font has finally been liberated on the web.

Good typography is essential to any design, and the new @font-face ability lets us embed fonts for browsers to use. Though technically not part of HTML5, this CSS3 property is much too important not to address.

Getting ready

For this recipe, let's find a fun font and embed it as a simple logo. Below you'll find links to several great sites to find both free and paid fonts for web use. For this example, let's look at a previous version of the author's personal portfolio at `http://dalejcruse.com`.

How to do it...

There are several methods to display custom fonts on the web, but we're going to examine and use the bulletproof way to get it working in modern, legacy, and even mobile browsers.

Let's head over to the @Font-Face Generator at
`http://fontsquirrel.com/fontface/generator`.

Using the @font-face Kit Generator wizard walks us through the process of uploading a font ("League Gothic" here) and ensuring that the font you use is legally authorized for use.

Once uploaded, the generator will convert your font to multiple file formats. Download all of these, and save them to the server where you want them to be displayed. All that's needed is two bits of styling:

1. Referencing the @font-face files

2. Assigning the new font to the element we want to use.

```
<!DOCTYPE html>
<html lang="en">
<head>
  <meta charset="UTF-8">
  <title></title>
  <!--[if lt IE 9]><script
    src=http://html5shiv.googlecode.com/svn/trunk/html5.js>
    </script>[endif]-->
  <meta name="viewport" content="width=device-width,
    initial-scale=1.0">
  <style>
    @font-face {font-family: 'LeagueGothic'; src:
      url('fonts/league_gothic-webfont.eot'); src: local(''),
      url('fonts/league_gothic-webfont.woff') format('woff'),
      url('fonts/league_gothic-webfont.ttf') format('truetype'),
      url('fonts/league_gothic-webfont.svg#webfontdrbhz05x')
      format('svg');
    h1 {font-family: 'LeagueGothic'; font-size: 124px;
      line-height: 124px; margin: 355px 0 -25px 0;
      text-transform: uppercase;}
  </style>
</head>
<body>
  <h1>Dale J Cruse</h1>
</body>
</html>
```

DALE J CRUSE

And boom goes the dynamite.

How it works...

The new @font-face ability allows us to save font files in various formats on our web servers and use CSS to reference them for display. In this way, the font files become another asset, just like an image.

There's more...

Browsers use their own proprietary font files for display on the web. By downloading and referencing each of the possible formats, we have ensured that modern browsers like Firefox, Chrome, and Safari, as well as legacy browsers like Internet Explorer and even mobile browsers can display our intended fonts.

Don't steal

Ensure that the font(s) you are using has been legally authorized to be used for online display. Stealing isn't cool.

Firefox note

Remember to store the fonts you want to use on the same server as your unique domain. Some browsers (I'm looking at you, Firefox) do not like it when you try to reference fonts across domains.

Paul Irish rocks

In the spirit of giving credit where it is due, the CSS method we used to call various locally stored font files was developed by Paul Irish in his post "Bulletproof @font-face Implementation Syntax" at: `http://paulirish.com/2009/bulletproof-font-face-implementation-syntax`.

See also

There are some terrific sources to find both free and paid fonts on the web, including:

- Fontdeck – `http://fontdeck.com`
- Kernest – `http://kernest.com`
- The League of Moveable Type – `http://theleagueofmoveabletype.com`
- Typekit – `http://typekit.com`
- Typotheque – `http://typotheque.com/fonts`
- Web Fonts – `http://webfonts.fonts.com`
- Webfonts.info – `http://webfonts.info`
- Webtype – `http://webtype.com`

Adding drop-shadow effects to fonts

Once upon a time, it seemed like web designers and developers added drop shadows to every visual element they could. It was almost like they were getting paid by the drop shadow. Luckily that time has come and gone. Today, only the most fashionable designers and developers know to add drop shadows very sparingly Let's take a look at how to do that using only CSS.

Getting ready

To get started, let us use the previous example, and simply add a very subtle drop shadow to the headline font from a previous version of the author's portfolio site at `http://dalejcruse.com`.

How to do it...

In this recipe we will use some careful styling to add a tasteful drop shadow effect to some of our text.

```
<!DOCTYPE html>
<html lang="en">
<head>
  <meta charset="UTF-8">
  <title></title>
  <!--[if lt IE 9]><script
    src=http://html5shiv.googlecode.com/svn/trunk/html5.js>
    </script>[endif]-->
  <meta name="viewport" content="width=device-width,
    initial-scale=1.0">
  <style>
    @font-face {
      font-family: 'LeagueGothic';
      src: url('fonts/league_gothic-webfont.eot');
      src: local(''), url('fonts/league_gothic-webfont.woff')
        format('woff'), url('fonts/league_gothic-webfont.ttf')
        format('truetype'), url('fonts/league_gothic-
        webfont.svg#webfontdrbhz05x') format('svg');
    }
    h1 {font-family: 'LeagueGothic'; font-size: 124px;
      line-height: 124px; margin: 355px 0 -25px 0;
      text-transform: uppercase; text-shadow: black 1px 1px 0;}
  </style>
</head>
<body>
  <h1>Dale J Cruse</h1>
</body>
</html>
```

How it works...

The text-shadow CSS attribute displays a subtle black drop shadow one pixel to the right and one pixel underneath our text in modern browsers. Though very subtle on the author's portfolio site, the effect can be seen much more dramatically if we set the background and font color both to white.

With the background and text color both set to white, all we see here is the black drop shadow one pixel to the right and one pixel underneath. Since IE does not support text-shadow, this would be rendered as pure white in that browser. That's probably not what you want.

There's more...

In addition to absolute color values like "black," we can also use hexadecimal values like "#000" or even RGBA values with a semi-transparent alpha channel.

Browser support

Modern browsers like Chrome 2+, Firefox 3.1+, Opera 9.5+, and Safari 1.1+ all support the text-shadow CSS property. This song is pretty worn out by now, but suffices to say Internet Explorer does not support it.

With great power...

Just because the ability to add drop shadows to text using only CSS exists, don't consider it a license to go and abuse it. We don't want to revert to the ugly days of the web when drop shadows were everywhere. Instead, use your powers for good.

A plea to all readers

For the sake of readability, consider applying drop shadow effects only to headline or header fonts. Applying it to body text becomes tiresome and unreadable. And you do not want to be the person known for overusing and killing drop shadows all over again.

See also

Google released the WebFont Loader open-source JavaScript library to better control the way browsers load web fonts. Check out the super-simple implementation at:
`http://code.google.com/apis/webfonts/docs/webfont_loader.html`.

Applying gradient effects to fonts

Let's take our previous example and add one more layer to it: A subtle gradient effect.

Getting ready

The only other extra thing we'll need is a portable network graphics image that we can reference via our CSS.

How to do it...

In this recipe we will add a `.png` image file with alpha transparency to create a slick gradient effect on our headline.

```
<!DOCTYPE html>
<html lang="en">
<head>
  <meta charset="UTF-8">
  <title></title>
  <!--[if lt IE 9]><script
    src=http://html5shiv.googlecode.com/svn/trunk/html5.js>
    </script>[endif]-->
  <meta name="viewport" content="width=device-width,
    initial-scale=1.0">
  <style>
    @font-face {font-family: 'LeagueGothic'; src:
      url('fonts/league_gothic-webfont.eot'); src: local(''),
      url('fonts/league_gothic-webfont.woff') format('woff'),
      url('fonts/league_gothic-webfont.ttf') format('truetype'),
      url('fonts/league_gothic-webfont.svg#webfontdrbhz05x')
      format('svg');
    }
    h1 {font-family: 'LeagueGothic'; font-size: 124px;
      line-height: 124px; margin: 355px 0 -25px 0;
      text-transform: uppercase; text-shadow: black 1px 1px 0;
      position: relative;}
    h1 span {background: url(gradient.png) repeat-x; display: block;
      height: 124px; position: absolute; width: 100%;}
  </style>
</head>
<body>
  <h1><span></span>Dale J Cruse</h1>
</body>
</html>
```

Notice that extra `<span>` in our `<h1>` tag. That is where we have put our image.

How it works...

By simply layering an image with some transparency over our text, we have subtly altered the text to appear to have a gradient.

There's more...

Your imagination is the only limitation to this effect. You could create fades, metallic effects, vertical or horizontal stripes—even zebra stripes!

Careful there

Remember: Just because you can, does not mean you should. Use text gradients sparingly. Please.

See also

For a beautiful example of a gradient effect over a font, check out the header on Alex Clarke's college project about Enceladus, one of Saturn's moons at: `http://hagablog.co.uk/demos/enceladus/index.html`. While you're enjoying the visual design, don't forget to check out the source code to see Alex's very well documented HTML5 code.

Annotating visual elements using the figure and figcaption tags

"The `<figure>` element represents some flow content, optionally with a caption, that is self-contained and is typically referenced as a single unit from the main flow of the document. The element can thus be used to annotate illustrations, diagrams, photos, code listings, etc, that are referred to from the main content of the document, but that could, without affecting the flow of the document, be moved away from that primary content, e.g. to the side of the page, to dedicated pages, or to an appendix." - WHATWG's HTML5 Draft Standard - `http://whatwg.org/html5`

"The first <figcaption> element child of the element, if any, represents the caption of the <figure> element's contents. If there is no child <figcaption> element, there is no caption." - WHATWG's HTML5 Draft Standard - `http://whatwg.org/html5`

Getting ready

You have seen it a million times: An image with some sort of text caption underneath. Usually it is on the side of a page. Previously, we'd just mark that up as an image with some sort of text container under it. Now, we have the more semantically rich new `<figure>` element to handle it for us. Let's find out how.

How to do it...

There are two ways to achieve this recipe:

1. Without a caption
2. With a caption

First let's try it without the caption:

```
<!DOCTYPE html>
<html lang="en">
<head>
  <meta charset="UTF-8">
  <title></title>
  <!--[if lt IE 9]><script
    src=http://html5shiv.googlecode.com/svn/trunk/html5.js>
    </script>[endif]-->
  <meta name="viewport" content="width=device-width,
    initial-scale=1.0">
</head>
<body>
  <figure>
    <img
      src="https://packtpub.com/sites/default/files/imagecache/
      productview/26880S_MockupCover.jpg"
      alt="Inkscape 0.48 for Web Designers">
  </figure>
</body>
</html>
```

Now let's add that caption:

```
<!DOCTYPE html>
<html lang="en">
<head>
  <meta charset="UTF-8">
  <title></title>
  <!--[if lt IE 9]><script
    src=http://html5shiv.googlecode.com/svn/trunk/html5.js>
```

```
      </script>[endif]-->
    <meta name="viewport" content="width=device-width,
      initial-scale=1.0">
  </head>
  <body>
    <figure>
      <img
        src="https://packtpub.com/sites/default/files/imagecache/
        productview/2688OS_MockupCover.jpg"
        alt="Inkscape 0.48 for Web Designers">
      <figcaption>Inkscape 0.48 for Web Designers</figcaption>
    </figure>
  </body>
</html>
```

Having one caption for multiple images is easy too. Notice multiple `img` tags and just one `<figcaption>`.

```
    <!DOCTYPE html>
    <html lang="en">
    <head>
      <meta charset="UTF-8">
      <title></title>
      <!--[if lt IE 9]><script
        src=http://html5shiv.googlecode.com/svn/trunk/html5.js>
        </script>[endif]-->
      <meta name="viewport" content="width=device-width,
        initial-scale=1.0">
    </head>
    <body>
      <figure>
        <img
          src="https://www.packtpub.com/sites/default/files/imagecache/
          productview/2688OS_MockupCover.jpg"
          alt="Inkscape 0.48 for Web Designers">
        <img
          src="https://www.packtpub.com/sites/default/files/imagecache/
          productview/bookimages/0042_MockupCover_0.jpg"
          alt="jQuery 1.4 Reference Guide">
        <figcaption>Recent bestsellers from Packt Publishing</figcaption>
      </figure>
    </body>
    </html>
```

How it works...

A bit of styling makes that `<figcaption>` display beneath those images in the new `<figure>` element.

Recent bestsellers from Packt Publishing

There's more...

Remember that the new `<figure>` element is used for inline content that you want to display to the side of its corresponding main text.

Grouping's good

The new `<figure>` element can contain text, images, audio, video, illustrations, diagrams, code listings, and just about anything else that deserves to be grouped together aside from the primary content.

Semantics are valuable too

Inline content with captions occurs all the time in books, newspapers, and magazines. Since some of the earliest days of the web, we have been able to accomplish the same thing, but now the new `<figure>` element gives us a much more semantic "hook" to style instead of resorting to class names.

<figure> vs <aside>

So what is the difference between `<figure>` and `<aside>`? We should use the new `<figure>` element for essential content whose position is not important. The new `<aside>` element, however, is for content that is related but not essential. Are we splitting hairs? Maybe. But you are the kind of web developer who lives and dies by the details, right?

See also

For an even more detailed description of how HTML5 differs from all previous versions of HTML, see the Wikipedia entry at: `http://en.wikipedia.org/wiki/HTML5`.

3

Styling with CSS

In this chapter, we will cover:

- ▸ Setting elements to `display:block`
- ▸ Styling a `nav` block element
- ▸ Using background-size to control background appearance
- ▸ Adding rounded corners with `border-radius`
- ▸ Including multiple background images
- ▸ Adding a box shadow to images
- ▸ Styling for Internet Explorer browsers

Introduction

"Thanks for all the good times, IE6. See you all at @Mix when we show a little piece of IE Heaven. - The Internet Explorer Team at Microsoft" – Eulogy from the Internet Explorer 6 Funeral seen online at `http://ie6funeral.com`*.*

You've risen to the challenge of thinking differently about HTML. Next up, you'll be challenged to expand your Cascading Style Sheets knowledge as well. Along with that, we're going to challenge some assumptions about cross-browser display. If you—and your clients—think websites should look the same in every browser, we're going to change some minds. But if you already know the fallacy of cross-browser display, you'll be the one helping to change other people's minds.

Before we do any of those things, we need to ask ourselves and our clients a simple question: Do websites need to look exactly the same in every browser? *Need?* For the concise, one-word answer, visit `http://dowebsitesneedtolookexactlythesameineverybrowser.com` in a modern browser such as Chrome, Firefox, Opera, or Safari.

Also check a legacy browser like Internet Explorer 6:

That, my friends, is what a dead browser looks like. Watching something die isn't very pretty, is it?

It's obvious that site displays differently across browsers. The question is: So what? Does that matter? Should it? Why?

Very few of us work in sterile labs where we have 100% creative control over the display of what we create. Even fewer of us have the time or inclination to create separate bespoke experiences for every browser. Surely there must be a middle way. There's an old phrase this author really likes:

> "The truth lies somewhere in between." - Avadhoot Patwardhan

In this case, the truth is you're going to have to work with your clients, be they business owners, project managers, or anyone who pays you to create a site for them. But the days of sitting idly by while those people tell us how to do our jobs is over. If you know a better, faster, more efficient way to develop, you must speak up. It is your duty. If you don't, no one else will speak up for you. That's bad for you, that's bad for your client, and that's bad for the industry. Don't be that guy.

Instead, you're going to have to educate your clients why some browsers display things slightly differently and why that's perfectly acceptable. Here are a few tactics the author has used in real business situations:

1. Demonstrate to the client that accommodating for older browsers (especially IE6) will take longer. Be ready to prove that developing for that browser alone could easily take one quarter of your time. Hit the client where it hurts (the pocketbook), and that person will usually back down.

2. Emphasize that the user experience can remain exactly the same even if IE doesn't have every rounded corner or transition effect that other browsers do.

 User experience *always* trumps eye candy.

CSS is not officially part of the HTML5 specification. In fact, it deserves its own book. But in this chapter, the author will show you real-world examples of how others have used CSS to apply visual treatments by displaying elements as block level, mocking up a navigation bar, working with multiple background images, applying rounded corners as well as advanced stylings like adding box shadows, and styling for Internet Explorer browsers.

Let's get cooking!

Setting elements to display:block

By default, modern browsers assign the new HTML5 elements to `display:block`. But also by default, older browsers and most versions of Internet Explorer fall back to `display:inline` natively. If you've worked with CSS before, you can see trouble coming a mile away. First thing we're going to do is fix it before it can become a problem.

Getting ready

First, let's identify all the new elements in HTML5. These include:

- `<article>`
- `<aside>`
- `<audio>`
- `<canvas>`
- `<command>`
- `<datalist>`
- `<details>`
- `<embed>` - not a new tag, but it finally validates in HTML5
- `<figcaption>`
- `<figure>`
- `<footer>`
- `<header>`
- `<hgroup>`
- `<keygen>`
- `<mark>`
- `<meter>`
- `<nav>`
- `<output>`
- `<progress>`
- `<rp>`
- `<rt>`
- `<ruby>`
- `<section>`
- `<source>`

- `<summary>`
- `<time>`
- `<video>`
- `<wbr>`

How to do it...

We'll start with our usual page framework and add a style to make all those new elements `display:block`.

```
<!DOCTYPE html>
<html lang="en">
<head>
  <meta charset="UTF-8">
  <title>Blog Title</title>
  <!--[if lt IE 9]><script
    src="http://html5shiv.googlecode.com/svn/trunk/html5.js">
    </script>[endif]-->
  <style>
    article, aside, audio, canvas, command, datalist, details,
    embed, figcaption, figure, footer, header, hgroup, keygen,
    mark, meter, nav, output, progress, rp, rt, ruby, section,
    source, summary, time, video, wbr {display:block;}
  </style>
</head>
<body>
</body>
</html>
```

There. That wasn't so bad. Much better, in fact. Of course, these could also be included in a CSS reset file as well.

How it works...

Using CSS, we've set all the new HTML5 elements to display as block-level elements, ensuring more predictable browser behavior.

There's more...

Even though modern browsers already display these new HTML5 tags as block-level elements, declaring them `display:block` once again in our stylesheet doesn't hurt anything. Better safe than sorry here.

No need to repeat and repeat and repeat and repeat and repeat

Note: We should include that short bit of style in an external stylesheet referenced by every page on our site rather than display it inline at the top of every page. Better to declare it once and have it carry through the rest of your site than repeat it over and over again.

Style once

Using that simple style declaration once, we can ensure that our modern, legacy, and mobile browsers will behave more predictably when displaying new HTML5 elements.

Echoes of the past

For some reason, some developers don't want to bother learning HTML5. You hear them spout all sorts of nonsense about how the spec isn't ready, it's not fully supported in all browsers, and how you need "hacks" like CSS or JavaScript to make it work. That's all just nonsense. Don't pay any attention to their whining. What you're really hearing is the sound of dinosaurs going extinct. If a dinosaur is bound and determined to will itself into extinction by its own inaction, we say let it. Only the strong survive.

It's helpful to remember that evolution occurs in stages. Not all beings suddenly evolve at once. Unlike the dinosaurs, you get to decide if you want to evolve now, later, or not at all. You can decide on which side of history you want to be.

See also

We didn't start the fire. It was always burning. Since the world's been turning. Jeffrey Zeldman's "*To Hell With Bad Browsers*" article sent shockwaves through the web development world when it was published *in 2001*. In it, Zeldman, now widely considered the godfather of the web standards movement, lit a fire under a generation of web designers and developers to use CSS for the web presentation layer and leave behind broken, legacy browsers. Read this seminal manifesto at: `http://alistapart.com/articles/tohell`.

Styling a nav block element

When creating the HTML5 spec, analysis was done and determined that one of the most used elements was `<div id="nav">` or `<div id="navigation">`. With HTML5 there's no more need for that. Instead we have the semantically rich `<nav>`. Now let's get to work styling it.

Getting ready

Let's examine how the `http://css3maker.com` site uses the new semantically rich `<nav>` element.

How to do it...

If we view the source of the homepage, we'll find this snippet:

```
<!DOCTYPE html>
<html>
<head>
  <meta http-equiv="Content-Type" content="text/html;
    charset=utf-8" />
  <title>CSS3.0 Maker | CSS3.0 Generator | CSS 3.0 Generator </title>
  <link href="style/style.css" rel="stylesheet" type="text/css" />
  <script type="text/javascript"
    src="js/CreateHTML5Elements.js"></script>
```

```
    </head>
    <body>
    <div class="main_wrapper">
      <div id="wrapper">
        <nav class="clearfix">
          <ul>
            <li class="frest"><a href="index.html" title="CSS 3.0 Maker"
              class="active">Home</a></li>
            <li><a href="border-radius.html" title="Border Radius">
              Border Radius</a></li>
            <li><a href="css-gradient.html"
              title="Gradient">Gradient</a></li>
            <li><a href="css3-transform.html"
              title="CSS 3.0 Transform">CSS Transform</a></li>
            <li><a href="css3-animation.html"
              title="CSS 3.0 Animation">CSS Animation</a></li>
            <li><a href="css3-transition.html"
              title="CSS 3.0 Transition">CSS Transition</a></li>
            <li><a href="css-3-rgba.html"
              title="CSS 3.0 RGBA">RGBA</a></li>
            <li><a href="text-shadow.html"
              title="Text Shadow">Text Shadow</a></li>
            <li><a href="box-shadow.html"
              title="Box Shadow">Box Shadow</a></li>
            <li><a href="text-rotation.html"
              title="Text Rotation">Text Rotation</a></li>
            <li><a href="font-face.html"
              title="@Font Face">@Font Face</a></li>
          </ul>
        </nav>
      </div>
    </div>
    </body>
    </html>
```

Notice that HTML markup is quite straightforward so far. The team at `http://css3maker.com` created a page wrapper and then used the new `<nav>` element to contain the unordered list that has all the typical navigation elements. Simple, right? Next let's turn our attention to how they styled it.

```
<style>
  nav {
    background: url("../images/box_bg.png")
      repeat scroll 0 0 transparent;
    border-radius: 5px;
    margin-bottom: 8px;
    margin-right: 5px;
  }
```

```
nav ul {
  display: block;
  list-style: none outside none;
  margin: 0;
  padding: 0 0 0 5px;
}
nav ul li.frest {
  border-left-width: 0;
}
nav ul li {
  border-right: 1px solid #1D1C1C;
  display: inline;
  float: left;
  margin: 0;
  padding: 0;
}
nav ul li a {
  color: #000;
  display: inline;
  float: left;
  font-size: 13px;
  height: 35px;
  line-height: 35px;
  padding: 0 10px;
  text-shadow: 0 -1px 2px #737373;
  -webkit-transition: All 0.50s ease;
  -moz-transition: All 1s ease;
  -o-transition: All 1s ease;
}
</style>
```

How it works...

The new <nav> element becomes not only a container for our unordered list, but it also provides additional meaning to the web browser as well as accessibility enhancements. By floating the <nav> element and displaying our unordered list without a list style, this allows us to display our navigation bar horizontally.

There's more...

We also saw the use of the new CSS3 transition property. Simply put, this is a new browser rollover effect that was previously only possible with Flash or JavaScript. Now, CSS can do the job of changing an element's appearance when the mouse moves over it.

Since the `transition` property only has experimental support among browser makers, you'll see vendor-specific prefixes that are prefaced by a single dash, such as:

- `-webkit` (for Safari and Chrome)
- `-moz` (for Firefox)
- `-o` (for Opera)

In addition, Internet Explorer has its own vendor prefix, which is `-ms`. Inexplicably, Chrome can handle both the `-webkit` prefix as well as its own `-chrome` prefix.

Those dashes simply indicate support is a work in progress by the browser manufacturers. Remember that HTML5—and CSS3—are evolving specifications. We can start using elements of them now, but full support isn't there yet. It's like we're cooking for the future.

Browser support

Web browsers that support the new `<nav>` element:

Apple Safari 5+   Google Chrome 7+   Microsoft Internet Explorer 9   Mozilla Firefox 3.5+

Text-shadow is cool

In the previous code sample, you'll also notice the clever use of the new CSS3 `text-shadow` property that we covered in depth in the previous chapter.

See also

The `http://cSS3maker.com` site is a terrific resource for any CSS3 developer needing browser-specific prefixes for these new CSS properties:

- border-radius
- gradient
- CSS transform
- CSS animation
- CSS transition
- RGBA
- text shadow
- box shadow
- text rotation
- @font-face

Using background-size to control background appearance

Using CSS3, we now have a way to specify the size of our background images. We can specify this size in pixels, width and height, or in percentages. When you specify a size as a percentage, the size is relative to the width or height of the area that we have designated using background-origin.

Getting ready

Let's take a look at a real-world example at `http://miessociety.org`, a gorgeous website by Simple Honest Work, an agency created by designer Scott Thomas and dedicated to preserving the legacy of architect Ludwig Mies van der Rohe.

How to do it...

If we view the source of the stylesheet, we'll see the authors created one rule for the `body` and then specified that any background image used would cover the entire `body`.

The authors also specified a background image for each page by attaching an `ID` to each `body` element.

How it works...

Here we see how the creators used some simple styling, including the new `background-size` property, to stretch a large background image all the way across the page, no matter your monitor size or resolution.

```
<style>
body {
    background: transparent no-repeat scroll 50% 50%;
    background-repeat: no-repeat;
    background-size: cover;
    margin: 0px;
    padding: 0px;
}
body#body_home {
    background-attachment: inherit;
    background-image:
        url(http://miessociety.org/site_media/library/
        img/crownhall_index.jpg);
    background-position: 50% 0%;
}
</style>
```

There's more...

The new `background-size` element is typically specified in pixels, width and height, or in percentages. In the Mies van der Rohe Society website example, we see the author has used the term "cover", which enables the background image to stretch to "cover" the entire canvas. Clever.

Browser support

Web browsers that support the new `background-size` property:

Apple Safari 3+

Microsoft Internet
Explorer 10 Preview

Mozilla Firefox 3.6+

Acceptable in IE

So what happens when we view a site using background-size in an unsupported browser? Here we can see how versions of Internet Explorer prior to 10 fail to stretch the background image and instead simply fills the rest of the canvas with black. This is a perfect example of not looking the same in every browser yet still providing a completely satisfactory user experience. No website viewer—even one using IE6—could legitimately complain that they weren't experiencing the site as the author intended.

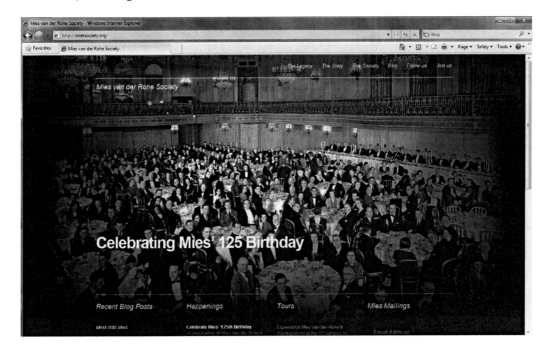

Simple Scott simply rocks

In this section we used the real-world example of the Mies van der Rohe Society website using the new CSS3 `background-size` property and noted how the site authors cleverly accommodated for the use of older browsers.

See also

The `http://html5rocks.com` site features interactive presentations, a code playground, samples, and step-by-step tutorials to develop and hone your new technical skills. The fun part is the site is an open source project you can contribute to. Learn it, share it, pay it forward!

Adding rounded corners with border-radius

Border-radius may very well become the most commonly used new attribute of CSS3. With so many buttons and rounded corners on containing elements used throughout the web, `border-radius` makes it easy to accomplish via CSS rather than rely on images. Here's how to do it.

Getting ready

Let's take a look at `http://devinsheaven.com`, featuring the work and writings of iPhone application designer and developer Devin Ross. Specifically, we're going to examine how Devin styled his search field.

How to do it...

Viewing the source of Devin's code, we see simple, straightforward form markup with all the typical elements: a wrapper, a form, a label, and two inputs.

```
<div id="search-form">
  <form role="search" method="get" id="searchform"
    action="http://devinsheaven.com/" >
    <div>
      <label for="s">Search for:</label>
      <input type="text" value="" name="s" id="s" />
      <input type="submit" id="searchsubmit" value="Search" />
    </div>
  </form>
</div>
```

But it's what Devin does next in his stylesheet that accomplishes the rounded corners in modern browsers:

```
<style>
#navigation-bar #search-form {
  background: none repeat scroll 0 0 white;
  border-radius: 4px;
  margin-left: 180px;
  margin-top: 12px;
  padding: 2px 6px;
  position: absolute;
  width: 250px;
}
</style>
```

How it works...

Devin specifies a four pixel `border-radius` to the search-form ID, which rounds all four of its corners by the same amount. It's also possible to specify the `border-radius` of each corner separately.

There's more...

Interestingly, the Opera browser will support the new CSS3 `border-radius` attribute without a browser-specific prefix. Good job, Opera! Thanks!

Browser support

Web browsers that support the new `border-radius` style:

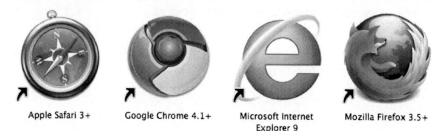

Apple Safari 3+   Google Chrome 4.1+   Microsoft Internet Explorer 9   Mozilla Firefox 3.5+

Acceptable in IE

So what happens when viewing Devin's well-designed site in an unsupported browser? Internet Explorer 8 and earlier simply ignore the `border-radius` attribute and squares the corners. Once again, this is perfectly acceptable, but will often require you educating your clients why pixel perfection is not always a realistic goal.

Devin's Heaven website viewed in Internet Explorer 8. Note square search form border.

Devin's Heaven goes to 11

In this section we demonstrated how `http://devinsheaven.com` uses the new CSS3 `border-radius` attribute to round the corners of a search field subtly. We also looked at the author's use of browser-specific prefixes and how the author chose to deal with legacy browsers like Internet Explorer 8 and before.

See also

For lots more great uses of the new CSS3 `border-radius` attribute, visit `http://houseofbuttons.tumblr.com`. It includes lots of design and development inspiration.

Including multiple background images

`http://benthebodyguard.com` had the Internet all abuzz when it debuted in December, 2010. The authors used a single-page layout to tell an interactive story of a fictional French bodyguard named Ben. As viewed scrolled down the long page, multiple backgrounds help tell the story of the then-soon-to-be-released iPhone application.

Getting ready

Let's check out `http://benthebodyguard.com` and scroll through the animation.

How to do it...

Let's focus on a snippet of the source code and see how the site authors utilized multiple backgrounds.

```
<!doctype html>
<html class="" lang="en">
<head>
  <meta http-equiv="Content-Type" content="text/html;
    charset=UTF-8"/>
  <title>Ben the Bodyguard. Coming soon to iPhone® and iPod
    touch®</title>
  <meta name="author" content="Ben the Bodyguard">
  <link rel="stylesheet" href="css/style.php?v=1">
</head>
<body class="index">
  <div id="container">
    <div id="hide-wrapper">
      <header>
        <img id="comingDecember" alt="Ben the Bodyguard is coming for
          iPhone and iPod touch in january 2011"
          src="http://benbodyguard1.s3.amazonaws.com/red_stamp.png">
        <h1>A Frenchman <br>protecting your secrets.<br> Yes,
            seriously.</h1>
        <h3>Ben the Bodyguard</h3>
        <p>Protecting your passwords, photos, contacts<br> and
            other sensitive stuff on your iPhone or iPod touch</p>
      </header>
        <div id="ben">
          <div id="speechBubbleWrapper">
            <div id='speechBubble'></div>
          </div>
          <div id="ben-img"></div>
        </div>
        <div id="hotel">
          <div id="hotelanimation"></div>
        </div>
        <div id="bridge"></div>
        <div id="train"></div>
        <div id="hideBenInBeginning"></div>
        <div id="city">
        <div id="thief"></div>
        <div id="stolen"></div>
        <div id="yakuza"></div>
      </div>
```

```
            </div>
          </div>
      </body>
      </html>
```

Nothing out of the ordinary so far, except for several empty `div`s. Those are containers for the multiple background images the authors used to storytell. Your containers can include text, images, video, and more.

How it works...

By specifying background images for each of those `div`s, the site author has used multiple PNG file background images to create a seamlessly interactive online experience.

There's more...

Friends of Mighty created a series of mini sites to demonstrate some of the new typographic possibilities we talked about in the last chapter. Frank Chimero created a one-page site at `http://lostworldsfairs.com/atlantis` that works in much the same way the `http://benthebodyguard.com` site works with multiple backgrounds. As you scroll through the long page, your avatar descends to the lost city of Atlantis.

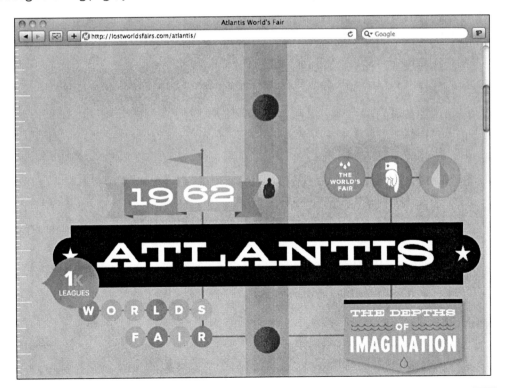

Where's the content?

Viewing the source of the Atlantis Lost Worlds Fair mini site, we see a similar approach with multiple empty divs.

```
<!doctype html>
<html lang="en" class="no-js">
<head>
  <meta charset="utf-8">
  <title>Atlantis World's Fair</title>
  <meta name="Author" content="Friends of Mighty">
  <link rel="stylesheet" href="css/all.min.css">
</head>
<body>
  <div id="back_to"><a href="http://lostworldsfairs.com">Lost World's
Fairs</a></div>
  <div id="header">
    <div id="img_doc"></div>
    <div id="img_ship"></div>
    <div class="container">
      <p id="txt_below">Below</p>
    </div>
    <div id="backwave"></div>
    <div id="frontwave"></div>
  </div>
  <div id="tube">
    <div class="tube_container">
      <div id="tube_dude" class="tube_container"></div>
    </div>
    <div class="tube_container">
      <div id="tube_overlay"></div>
      <div id="tube_backtop"></div>
      <div id="tube_back"></div>
      <div id="tube_fronttop"></div>
      <div id="tube_frontbottom"></div>
      <div id="tube_front"></div>
    </div>
  </div>
  <div id="depthfinder"><span id="depth-o-meter">0</span>
    <span id="txt_k">k</span> Leagues</div>
  <div id="depthscale"></div>
  <div id="content">
    <section id="depth1">
      <div class="container">
        <div id="welcomesign" class="bringFront">
```

```
<header>
  <h1><span id="txt_date">1962</span>
    <span id="txt_atlantis">Atlantis</span>
    <span id="txt_worldsfair">Worlds Fair</span></h1>
    <p id="txt_taglines"><span id="txt_worldsfaircircle">The
    World's Fair</span> <span id="txt_imaginationflag">The
    Depths Of Imagination</span></p>
</header>
      </div>
      <aside id="info_1" class="dyk-right">
        <div class="didyouknow">
          <img src="img/dyk-info.png" alt="info" height="30"
            width="30"/>
          <h4>Did You Know</h4>
          <p>Atlantis was<br/> originally built on<br/> the floor
            of the<br/> sea in 722 BCE<br/> by amphibious<br/>
            herbivores</p>
        </div>
      </aside>
    </div>
  </section>
</div>
</body>
</html>
```

Let's be Frank

Chimero uses a similar approach to the `http://benthebodyguard.com` site by specifying background images for each of those otherwise empty `div`s to create a seamless experience.

See also

There are so many new things in HTML5 that it's like the best technology Christmas ever. Keep track of which elements your browsers support by visiting `http://html5test.com`. Visiting the site via a host of browsers yields sobering results.

Adding a box shadow to images

Previously, a visual effect like a shadow under or around an image was only possible by using a second image for the shadow or making the shadow itself part of the image. The problem was that if you ever wanted to adjust the shadow, you had to recut it. Let's look at a modern, smart way to do it using CSS3.

Getting ready

Check out the attractive and subtle shadow around the visual elements at
http://thebox.maxvoltar.com. Author Tim Van Damme has applied the
new CSS3 box-shadow attribute.

How to do it...

Let's examine the styles to see how Tim achieved that beautifully simple effect:

```
<style>
section {
  background: none repeat scroll 0 0 #EAEEF1;
  border: 1px solid #FFFFFF;
  box-shadow: 0 2px 10px rgba(0, 0, 0, 0.5);
  margin: 0 auto;
  padding: 49px;
  position: relative;
  width: 300px;
  z-index: 50;
}
</style>
```

In addition to other styles, we can clearly see the box-shadow attribute specifying a color
and spread distance for the shadow.

How it works...

The syntax for the new CSS3 `box-shadow` attribute is the same as the `text-shadow` attribute. That is, the site author applied a shadow around the photo that is two pixels to the right and ten pixels on the bottom at 50% opacity.

Browser support

Web browsers that support the new `box-shadow` style.

| Apple Safari 5+ | Google Chrome 7+ | Microsoft Internet Explorer 9 Beta | Mozilla Firefox 3.5+ |

Ignorance is bliss

Browsers that don't support the new CSS `box-shadow` attribute simply ignore the rule and won't display the shadow. The appearance is slightly altered but the user experience is not. No harm, no foul.

Box-shadow for The Box

In this section, we demonstrated how author Tim Van Damme is using the new CSS3 `box-shadow` attribute to create a subtle shadow effect around his interview website.

See also

When creating stylesheets for your own projects, you have total control to create one CSS to rule them all, or create separate bespoke experiences for mobile and/or printer friendly pages. But what happens when you don't have that full control? Then it's good to know we have tools like `http://printfriendly.com` to do it for us.

Styling for Internet Explorer browsers

It should be obvious by now the author is a strong advocate of serving optimal CSS3 experiences to modern browsers and letting old versions of IE do what it wants. If an element is missing a rounded corner or shadow in an old browser, this author certainly doesn't care. But the fact is your clients might. Let's open a can of worms and talk about how to accommodate dead browsers.

Getting ready

We're going to look at a series of specific methods to make IE behave when using new CSS3 attributes like `border-radius`, `box-shadow`, and `text-shadow`.

Border-radius

It's possible to achieve rounded corners in old versions of IE. Let's visit `http://htmlremix.com/css/curved-corner-border-radius-cross-browser` to find out how. There we'll learn how to include an `.htc` behavior in our stylesheet:

```
<style>
.curved {
  -moz-border-radius: 10px;
  -webkit-border-radius: 10px;
  behavior: url(border-radius.htc);
}
<style>
```

Note that `.htc` file is code bloat, and the behavior will cause your CSS to not validate.

Box-shadow

We can force IE to display `box-shadow`s by using a proprietary filter:

```
<style>
.box-shadow {
  -moz-box-shadow: 2px 2px 2px #000;
  -webkit-box-shadow: 2px 2px 2px #000;
  filter: progid:DXImageTransform.Microsoft.Shadow(color='#000',
Direction=145, Strength=3);
}
</style>
```

Unfortunately you'll have to fiddle with that filter to achieve the direction and darkness of the shadow. Note this filter is not as powerful as the new CSS3 `box-shadow` attribute.

Text-shadow

It seems the only way to make `text-shadow` work in versions of Internet Explorer before version 9 is to use a jQuery plugin like the one at `http://scriptandstyle.com/submissions/text-shadow-in-ie-with-jquery-2` to achieve the look through JavaScript. Note that forcing JavaScript to do CSS' job is never a good approach, and this technique only leads to code bloat.

Note

While several CSS3-like effects are possible in legacy versions of IE, none are recommended. Each one takes additional development type and can have an effect on browser performance. Use at your—and your clients—own risk.

See also

Kyle Weems has created a hilariously terrific weekly comic strip lampooning the goings on in the web standards world at `http://cssquirrel.com`. HTML5, CSS3, Twitter, accessibility, and the major voices that matter in those worlds are ripe for Kyle's often twisted sense of humor.

4
Creating Accessible Experiences

In this chapter, we will cover:

- ▸ Testing browser support
- ▸ Adding skip navigation
- ▸ Adding meta tags
- ▸ Using semantic descriptions in tags for screen readers
- ▸ Providing alternate site views
- ▸ Using `hgroup` to create accessible header areas
- ▸ Displaying alternate content for non-supported browsers
- ▸ Using WAI-ARIA

Introduction

"Good accessibility design is good web design."

So far we have talked a lot about semantic web coding and the way HTML5 allows us to take this naming approach to a new level we have not previously been able to reach. Much of our discussion has centered on how semantic web coding makes our job as web developers easier, faster, and more meaningful.

In this chapter, we will turn our attention to how semantic web coding can improve the online experiences our audiences have. Now, applying semantic tags—tags that are meaningful rather than just presentational—become even more important to screen readers and those who rely on them to navigate the websites and applications and interfaces we create.

If you have ever coded a website, application, or interface for the military, an academic institution, or just about anyone who gets money from the United States federal government, you have heard of Section 508.

Unlike HTML or CSS validation, Section 508 validation works differently. In HTML or CSS, code is either valid or it is not. It is binary. Not so with Section 508. In this case, there are three different levels of validation, each ever more difficult to reach.

In this chapter we will examine how to use HTML5 to test browser support, add skip navigation and meta tags, use semantic descriptions in tags for screen readers, provide alternate site views, use the new HTML5 `hgroup` element to create accessible header areas, display alternate content for non-supported browsers, and use WAI-ARIA.

Now. let's get cooking!

Testing browser support

Let's start by using the open source Modernizr project at: `http://modernizr.com` created by developers Faruk Ates and Paul Irish. According to the website, Modernizr uses feature detection to test the current browser against upcoming features.

The Modernizr concept aims at feature detection instead of browser detection. It is a subtle but important differentiation. Instead of making broad assumptions, the Modernizr approach detects features that browsers support.

How to do it...

Download the Modernizr JavaScript file and reference it in the `head` section of your markup. You will then add the class of "no-js" to your `body` element, like this:

```html
<!DOCTYPE html>
<html lang="en">
<head>
  <meta charset="UTF-8">
  <title>Title</title>
  <!--[if lt IE 9]><script
    src="http://html5shiv.googlecode.com/svn/trunk/html5.js">
    </script>[endif]-->
  <script src="modernizr-1.6.min.js"></script>
</head>
<body class="no-js">
</body>
</html>
```

How it works...

Including that script and simple body class in your markup enables Modernizr to detect which of the following items the web browser supports. It will then add classes and a JavaScript API to detect support for certain features. If the features aren't supported in the given browser, Modernizr simply won't add them.

- @font-face
- Canvas
- Canvas Text
- HTML5 Audio
- HTML5 Video
- rgba()
- hsla()
- border-image:
- border-radius:
- box-shadow:
- text-shadow:
- opacity:
- Multiple backgrounds
- Flexible Box Model

- ► CSS Animations
- ► CSS Columns
- ► CSS Gradients
- ► CSS Reflections
- ► CSS 2d Transforms
- ► CSS 3d Transforms
- ► CSS Transitions
- ► Geolocation API
- ► localStorage
- ► sessionStorage
- ► SVG
- ► SMIL
- ► SVG Clipping
- ► Inline SVG
- ► Drag-and-Drop
- ► hashchange
- ► X-window Messaging
- ► History Management
- ► applicationCache
- ► Touch events
- ► Web Sockets
- ► Web Workers
- ► Web SQL Database
- ► WebGL
- ► IndexedDB
- ► Input Types
- ► Input Attributes

There's more...

New in Modernizr 2 Beta is the ability to customize your JavaScript download. So now if you do not care about a particular feature (let's say Drag and Drop), you can unclick it and not have Modernizr check for it. Read all about it at: `http://modernizr.github.com/Modernizr/2.0-beta`.

With an eye to the future

From the website:

> *"Modernizr is a small and simple JavaScript library that helps you take advantage of emerging web technologies (CSS3, HTML5) while still maintaining a fine level of control over older browsers that may not yet support these new technologies."*

What Modernizr really does

What Modernizr does not do is add or enable functionality that does not natively exist in browsers. If your browser doesn't support Input Attributes, for example, Modernizr does not somehow automatically add that ability to your browser. That is not possible. It simply lets you as the developer know with what you can work.

Do it for the right reasons

There are some web developers using Modernizr because they read in an article somewhere that they were supposed to use it. That is fine, but you are smarter than they are. You see how detecting these abilities in the browser better informs you of how to serve accessible experiences if a browser does not natively support certain attributes. Clever and handsome you are!

See also

For further reading, author Gil Fink wrote the simple but concise *"Detecting HTML5 Features Using Modernizr"* article for Microsoft at `http://blogs.microsoft.co.il/blogs/gilf/archive/2011/01/09/detecting-html5-features-using-modernizr.aspx`.

Adding skip navigation

The ability to skip repeated elements like navigation is beneficial to those who use screen readers. Imagine when visiting a website, you read every single navigation element before you could proceed to the main content. That would be annoying, wouldn't it? Well, it can be for those using screen readers too. Let us take a look at an easy way to not annoy a part of our audience.

Getting ready

What we are going to do in this example is create a simple but special invisible anchor that will give our screen reader friends the option to skip over our navigation and get right to the good stuff: our site content.

How to do it...

If you have been around HTML for a while, you have no doubt created a skip navigation at some point. It probably looked something like this:

```
<a class="skip" href="#content">Skipnav</a>
```

Your CSS would include something like this to make the anchor invisible:

```
.skip {display: none}
```

The first `div` that contained your primary content then included another invisible anchor that looked something like this:

```
<h2><a name="content"></a></h2>
```

That was all well and good for years. It worked just fine. And it should work in HTML5 too, right? Well, guess what? It does not. Let us take a look at why.

How it works...

In HTML5, the `name` attribute for anchor tags is no longer valid. Remember all that stuff I said in the first chapter about the approach to creating the HTML5 spec is to "pave the cowpaths?" Well, not this time. This time the cowpath has been removed. So here is what we are going to do about it for now:

We will keep the initial bit of markup:

```
<a class="skip" href="#content">Skipnav</a>
```

And we will keep that bit of CSS that hides the anchor:

```
.skip {display: none}
```

But here is what we are going to do differently with that second bit of markup:

```
<h2 id="content"></h2>
```

When we removed the anchor, we renamed the `name` attribute it had from an `ID` and added it to the `h2` instead. Now it works and is valid in the HTML5 spec. Easy!

There's more...

The ability to skip navigation is one of the most common—and easy to accomplish—things we developers can do to support our differently abled audiences. Consider revisiting old sites you have developed, updating (or adding) the skip navigation, switch the `DOCTYPE` to HTML5, and you are well on your way to using the latest technologies while still supporting accessibility.

Full browser support

Skip navigation is one change that is fortunately supported by all major web browsers. The author does not get to say that very often in a book like this, so this is quite a relief!

Less equals more

In the near future when screen readers are updated, instead of creating the ability to skip navigation via an explicit link, we will be able to use Web Accessibility Initiative-Accessible Rich Internet Applications roles and use the new `nav` element to achieve the same thing. Less markup equals more gooder!

The Web Standards Project site at `http://webstandards.org` takes an interesting approach by only displaying the skip `nav` when the sighted user hovers over it.

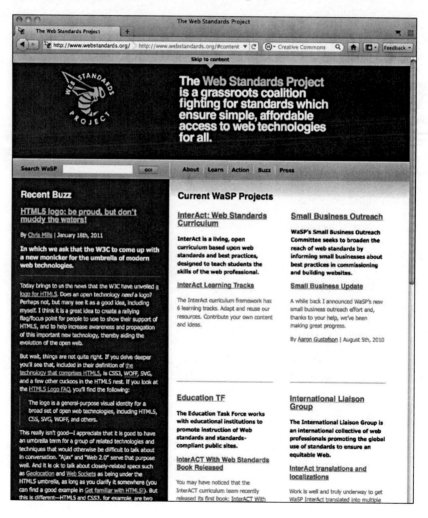

See also

`http://html5accessibility.com` is a terrific resource, providing information about which new HTML5 elements are accessibly supported in web browsers as well as for those who use assistive technologies.

Adding meta tags

"A language tag identifies a natural language spoken, written, or otherwise conveyed by human beings for communication of information to other human beings. Computer languages are explicitly excluded. HTTP uses language tags within the Accept-Language and Content- Language fields." - World Wide Web Consortium's Hypertext Transfer Protocol specification

Getting ready

If you are thinking about accessibility for your or your client's website (and you should be!) you will want to ensure that those using a screen reader are able to have your information read to them in the language(s) you intended. We are going to take a look at how to do this.

How to do it...

First, determine the language in which you want your website read. It could be English, French, Klingon, or any combination. See this list of the most popular content-languages: `http://devfiles.myopera.com/articles/554/httpheaders-contentlang-url.htm`.

How it works...

We already have an English content-language meta tag in our common template:

```
<!DOCTYPE html>
<html lang="en">
<head>
  <meta charset="UTF-8">
  <title>Title</title>
  <!--[if lt IE 9]><script
    src="http://html5shiv.googlecode.com/svn/trunk/html5.js">
    </script>[endif]-->
  <script src="modernizr-1.6.min.js"></script>
</head>
```

```
<body class="no-js">
</body>
</html>
```

The simple `<html lang="en">` is all we need to ensure our site will be read in English. Changing that for other languages could not be simpler. Use `<html lang="fr">` for French and `<html lang="x-klingon">` if you are a huge Star Trek fan. Note, the `x-` prefix in the Klingon example indicates an experimental language.

There's more...

You could also specify more than one language by using something like: `<html lang="en, fr">` for both English and French. Note the use of quotes around the values since we are referencing more than one.

Whatchu talkin' 'bout?

> Note: "If no Content-Language is specified, the default is that the content is intended for all language audiences. This might mean that the sender does not consider it to be specific to any natural language, or that the sender does not know for which language it is intended." - World Wide Web Consortium's Hypertext Transfer Protocol specification

It all comes back to SEO

Specifying a content-language is also beneficial to search engines and enables them to parse our content in the language we intend. And who among us couldn't use some more search-engine optimization?

Did I do that?

If you do not specify a meta language, what is the worst that could happen? Nothing, right? Wrong. It turns out if we do not specify that meta language, old versions of our nemesis Internet Explorer will attempt to guess what language you intended. And as we have seen already, sometimes IE guesses wrong. According to this article, harmless user input can become active HTML and may execute, leading to security vulnerability: `http://code.google.com/p/doctype/wiki/ArticleUtf7`.

See also

`http://section508.gov` is the official website for the Section 508 specification of the U.S. Code. Though we web developers focus primarily on how Section 508 applies to the web, it is actually a much broader set of laws that define how those of us in the United States of America accommodate for those with different abilities both virtually and in the real world.

Using semantic descriptions in tags for screen readers

The approach of semantic web development makes sense not just for those of us who develop websites and applications and interfaces, but also for those who use and interact with those experiences we create.

Getting ready

Let's review some of the new, more-semantic tags in the HTML5 specification.

How to do it...

New HTML5 tags include:

- `<article>`
- `<aside>`
- `<audio>`
- `<canvas>`
- `<datalist>`
- `<details>`
- `<embed>` – not a new tag, but it finally validates in HTML5
- `<figcaption>`
- `<figure>`
- `<footer>`
- `<header>`
- `<hgroup>`
- `<keygen>`
- `<mark>`
- `<meter>`
- `<nav>`
- `<output>`
- `<progress>`
- `<rp>`
- `<rt>`
- `<ruby>`

- `<section>`
- `<source>`
- `<summary>`
- `<time>`
- `<video>`
- `<wbr>`

How it works...

Of that list, the following new tags can support text:

- `<article>`
- `<aside>`
- `<datalist>`
- `<details>`
- `<figcaption>`
- `<figure>`
- `<footer>`
- `<header>`
- `<hgroup>`
- `<keygen>`
- `<mark>`
- `<nav>`
- `<output>`
- `<section>`
- `<source>`
- `<summary>`
- `<time>`
- `<wbr>`

That list represents the vast majority of new HTML5 tags available. The simple act of using these more semantic tags will add additional meaning and intelligence to screen readers.

There's more...

The following new tags also present us with the opportunity to create richer and more semantically meaningful experiences:

- `<audio>`
- `<embed>`
- `<progress>`
- `<video>`

Always improve

Survey the projects you have already launched that had accessibility requirements. If you are still able to update them, this is a golden opportunity to revisit them to add more semantically meaningful markup. Remember: Just because a site or application or interface is already launched does not mean you cannot revisit it later. If a project was a dud when it launched, this is the perfect time to update it and then relaunch it. Who knows? It might turn into that perfect portfolio piece that could land you another job! Score!

Semantics for good SEO

Using increasingly more semantic and meaningful tags can have a benefit not just to those using screen readers, but also to search engine optimization because search engines will be able to more intelligently parse and understand your code.

Greg finally learned

Semantic web development also has a benefit to other developers. If you code an area with a `<nav>` tag, another developer currently on your team or working on your project in the future will instantly understand what your intention is. The author once worked with a developer who used nonsensical naming like `<div id="banana">` for something that had nothing to do with bananas. That developer thought it was a kind of job security by being the only one to know what certain tags meant. Unfortunately that approach became painful for him years later when editing something he had previously created, and he could not remember the meaning of it. The lesson? Do not tick your future self off!

See also

`http://caniuse.com` provides compatibility tables for HTML5, CSS3, SVG and more in both desktop and mobile browsers. The site is an invaluable aid for understanding which of the new tags can be supported. It is constantly updated and worth not only bookmarking but referring to over and over again.

Providing alternate site views

Cambridge, Massachusetts-based website developer Ethan Marcotte created an approach he refers to as "responsive web design" to support desktop computers with different sized displays as well as mobile devices—all with one code base. Though this approach is not required, it can be viewed as another step toward creating accessible experiences. Let's take a closer look at his approach.

Getting ready

Marcotte published the article in the May 25, 2010 issue of A List Apart at: `http://alistapart.com/articles/responsive-web-design`. Reading the article will give you a head start toward understanding the rest of this section.

How to do it...

Let's take a close look at Jon Hicks' portfolio at `http://hicksdesign.co.uk` for a spectacular example of Marcotte's approach at work.

Hicks' portfolio seen at full width on a 27" monitor.

Resizing the window causes the site to collapse from four to three columns:

Resizing the window further causes the site to collapse from three to two columns:

Resizing the window even further causes the site to collapse from two to one column:

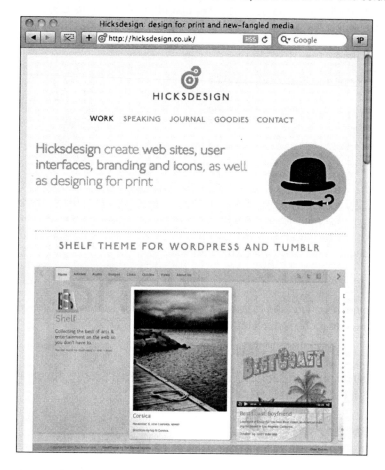

How it works...

By using a flexible grid as well as `min-width` and `max-width` values in his stylesheet, Hicks creates an experience that adjusts to different display sizes with ease. Let's take a look at how it is done.

There's more...

This new way of flexible front-end web development allows us to create experiences that work despite the device resolution. Thanks to Marcotte, we are no longer forced to create separate experiences for every device. Current status: Code once, display everywhere.

We start with a fluid grid with columns that can adapt to whatever screen space is available, flexible images, and letting media queries serve up unique stylesheets depending on the resolution and viewport.

Here is a sample media query:

```
@media screen and (max-width: 600px) {
    body {
        font-size: 80%;
    }
    #content-main {float: none; width: 100%;}
}
```

You can easily see we are saying that when the device has a maximum width of 600 pixels, we are telling the `body` to display fonts at 80% of their height. We also specify the content-main `div` will be a single column with 100% width. If the device's maximum width is 601 pixels or more, these rules will be ignored. Note that since this media query specifies the screen, if the user prints the page, these rules will be ignored also.

Min-width

As you can imagine, if we are able to specify styles for narrow widths like this, you can also specify other styles for much wider widths, such as:

```
@media screen and (min-width: 1024px)
```

Notice we are still targeting the screen in our media query, but now we are saying to apply some styles only if the viewport is *larger* than 1024 pixels.

My math teacher was right

Those who are used to working with a rigid, fixed grid layout system like Grid960 may find using a flexible grid a mental challenge at first. As Marcotte explains:

> "Every aspect of the grid—and the elements laid upon it—can be expressed as a proportion relative to its container."

We can convert our pixel-based widths into percentages in order to keep our proportions intact no matter the size displayed. Let us start with an easy example: Let us say our `header` is 600 pixels wide and we want to display it on a device that is 1200 pixels wide. If the equation is target ÷ context = result, then 600 ÷ 1200 = .5. Our CSS would look like this:

```
header {width: 50%; /* 600px / 1200px = .5 */}
```

That was easy. But what if you want to display a different `header` at 510 pixels wide in a 960 pixel width? Simple division leaves us with this: 510 ÷ 960 = .53125. We can adjust our CSS this way:

```
header {width: 53.125%; /* 510px / 960px = .53125 */}
```

Repeat this process by defining each of your widths as a part of the overall whole and you will be well on your way toward a responsive display for many devices.

Is bigger always better?

Fluid images are even easier because there is no math to do. Instead, simply include:

```
img {max-width: 100%;}
```

in your stylesheet and those images will never escape the width of your display or device.

Putting these three techniques together can create a virtually seamless site experience for users on multiple platforms, browsers, and even screen readers.

See also

In 2011, Marcotte published the authoritative book on the subject of Responsive Web Design at `http://books.alistapart.com/products/responsive-web-design`.

Using hgroup to create accessible header areas

Remember `hgroup`s? Sure you do. We looked at those in a previous chapter as a way to group related heading tags logically. Now, we will look at how that new HTML5 element can have added accessibility benefits.

Getting ready

Previously, we looked at Roxane's portfolio as an example:

```
<!DOCTYPE html>
<html lang="en">
<head>
  <meta charset="UTF-8">
  <title>Roxane</title>
  <!--[if lt IE 9]><script
    src="http://html5shiv.googlecode.com/svn/trunk/html5.js">
    </script>[endif]-->
</head>
```

```
<body>
  <header>
    <hgroup>
      <h1>Roxane is my name.</h1>
      <h2>Developing websites is my game.</h2>
    </hgroup>
  </header>
</body>
</html>
```

In the past, we might have coded the body area of her site this way:

```
<body>
  <div>
    <div>
      <h1>Roxane is my name.</h1>
      <h2>Developing websites is my game.</h2>
    </div>
  </div>
</body>
```

How to do it...

To a screen reader, the outdated second example is semantically meaningless. It does not know that those heading tags are related in any way other than being in the same `div`.

How it works...

Now, thanks to the WHATWG's HTML5 Draft Standard at `http://whatwg.org/html5` we—and screen readers—understand that the `hgroup` is a grouping of related headings. So what, you ask? If you could not rely on sight to know those headings were related, wouldn't you want some other mechanism—like a screen reader—to let you know they are?

See also

`http://diveintoaccessibility.org` is terrific 30-day step-by-step resource to learning more about Section 508 and accessibility standards. Author Mark Pilgrim (also author of *Dive Into HTML5* at `http://diveintohtml5.org`) provides easy to understand tips by person, disability, design principle, web browser, and publishing tool. The site is a few years old, but because accessibility standards have not changed that much over the years, it is still an invaluable free resource.

Displaying alternate content for non-supported browsers

Some of the new HTML5 elements are so new that not all desktop browsers support them yet. So how can we assume all screen readers will support them?

Getting ready

Fortunately we can rest assured that screen readers will support common text tags such as:

- `<h1>`
- `<h2>`
- `<h3>`
- `<h4>`
- `<h5>`
- `<h6>`
- `<p>`
- `<ul>`
- `<ol>`
- `<li>`
- `<dl>`
- `<dt>`
- `<dd>`

and more as intended. But what about those new HTML5 elements such as:

- `<article>`
- `<aside>`
- `<audio>`
- `<canvas>`
- `<datalist>`
- `<details>`
- `<figcaption>`
- `<figure>`
- `<footer>`
- `<header>`
- `<hgroup>`

- `<mark>`
- `<meter>`
- `<nav>`
- `<output>`
- `<progress>`
- `<section>`
- `<summary>`
- `<time>`
- `<video>`

Are those going to convey the meaning to the user as we intend? If so, terrific. But if not, what information does the user get? Is it meaningful at all? Certainly we would agree the last thing we would want is to provide less meaning through our new tags. Even the blind could see that would be an epic fail.

How to do it...

At the time of this writing, many HTML5 elements provide at least the same amount of semantic information as a `div` to a screen reader. Let us look at each new element more specifically:

- `<article>` – same semantic information as a `div`.
- `<aside>` – same semantic information as a `div`.
- `<details>` – same semantic information as a `div`.
- `<figcaption>` – same semantic information as a `div`.
- `<figure>` – same semantic information as a `div`.
- `<footer>` – same semantic information as a `div`.
- `<header>` – same semantic information as a `div`.
- `<hgroup>` – same semantic information as a `div`.
- `<meter>` – same semantic information as a `div`.
- `<nav>` – same semantic information as a `div`.
- `<output>` – same semantic information as a `div`.
- `<progress>` – same semantic information as a `div`.
- `<section>` – same semantic information as a `div`.
- `<summary>` – same semantic information as a `div`.

For other new HTML5 elements however, their meaning is not so clear to a screen reader:

- ▶ `<audio>` – semantic information seems consistent but Firefox has a problem with built-in slider controls, Internet Explorer 9 has only partial play/pause support, and Opera has good keyboard support but no actual assistive technology support.

- ▶ `<canvas>` – provides virtually no usable semantic information to assistive technologies. Extreme caution must be used by anyone relying on the new HTML `<canvas>` element to convey information. Using it intentionally leaves members of the audience at the door, unable to get in.

- ▶ `<datalist>` – keyboard accessible only in Opera.

- ▶ `<mark>` – provides no additional semantic information.

- ▶ `<time>` – buggy keyboard accessibility only in Opera.

- ▶ `<video>` – semantic information seems consistent, but Firefox has a problem with built-in slider controls, Internet Explorer 9 has only partial play/pause support, and Opera has good keyboard support but no actual assistive technology support.

How it works...

For now, until screen readers can catch up to all the new HTML5 elements, care must be taken when deciding which of these new tags we intend to use and what meaning we intend to convey with them to those using assistive technologies.

See also

Emily Lewis is excited not just about HTML and CSS, but usability, semantics, and accessibility too. She is the kind of passionate advocate we need more of for the front-end web development world to thrive. See her excellent "Web Accessibility and WAI-ARIA Primer" for information on how to get started thinking about the future of accessibility at `http://msdn.microsoft.com/en-us/scriptjunkie/ff743762.aspx`.

Using WAI-ARIA

Through the use of technology, we have developed methods to update information in the browser window dynamically without manually refreshing the page from the server. For a person gifted with sight, this a boon, retrieving information quicker and in a more useful way. But what happens when a person cannot see? How will they know information on the page has been updated in any way without refreshing the page, redisplaying its contents, and having the assistive technology read it to them again in its entirety?

Getting ready

Accessible Rich Internet Applications (WAI-ARIA) is an emerging technical specification that, like many of HTML5's new semantic tags, forces us to really think about our content and how we want to present it to our audiences. We can use WAI-ARIA to define roles, properties, and states to help us define what our elements are supposed to do.

The WAI-ARIA Overview at `http://w3.org/WAI/intro/aria`, based on Marcotte's Responsive Web Design approach.

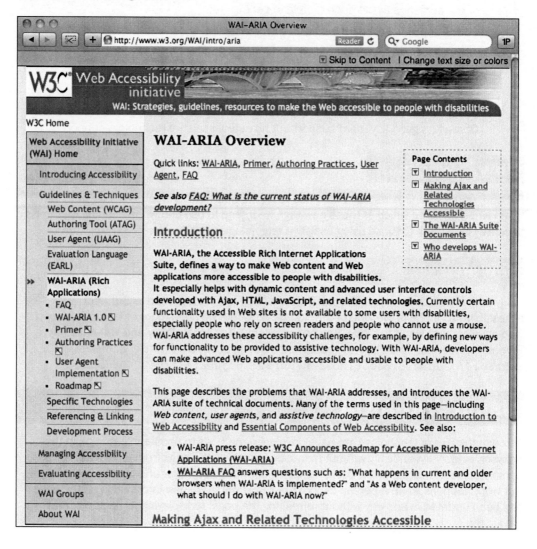

How to do it...

Remember how we included the new HTML5 `nav` element on Roxane's portfolio? Here is how we can use WAI-ARIA to add additional meaning:

```html
<!DOCTYPE html>
<html lang="en">
<head>
  <meta charset="UTF-8">
  <title>Roxane</title>
  <!--[if lt IE 9]><script
    src="http://html5shiv.googlecode.com/svn/trunk/html5.js">
    </script>[endif]-->
</head>
<body>
  <header>
    <hgroup>
      <h1>Roxane is my name.</h1>
      <h2>Developing websites is my game.</h2>
    </hgroup>
  </header>
  <nav role="navigation">
    <ul>
      <li><a href="#About">About</a></li>
      <li><a href="#Work">Work</a></li>
      <li><a href="#Contact">Contact</a></li>
    </ul>
  </nav>
</body>
</html>
```

Because not every browser understands the `nav` tag, not every browser will understand its role either. WAI-ARIA provides us with the method to do so. That `role="navigation"` is named a "landmark role", and does for a non-sighted person what an actual landmark does for a sighted person in the real world: It lets them know where they are.

How it works...

Now, even those without site can be made aware when something on the page changes via these landmark roles. WAI-ARIA informs the user of those dynamic page changes by "watching" for updates. Instead of re-reading the entire screen, only the new information is presented.

e's more...

allows us to create the complex, data-driven objects like pulldown menus, tabs,
ile trees, and more that sighted users have become used to over the years and
through the use of these roles that even those who cannot see the content as it
s will be notified that it has done so.

Still awaiting browser support

There is always a catch, right? The catch in this case is that, like many of the other HTML5
features described in this book, WAI-ARIA is not fully supported by all assistive-technology
browsers. No matter how diligent and well-meaning we as developers are, if members of our
target audience do not have the latest browsers with WAI-ARIA support, they will not receive
the information we desire them to have.

That's how I role

There is another catch: Using WAI-ARIA incorrectly can actually make the situation worse.
If a lesser developer than you assigned `role="navigation"` to some content that was
frequently updated but gave the user the ability to skip the navigation, that user would never
know information was being updated. Luckily that would probably never happen to you
because you would have caught that mistake in a peer code review. With great power
comes great responsibility.

Accessibility first

If you have a website under development and you have to support differently abled people,
great care must be taken from the initial kickoff meeting to ensure their needs are being met.
The most accessibly successful projects are ones that take people's needs into consideration
from the outset. Trying to glom a set of features on at the end is just another way of setting
yourself—and your project—up to fail. We either set people and projects up to succeed, or we
set them up to fail. Which will you do?

See also

For further reading on how to use WAI-ARIA to build a more accessible web, see this excellent
WebMonkey article by Scott Gilbertson: `http://webmonkey.com/2010/11/can-wai-aria-build-a-more-accessible-web`.

Gilbertson was on a roll by later penning a terrific resource for styling websites using the
ARIA roles at: `http://webmonkey.com/2011/01/styling-webpages-with-arias-landmark-roles`.

5

Learning to Love Forms

In this chapter, we will cover:

- ▶ Displaying placeholder text
- ▶ Adding autofocus to form fields
- ▶ Styling forms using HTML5 and CSS3
- ▶ Using the email input type
- ▶ Adding a URL using the URL input type
- ▶ Using the number tag
- ▶ Using the range tag
- ▶ Creating a search field
- ▶ Creating a picker to display date and time

Introduction

"We have met the enemy and he is us." – Pogo

Boring. Tedious. Mindless. Why do web users' eyes glaze over and minds go numb when presented with an interactive form online? This author believes at least part of the problem lies with the information architect who arranged the form fields and—to a lesser degree—with the front-end developer who coded it.

Admittedly, forms aren't sexy. But if you're a web developer (and chances are, if you're reading this, you are) then odds are at some point in your career you were asked to mark up and style some sort of form. If you dreaded coding that form, imagine the amount of dread you aided in creating in your user. That ends now.

You're mature and seeking new challenges worthy of that maturity. And if we can stop worrying and learn to love the form, the odds are better that our audiences will actually enjoy them too.

In this chapter we'll look at real-life examples of how HTML5 is used for interactive forms, including displaying placeholder text, adding autofocus to form fields, styling forms using HTML5 and CSS3, using the e-mail input type, adding a URL using the URL input type, using the number tag, using the range tag, creating a search field, and creating a picker to display date and time.

Now let's get cooking!

Displaying placeholder text

The first new HTML5 form ability we want to check out is the native ability to display placeholder text.

How to do it...

We have all used—and even created—form placeholder text before. But now with HTML5 we're going to do it a bit differently and more efficiently. The Packt Publishing website features the ability to search the entire site or search only book/eBooks.

Once the user clicks on one of those two form fields, the placeholder text disappears.

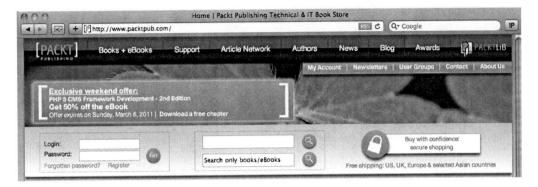

This is accomplished via a traditional method of using the value attribute to display the placeholder text:

```
<form action='/search'>
  <div id="search-site">
    <input type="text" class="form-text" name='keys'
      value="Search entire site" onclick='clearIf(this, "Search
      entire site")'/>
  </div>
  <div id="search-button-site">
    <input type="image"
      src="/sites/all/themes/pixture_reloaded/images/pp/search-
      button.png">
  </div>
</form>
<form action='/books'>
  <div id="search-books">
    <input type="text" class="form-text" name='keys' value="Search
      only books/eBooks" onclick='clearIf(this, "Search only
      books/eBooks")'/>
  </div>
  <div id="search-button-books">
    <input type="image"
      src="/sites/all/themes/pixture_reloaded/images/pp/search-
      button.png">
  </div>
</form>
```

Using the `placeholder` attribute instead of `value` results in:

```html
<form action='/search'>
  <div id="search-site">
    <input type="text" class="form-text" name='keys'
    placeholder="Search entire site" onclick='clearIf(this, "Search
    entire site")'/>
  </div>
  <div id="search-button-site">
    <input type="image"
      src="/sites/all/themes/pixture_reloaded/images/pp/search-
      button.png">
  </div>
</form>
<form action='/books'>
  <div id="search-books">
    <input type="text" class="form-text" name='keys'
    placeholder="Search only books/eBooks" onclick='clearIf(this,
    "Search only books/eBooks")'/>
  </div>
  <div id="search-button-books">
    <input type="image"
      src="/sites/all/themes/pixture_reloaded/images/pp/search-
      button.png">
  </div>
</form>
```

How it works...

The `placeholder` attribute can take the place of the `value` attribute to display placeholder text in a form. In this case, developers added an `onclick` event handler to accommodate older browsers. This is another case of superior semantics adding additional meaning to a tag.

There's more...

Remember—and plan for—the fact that the placeholder text itself will disappear when the user clicks into each form field. If the user clicks away without filling out the form field, the `placeholder` will reappear.

Text only

The `placeholder` attribute can contain only text. We cannot include additional markup, images, or any other element there.

Embrace italics

By default, the placeholder text will appear in italics. There's no good way to change this, unfortunately. Rather than beat your head against the wall, know this up front and convince your designer that text *should* be italics and have that person concentrate and focus on things that really matter.

Browser support

Web browsers that support the new `placeholder` attribute.

Apple Safari 4+   Google Chrome 4+   Mozilla Firefox 3.7+

See also

Build Guild is monthly gathering of web people around the nation. Built with HTML5 (and using the placeholder attribute!) at `http://buildguild.org`, developers can get together and chat over drinks every few weeks. There are already local chapters in cities such as: Abilene, TX; Albany, NY; Billings, MT; Grand Rapids, MI; Hartford, CT; Louisville, KY; Milwaukee, WI; New York City, NY; Philadelphia, PA; Pittsburgh, PA; Saint Louis, MO; Salem, MA.

If there isn't a Build Guild in your area yet, create one! Contact the site owners at `http://buildguild.org` about getting started! Mustaches optional.

Adding autofocus to form fields

In the past, we have had to rely on JavaScript to add input focus to specific form fields, but not anymore! Now we have the ability to do it natively in HTML5!

How to do it...

Ally Creative at `http://allycreative.net/contact` effectively uses the `autofocus` ability in their contact form.

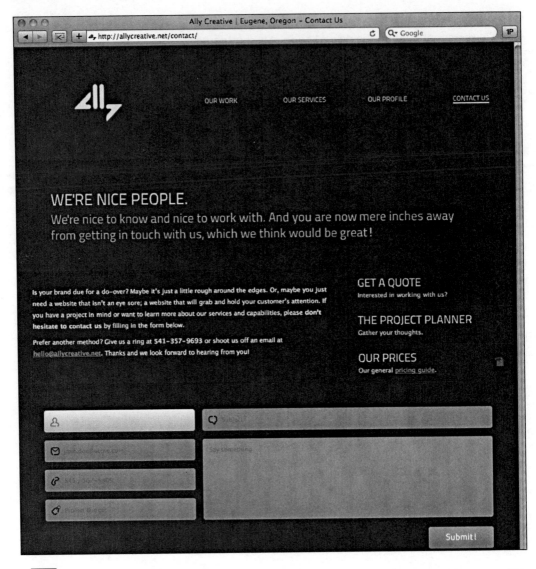

How it works...

Here's how they did it:

```
<form action="" method="post">
  <ol id="left">
    <li>
      <label for="contact-name" class="label-fade">Jane Doe of ACME
        Corporation</label>
      <input type="text" id="contact-name" name="contact-name"
        title="Name / Business" autofocus /></li>
    <li>
      <label for="contact-mail" class="label-
        fade">jane.doe@acme.com</label>
      <input type="text" id="contact-mail" name="contact-mail"
        title="E-mail Addy" /></li>
    <li>
      <label for="contact-phone" class="label-fade">541 / 567-
        5309</label>
      <input type="text" id="contact-phone" name="contact-phone"
        title="Phone Number" /></li>
    <li>
      <label for="contact-budget" class="label-fade">Project
        Budget</label>
      <input type="text" id="contact-budget" name="contact-budget"
        title="Budget" /></li>
    <li><input type="hidden" id="contact-human" name="contact-human"
      title="Human" /></li>
  </ol>
  <ol id="right">
    <li>
      <label for="contact-subject" class="label-fade">Subject</label>
      <input type="text" id="contact-subject" name="contact-subject"
        title="Budget" /></li>
    <li>
      <label for="contact-body" id="textarea-label" class="label-
        fade">Say something.</label>
      <textarea id="contact-body" name="contact-body" title="Contact
        Copy"></textarea></li>
    <li class="f-right"><span id="required"></span> <input
      type="image" src="http://allycreative.net/images/button.png"
      id="submit-button" alt="Submit!" /></li>
  </ol>
</form>
```

Simply by applying the `autofocus` attribute to the form field for the contact name and adding an appropriate style to change the background color, developers at Ally Creative created a slick, interactive form that's easy for users to complete.

There's more...

The new HTML5 `autofocus` attribute is intended to work on all form controls. So no matter whether you are collecting a user's name, address, phone number, or some other bit of data, use the ability to `autofocus` smartly!

One per page

Remember that you can only set one form field per page to `autofocus`.

Older browsers

In a moment, you'll see only two modern browsers currently support `autofocus`. Luckily, older browsers simply ignore the attribute. Consider tools like `autofocus` as enriching the user experience for those who can see it without harming or degrading the user experience for those using lesser browsers. No harm, no foul.

Browser support

Web browsers that support the new `autofocus` attribute:

Apple Safari 4+   Google Chrome 3+

See also

Mozilla's "People of HTML5" video series featured many of the leading voices of the HTML5 movement. Remy Sharpe, author of the "*HTML5 Shim*" we've examined and used elsewhere, is a JavaScript craftsman. It should come as no surprise when he described his favorite aspects of the new HTML5 specification:

"For me, the most exciting aspects of HTML5 is the depth of the JavaScript APIs. It's pretty tricky to explain to Joe Bloggs that actually this newly specced version of HTML isn't mostly HTML; it's mostly JavaScript."

Read and watch the full interview at: `http://hacks.mozilla.org/2011/01/people-of-html5-remy-sharp`.

Styling forms using HTML5 and CSS3

One of the most simple but beautiful examples of using HTML5 and CSS3 for a form the author has seen is by Canada-based FoundationSix at: `http://foundationsix.com/contact`. Here's how they did it.

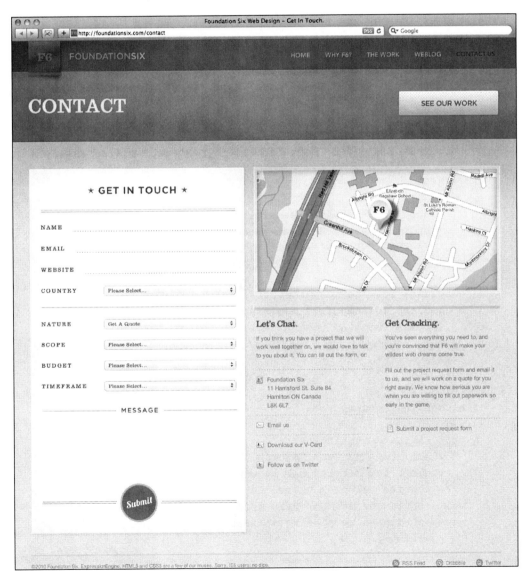

How to do it...

The team at FoundationSix starts with a fairly straightforward contact form markup. Note the lengthy country drop-down list was omitted from this example for the sake of space.

How it works...

```html
<form id="contactf6" method="post" action="http://foundationsix.com/
index.php"  enctype="multipart/form-data" >
  <fieldset id="contactinfo">
    <ul>
      <li>
        <label for="name">Name</label>
        <input id="name" name="name" type="text" class="required">
      </li>
      <li>
        <label for="email">Email</label>
        <input id="email" name="email"  type="text" class="required
          email">
      </li>
      <li>
        <label for="website">Website</label>
        <input id="website" name="website"  type="text"
          class="required">
      </li>
      <li>
        <label for="country">Country</label>
        <select id="country" name="country" class="selectors">
        <option selected value="">Please Select...</option>
        </select>
      </li>
    </ul>
  </fieldset>
  <fieldset id="natureinfo">
    <ul>
      <li class="selectli">
        <label for="nature">Nature</label>
        <select id="nature" name="nature" class="selectors">
          <option selected value="Get A Quote">Get A Quote</option>
          <option value="Get More Info">Get More Info</option>
          <option value="Say Hello">Say Hello</option>
        </select>
      </li>
      <li class="selectli showmore">
```

```
      <label for="scope">Scope</label>
      <select id="scope" name="scope" class="selectors">
        <option selected value="">Please Select...</option>
        <option value="Complete Website Design">Complete Website
          Design</option>
        <option value="Design Only">Design Only</option>
        <option value="Coding Only">HTML / CSS Coding Only</option>
        <option value="Other">Other</option>
      </select>
    </li>
    <li class="selectli showmore">
      <label for="budget">Budget</label>
      <select id="budget" name="budget" class="selectors">
        <option selected value="">Please Select...</option>
        <option value="$2,500-$5,000">$2,500-$5,000</option>
        <option value="$5,000-$7,500">$5,000-$7,500</option>
        <option value="$7,500-$10,000">$7,500-$10,000</option>
        <option value="$10,000-$15,000">$10,000-$15,000</option>
        <option value="$15,000-$20,000">$15,000-$20,000</option>
        <option value="$20,000-$50,000">$20,000-$50,000</option>
        <option value="$50,000+">$50,000+</option>
      </select>
    </li>
    <li class="selectli showmore">
      <label for="timeframe">Timeframe</label>
      <select id="timeframe" name="timeframe" class="selectors">
        <option selected value="">Please Select...</option>
        <option value="Right Away">Right Away</option>
        <option value="Within 1 Month">Within 1 Month</option>
        <option value="Within 2 Months">Within 2 Months</option>
        <option value="Within 3 Months">Within 3 Months</option>
        <option value="Within 6 Months">Within 6 Months</option>
        <option value="Don't Know Yet">Don't Know Yet</option>
      </select>
    </li>
  </ul>
</fieldset>
<fieldset id="message">
  <ul>
    <li>
      <label for="messagetext">Message</label>
      <textarea id="messagetext" name="message"></textarea>
    </li>
  </ul>
```

```
    </fieldset>
    <div id="submitbutton"><input type="submit" name="submit"></div>
  </form>
```

The team provides a special stylesheet just for this contact page. Notice how clean it is, defining only the necessary values while omitting any cruft.

```
html {
  background: url(../img/sitebg.jpg) repeat; -webkit-font-smoothing:
    antialiased;
}
body {
  color: #8a8a8a; font: 13px/19px "Helvetica Neue", Arial, Helvetica,
    Geneva, sans-serif; background: url(../img/subbg.jpg) repeat-x;
}

#contactform {
  float: left; width: 498px; margin-bottom: 40px;
}
#formtop {
  height: 97px; width: 498px; background: url(../img/formtop.png)
    no-repeat;
}
#formtop h1 {
  text-indent: -9999px; width: 445px; height: 57px; margin: 0 auto;
    background: url(../img/formheader.png) no-repeat; position:
    relative; top: 39px;
}
#formcontent {
  background-image: url(../img/formrepeat.png); width: 498px;
    background-position: 1px;
}
form {
  width: 445px; margin: 0 auto;
}
form label {
  font: 13px "ClarendonRoman", Georgia, Times, serif; color: #525250;
    letter-spacing: 2px; text-transform: uppercase; float: left;
    position: relative; top: 4px;
}
form label.error {
  text-transform: none; letter-spacing: 0; color: #a21714;
    font: 15px "SeanRegular", Courier New, Courier New, Courier6,
    monospace; margin-top: -10px; clear: both; padding: 0px 0px 10px
    21px; background: url(../img/errow.png) no-repeat 0 0;
}
```

```
form ul {
  padding-top: 10px;
}
form ul li {
  padding-top: 10px; clear: both; overflow: hidden;
}
form ul li.selectli {
  padding-bottom: 10px;
}
form select, form input {
  float: right;
}
form input {
  border-bottom: 1px dashed #989895; border-right: none; border-left:
    none; border-top: none; color: #4f4f4f; background: none;
    outline: none; position: relative; bottom: 13px;
    font: 16px "SeanRegular", Courier New, Courier New, Courier6,
    monospace; letter-spacing: 1px;
}
form input:focus {
  border-bottom: 1px dashed #000; -webkit-transition:border 0.3s
    ease-in; -moz-transition:border 0.3s ease-in;
    -o-transition:border 0.3s ease-in; transition:border 0.3s
    ease-in;
}
form select {
  width: 300px;
}
input#name {
  width: 370px;
}
input#email {
  width: 360px;
}
input#website {
  width: 340px;
}
fieldset#contactinfo {
  padding-bottom: 23px; border-bottom: 1px solid #a7a7a4;
}
fieldset#natureinfo {
  margin-top: 4px;
}
fieldset#message {
  background: url(../img/messagebar.png) top no-repeat; width: 445;
```

```
        margin-top: 25px;
}
fieldset#message label {
  display: none;
}
textarea#messagetext {
    margin-top: 4px; width: 445px; height: 150px; border: none;
        background: none; outline: none; resize: none; overflow: auto;
        color: #4f4f4f; font: 16px "SeanRegular", Courier New,
        Courier New, Courier6, monospace; letter-spacing: 1px;
        float: left; display: block;
}
#submitbutton {
  float: right;
}
#submitbutton input {
    cursor: pointer; background: url(../img/submit.png) no-repeat;
        width: 445px; height: 86px; border: none; text-indent: -9999px;
        position: relative; bottom: 10px;
}
#submitbutton input:hover {
  background-position: 0 -86px;
}
span#formbottom {
    background: url(../img/formbottom.png) no-repeat; width: 498px;
        height: 108px; display: block;
}


#othercontact {
    float: right; width: 566px; margin-bottom: 40px;
}
#map {
    width: 552px; height: 269px; background: url(../img/map.jpg) center
        no-repeat rgb(233,233,228); background: url(../img/map.jpg)
        center no-repeat rgba(255,255,255,0.3); padding: 6px;
        border: 1px solid rgb(249,249,248); border: 1px solid
        rgba(255,255,255,0.7); margin-bottom: 28px; position: relative;
}
span#mappointer {
    width: 77px; height: 80px; display: block; position: absolute; top:
        66px; left: 257px; background-image: url(../img/map-pin.png);
}
section.subcontact {
    float: left; width: 267px; position: relative; padding-left: 3px;
        border-top: 6px solid #d3d2c5; -webkit-transition:border 0.4s
        ease-in; -moz-transition:border 0.4s ease-in;
```

```
      -o-transition:border 0.4s ease-in; transition:border 0.4s
      ease-in;
  }
section.subcontact:hover {
    border-top: 6px solid #cc7b58; -webkit-transition:border 0.3s
      ease-in; -moz-transition:border 0.3s ease-in;
      -o-transition:border 0.3s ease-in; transition:border 0.3s
      ease-in;
  }
section.subcontact h2 {
    padding-top: 17px; color: #5a5a5a; font: 20px "ClarendonRoman",
      Georgia, Times, serif; margin-bottom: 10px;
      letter-spacing: -0.05em;
  }
section.subcontact p {
    margin-bottom: 16px; width: 260px;
  }
section.subcontact.subright {
    position: relative; left: 25px;
  }
ul.iconlist {
    padding-top: 6px;
  }
ul.iconlist li {
    padding: 12px 25px; border-top: 1px dashed #b2b2ab;
  }

li#mapicon {
    background: url(../img/icons/map.png) no-repeat 0 14px;
  }
li#emailicon {
    background: url(../img/icons/mail.png) no-repeat 0 13px;
  }
li#vcardicon {
    background: url(../img/icons/card.png) no-repeat 0 13px;
  }
li#twittericon {
    background: url(../img/icons/twitter.png) no-repeat 0 13px;
  }
li#docicon {
    background: url(../img/icons/doc.png) no-repeat 3px 13px;
  }
```

There's more...

For the most part, adding Cascading Style Sheets to HTML5 is just like adding CSS to XHTML or previous versions of HTML. It's just that now we have additional tags of which to keep track.

 Remember that HTML5 and CSS3 are two different things. People often lump them together—just like they did with the term "Web 2.0" until that term finally lost all its meaning (if indeed it ever had any). Will we abuse the term "HTML5" so badly that it eventually loses all meaning? Or has it already happened? Only you can prevent forest fires.

Older browsers

We do need to be mindful of two things when styling HTML5:

1. How to style new elements when they are not supported by all browsers yet.
2. What the fallback looks like when a new HTML5 element is not supported in any given browser.

Test, test, test

When styling HTML5, the key is to test, test, test in browsers. For the good of our clients and the good of web development as a whole, we are compelled to understand what happens in browsers and adjust based on what we experience.

About pseudo classes

CSS3 offers a few new pseudo classes used to differentiate required form fields from ones that aren't. We'll tie these in with built-in HTML5 form validation:

- `:required` – lets us style fields based on what's required or not
- `:optional` – lets us style fields based on what's required or not
- `:valid` – will work with form validation
- `:invalid` – will work with form validation
- `:in-range` – works with minimum and maximum characters like a phone number
- `:out-of-range` – works with minimum and maximum characters like a phone number

See also

If you'd like to play with the ability to use CSS3 to style HTML5, the folks at Blue Griffon created `http://bluegriffon.org`, a new What-You-See-Is-What-You-Get content editor for the web. Available in multiple languages, the tool allows users to work with web standards without having to think about code too much.

Using the e-mail input type

One of the many new input types that HTML5 supports is `email`. How many times have you built a form using `<input type="text" />` intending to collect an e-mail address? Now we can use something much more semantically correct! Later, we'll see how this supports form validation as well.

How to do it...

The previous FoundationSix example could be easily converted to this new input type. Instead of:

```
<li>
  <label for="email">Email</label>
  <input id="email" name="email"  type="text" class="required email">
</li>
```

We could simply change the input type and end up with:

```
<li>
  <label for="email">Email</label>
  <input id="email" name="email"  type="email"
    class="required email">
</li>
```

Visually, the `<input type="email" />` tag looks identical to `<input type="text" />`. The difference is what the browser does with the information.

How it works...

Changing the type from `"text"` to `"email"` allows newer browsers to validate whether what the user has input is actually a valid e-mail address. Note that the server can't determine whether the email account is active, only if the address itself is well formed.

There's more...

So what happens if the e-mail address submitted isn't valid? The truth is the jury is still out. The Opera browser has an experimental error message, and Firefox has its own experimental add-on. Unfortunately this is a gray area with which we're going to have to be patient until browsers handle it in a consistent manner.

Browser support

But here's the cool thing about `<input type="email" />`: Browsers support it! Well, sort of. Even browsers that don't understand `<input type="email" />` will default back to `<input type="text" />`, so it still works. Brilliant!

No JavaScript

As we'll see in other instances, `<input type="email" />` in HTML5 allows us to stop using JavaScript hacks to achieve a similar result. We're all done using the behavior layer to make up for deficiencies in the markup or presentation layers.

Validation evolution

Form validation has evolved from the beginnings of the Internet. In the earliest days, developers were forced to use technology like CGI scripts to submit forms and completely redraw the results page. It was only then, after the page had been submitted to the server, that the user had any idea of their information was accepted. If it wasn't, they had to start over again.

After time, developers learned to use AJAX to perform client-side validation for forms. This worked but the heavy lifting fell to JavaScript. This presented challenges when JavaScript was turned off or accessibility was a requirement.

Now with HTML5, some validation can occur in the browser without sending information to the server or relying on JavaScript. Though not as robust as an AJAX solution, this type of validation traps many of the most common types of errors before they occur.

Adding a URL using the URL input type

Another of the many new input types that HTML5 supports is URL. How many times have you built a form using `<input type="text" />` intending to collect a website address? Now we can use something much more semantically correct! Later we'll see how this supports form validation as well.

How to do it...

The previous FoundationSix example could be easily converted to this new input type as well. Instead of:

```
<li>
  <label for="website">Website</label>
  <input id="website" name="website" type="text" class="required">
</li>
```

We could simply change the input type and end up with:

```
<li>
  <label for="website">Website</label>
  <input id="website" name="website"  type="URL" class="required">
</li>
```

Like `<input type="email" />` visually, the `<input type="URL" />` tag looks identical to `<input type="text" />`. Again, the difference is what the browser does with the information entered.

How it works...

Changing the type from `"text"` to `"URL"` allows newer browser to validate whether what the user has input is actually a valid website address. Note that the server can't determine whether the website is active, only if the address itself is well formed.

There's more...

So what happens if the website address submitted isn't valid? The truth is the jury is still out here too. Unfortunately this is a gray area with which we're going to have to be patient until browsers handle it in a consistent manner.

Browser support

But here's the cool thing about `<input type="URL" />`: Browsers support it! Well, sort of. Even browsers that don't understand `<input type="URL" />` will default back to `<input type="text" />`, so it still works. Brilliant!

No JavaScript

As we'll see in other instances, `<input type="URL" />` in HTML5 allows us to stop using JavaScript hacks to achieve a similar result. We're all done using the behavior layer to make up for deficiencies in the markup or presentation layers.

What's next?

As browsers evolve, in the future we may see implementations that allow browsers to do something even smarter with `<input type="URL" />`, like pre-fetching a favicon for display in a comment field. Time will tell.

See also

The band Arcade Fire teamed with film maker Chris Milk to create "The Wilderness Downtown" at `http://thewildernessdowntown.com`, an interactive online movie based on the band's song "*We Used To Wait*" entirely in HTML5 and CSS3 for the Chrome browser. The site instantly became one of the most talked-about HTML5 experiences ever created due to its use of canvas, HTML5 video, Google Maps, and so much more.

Using the number tag

HTML5 now allows users to select among a range of numbers. If, for instance, you want your viewers to make a purchase, you'll probably want them to use whole numbers. After all, who orders 2 ½ shoes?

How to do it...

If we continue the shoe-buying example, we could develop a form like this:

```
<form>
  <label>How many shoes would you like to purchase?<label>
  <input type="number" name="quantity" min="2" max="6" step="2"
    value="2" size="4" />
</form>
```

Notice that in the `input`, we have optionally specified a minimum number that can be ordered (2) and a maximum that can be ordered (6). `Step` allows us in this case to make sure users can only order shoes in pairs while `value` sets the initial number of items displayed. `Size` then controls how wide the `input` box will be.

How it works...

Specifying `<input type="number">` will display the new form control with up and down arrows, allowing the user to increase and decrease the value in the field. These are often called "spinners" or "spin boxes." You can also set the increments of this field:

How many shoes would you like to purchase? 2 ⊕

There's more...

The new `<input type="number" />` tag has uses beyond online e-commerce. For instance, we could imagine a non-profit organization using it to set up a form allowing users to donate fixed amounts of money. Since organizations sometimes offer premiums for different donation amounts, the form could be created to allow input only at that those minimum increments.

Browser support

Currently `<input type="number" />` is only supported by Opera as well as Webkit-based browsers like Chrome and Safari. But here's the cool thing about `<input type="number" />`: Like `<input type="email" />` and `<input type="URL" />` other browsers support it! Well, sort of. Like those tags, even browsers that don't understand `<input type="number" />` will default back to `<input type="text" />`, so it still works. Brilliant!

No JavaScript

As we'll see in other instances, `<input type="number" />` in HTML5 allows us to stop using JavaScript hacks to achieve a similar result. We're all done using the behavior layer to make up for deficiencies in the markup or presentation layers.

Using the range tag

HTML5 now allows us to create a whole new kind of input. The range tag creates a slider control, allowing the user to choose among a range of values. This used to be difficult, but not anymore! Check it out!

How to do it...

Interestingly, we can use virtually the same code as we did in the number example, but change the input type to `"range"`. Here's how to do it:

```
<form>
  <label>How many shoes would you like to purchase?<label>
  <input type="range" name="quantity" min="2" max="6" step="2"
    value="2" />
</form>
```

Notice we can use the same optional `min`, `max`, `step`, `value`, and `size` attributes.

How it works...

Specifying `<input type="range">` will display the new form control with a slider, allowing the user to increase and decrease the value in the field:

How many shoes would you like to purchase?

There's more...

There are certainly plenty of other uses for the `<input type="range">` tag well beyond e-commerce. In fact, since we can't see the currently selected value, shopping probably isn't the best use of this new tag. The author could imagine using `<input type="range">` for a web-based music listening application where the user could visually increase or decrease the volume without having to see the specific volume number.

Use caution

Unfortunately, there's no non-JavaScript way to show the currently selected value for the range input tag. Here's hoping that as HTML5 gets further defined and more browsers support its native controls, we'll be able to better control that. Until then, use with caution.

No JavaScript

As we'll see in other instances, `<input type="range" />` in HTML5 allows us to stop using JavaScript hacks to achieve a similar result. We're all done using the behavior layer to make up for deficiencies in the markup or presentation layers.

Browser support

Like `<input type="number" />`, currently `<input type="range" />` is only supported by Opera as well as Webkit-based browsers like Chrome and Safari. But here's the cool thing about `<input type="range" />`: Like `<input type="email" />` and `<input type="URL" />` and `<input type="number" />`, other browsers support it! Well, sort of. Like those tags, even browsers that don't understand `<input type="range" />` (Firefox, I'm lookin' at you!) will default back to `<input type="text" />`, so it still works. Brilliant!

See also

Mozilla's "People of HTML5" video series featured many of the leading voices of the HTML5 movement. Author Bruce Lawson is entertainingly authoritative, especially when he skewers the use of HTML5 as a blanket term referring to related but different technologies:

> *"Clients and journalists will use 'HTML5' to mean CSS 3/video-that-runs-on-iThings/Geo-enabled applications. It's the new 'Web 2.0'. But we practitioners need to get our nomenclature straight. There are no HTML5 image transitions, just as there are no CSS semantics — and to say there are shows that you didn't get the 2001 memo about separating style and content."*

Read and watch the full interview at: `http://hacks.mozilla.org/2011/01/people-of-html5-bruce-lawson`.

Creating a search field

Another of the many new input types that HTML5 supports is `search`. How many times have you built a form using `<input type="text" />` intending to allow the user to search the site? Now we can use something much more semantic.

How to do it...

Let's build a quick search field using the placeholder attribute too. By now you're familiar with this outdated approach:

```
<form>
  <input name="something" type="text" value="keyword" />
  <input type="submit" value="Search" />
</form>
```

We've all done that a million times, right? Well, let's try this on for size instead:

```
<form>
  <input name="something" type="search" placeholder="keyword" />
  <input type="submit" value="Search" />
</form>
```

Spot the differences? Our type has changed from `text` to `search` and the placeholder text no longer uses the value tag. Makes more sense for us developers as well as search engines and assistive technologies.

How it works...

Specifying `<input type="search">` will display the new form field with rounded corners in Opera as well as Webkit-based browsers like Chrome and Safari:

There's more...

The rounded corner search box is a design approach made popular by Apple in OSX, as well as on the iPad and iPhone. Apple is slowly but surely emerging as the thought leader when it comes to the mobile experience, as well as one of the most vocal proponents of HTML5.

Why fix perfection?

Sure, it's possible to override the default rounded corner styling of the new HTML5 search field, but why? It looks so cool already!

Browser support

This has become a familiar refrain, but like `<input type="email" />` and `<input type="URL" />` and `<input type="number" />` and `<input type="range" />` you can rest assured that if a browsers doesn't natively understand `<input type="search" />` it will proceed as if `<input type="text" />` was there instead.

Search results

The new `search` specification also supports the new `results` attribute to display already searched terms in a drop-down list.

See also

Never Mind The Bullets at `http://nevermindthebullets.com` is an interactive online game built specifically to demonstrate the HTML5 and CSS3 features that Microsoft Internet Explorer 9 is capable of handling, including: @font-face; `<canvas>` animation; `<header>` and `<section>` layout; JavaScript acceleration; CSS3 2D transform; CSS3 multi-background; Editable content; `<audio>` soundtrack player; `<video>` player.

Creating a picker to display date and time

Every plane, train, and automobile rental website is going to have some sort of time/date picker. It's great to finally have a semantic method to approach this so let's look at how to create these `input` types using HTML5.

 As of this writing, only the Opera browser offers full support for each of these new `input` tags.

How to do it...

HTML5 actually has six different new `inputs` that can control date and time. Briefly, they are:

- ► `<input type="date" />`
- ► `<input type="datetime" />`
- ► `<input type="datetime-local" />`
- ► `<input type="month" />`

- ▶ `<input type="time" />`
- ▶ `<input type="week" />`

Each of these `input` types can be thought of as variations of one another. It's our job as developers to choose to the one that best fits the data you're collecting.

How it works...

For a date picker:

```
<form>
   <input type="date"/>
</form>
```

For a date/time picker:

```
<form>
   <input type="datetime"/>
</form>
```

For a local date/time picker:

```
<form>
   <input type="datetime-local"/>
</form>
```

For a month/year picker:

```
<form>
   <input type="month"/>
</form>
```

For a time picker:

```
<form>
   <input type="time"/>
</form>
```

For a week picker:

```
<form>
   <input type="week"/>
</form>
```

There's more...

You're encouraged to try each of the new calendar-based `input` tags to determine which works best for your particular website or application.

Browser support

As of this writing, only Opera offers full support for each of these new `input` tags. As time goes on, other browsers are expected to catch up. Once we have fully stylable date/time-based `input` methods, it'll be a truly happy day.

Meanwhile, those other browsers will default to displaying these `input` types as plain-text boxes. They'll still work, but they won't be as pretty as we'd like. Patience, grasshopper. Remember that we're dealing with the latest technologies—not fully baked, tried and true, approved methods.

If all else fails

User Agent Man created a great article about what to do when you need a fallback plan when these various new HTML5 `input` tags don't function the way you want or expect them to. Check out the full article at: `http://useragentman.com/blog/2010/07/27/cross-browser-html5-forms-using-modernizr-webforms2-and-html5widgets`.

See also

`Forrst.com` is a terrific online resource created by Kyle Bragger using HTML5. Forrst is a vibrant community of web developers and designers who believe they all increase their knowledge, skill and passion for the craft of website creation by sharing and constructively critiquing each other's work. We like the cut of their jib.

6
Developing Rich Media Applications Using Canvas

In this chapter, we will cover:

- ▶ Setting up the `canvas` environment
- ▶ Understanding the 2d rendering context
- ▶ Processing shapes dynamically
- ▶ Drawing borders for images using `canvas`
- ▶ Rounding corners
- ▶ Creating interactive visualizations
- ▶ Bouncing a ball
- ▶ Creating fallback content

Introduction

"I prefer drawing to talking. Drawing is faster, and leaves less room for lies."
– Le Corbusier

This might be the most experimental chapter of this entire book. In the recipes that follow, we will really push the limits of what is possible throughout this group of recipes.

Please note that over the course of time, the experimental new `canvas` element specifications are likely to change. Consider this group of recipes to be a snapshot of what is possible at the time of publication.

Putting an image on a website is so easy we take it for granted now. Through code, you simply tell the browser to display an image and, it's done. All that seems like child's play. Currently, some browsers can actually create dynamic images on the fly using the new `canvas` element. All the heavy lifting is up to JavaScript.

The cool thing with the new open-source `canvas` element is that not only can you create dynamic images on the fly, but the users' actions can create new images in real time as well—all without requiring a plugin. Sounds great, right? In many ways it is, but it also leaves our friends using assistive technologies out in the cold.

 What will happen if you're using a browser that doesn't support the new `canvas` element? Pretty much nothing. The browser just won't display it. That's why you'll need to be especially careful with this technology and not place anything inside the new `canvas` element on which your site or application absolutely depends. You must also consider fallback content.

Browsers that support `canvas` include:

| Apple Safari 3+ | Google Chrome 3+ | Microsoft Internet Explorer 9 | Mozilla Firefox 3+ | Opera 10+ |

 Before proceeding with developing with the new `canvas` element, make sure you have a good foundation of skills with HTML and JavaScript. Being comfortable with object-oriented programming sure wouldn't hurt either.

In this chapter, we'll look at real-life examples of setting up the `canvas` environment, understanding the 2d rendering context, processing shapes dynamically, drawing borders for images using `canvas`, rounding corners, creating interactive visualizations, bouncing a ball, and creating fallback content.

Now, let's get cooking!

Setting up the canvas environment

Creating the new `canvas` element is easy.

How to do it...

Check out how simple this is:

```
<!DOCTYPE html>
<html>
<head>
  <title>Canvas</title>
  <meta charset="utf-8" />
</head>
<body>
  <canvas id="FirstCanvas" width="800" height="600">
    <!-- Fallback code goes here -->
  </canvas>
</body>
</html>
```

How it works...

Of course, we can use whatever height and width dimensions we need, but that simple set of tags is what we need to start.

 You're probably thinking we could use CSS to control the height and width, but resist that temptation. Because the new `canvas` element contains a 2d rendering context, that approach can cause unpredictable behavior.

There's more...

Next, we'll call the new `canvas` element JavaScript API while calling jQuery:

```
<!DOCTYPE html>
<html>
<head>
  <title>Canvas</title>
  <meta charset="utf-8" />
  <script
    src="http://ajax.googleapis.com/ajax/libs/jquery/1/
    jquery.min.js"></script>
  <script>
```

```
    $(document).ready(function() {
    var canvas = document.getElementById("FirstCanvas");
    var ctx = canvas.getContext("2d");
    });
  </script>
</head>
<body>
  <canvas id="FirstCanvas" width="800" height="600">
    <!-- Fallback code goes here -->
  </canvas>
</body>
</html>
```

He's smart

"Let me make one thing completely clear: When you use `canvas`*, you're not drawing on the* `canvas` *element itself. Instead, you're actually drawing on the 2d rendering context, which you're accessing through the* `canvas` *element via the JavaScript API." – Rob Hawkes*

What am I sayin'?

Apple first introduced the new `canvas` element for the OSX Dashboard years ago. It was later implemented in web browsers Safari and then Chrome, with other browsers following suit. Since then it's become an official part of the HTML5 specification.

What's next for <canvas>?

Right now, we're barely scratching the surface of what the new `canvas` element can do. Now and in the future we'll use it to create animations, charts, diagrams, drawing apps, graphs, and user interfaces. What will you dream up?

See also

Developer Martin Angelov penned a great how-to guide titled, *"An HTML5 Slideshow w/ Canvas & jQuery"* for Tutorial Zine at: `http://tutorialzine.com/2010/09/html5-canvas-slideshow-jquery`. In it, Martin demonstrates how to combine the new canvas element with jQuery, the most popular JavaScript framework, to create an intensely interactive image slideshow.

Understanding the 2d rendering context

It's important to understand that the new `canvas` element is really a "surface" on which to draw bitmapped images in the browser.

How to do it...

Defining a `canvas` tag like this only tells half the story:

```
<!DOCTYPE html>
<html>
<head>
  <title>Canvas</title>
  <meta charset="utf-8" />
</head>
<body>
  <canvas id="FirstCanvas" width="800" height="600">
    <!-- Fallback code goes here -->
  </canvas>
</body>
</html>
```

How it works...

By itself that HTML5 code does nothing. We have to use JavaScript to make the Document Object Model retrieve the 2d rendering context in order to get something to happen:

```
<script>
  $(document).ready(function() {
  var canvas = document.getElementById("FirstCanvas");
  var ctx = canvas.getContext("2d");
  });
</script>
```

To be fair, that bit of JavaScript won't do anything without the `canvas` tag in the HTML either.

There's more...

You may be wondering about the name. If there's a 2d rendering context, isn't there probably a 3d rendering context too? The short answer is yes. But the more detailed answer isn't so simple.

While a 3d rendering context does exists in theory, at the time of this publication no browser supports it. So if the new `canvas` element renders in 3d but nobody sees it, did it really do anything?

You can master <canvas>

The 2d context uses a number of different drawing contexts for the new `canvas` element that use syntaxes that should look quite familiar if you're experienced with CSS and JavaScript.

X, meet Y

When drawing, remember the X and Y axis in the top left corner of your browser window. Values increase going down the page.

Respect my authority!

The World Wide Web Consortium's HTML5 `Canvas` 2d Context specification is online at: `http://dev.w3.org/html5/2dcontext`. There we can dig even deeper into information like conformance requirements, the `canvas` state, transformations, compositing, colors and styles, line styles, shadows, simple shapes, complex shapes, focus management, text, images, pixel manipulation, drawing model, examples, and more.

See also

Steve Fulton and Jeff Fulton penned the book *HTML5 Canvas* for O'Reilly Books. While this chapter will give you 30 or so pages of valuable new `canvas` element recipes, the Fulton's book weighs in at roughly 400 pages. Consider it the resource that picks up where this chapter leaves off. Check it out at: `http://oreilly.com/catalog/0636920013327`.

Processing shapes dynamically

Let's look at the JavaScript functions that allow the new `canvas` element to draw rectangles.

How to do it...

```
fillRect(x,y,width,height)
strokeRect(x,y,width,height)
```

In order:

```
fillRect(x,y,width,height)
```

draws a filled rectangle. Next,

```
strokeRect(x,y,width,height)
```

draws an outline around the rectangle.

Now, let's draw some shapes.

How it works...

We'll start with our basic `canvas` code and incorporate our new functions:

```
<!DOCTYPE html>
<html>
<head>
  <title>Canvas</title>
  <meta charset="utf-8" />
  <script
    src="http://ajax.googleapis.com/ajax/libs/jquery/1/
    jquery.min.js"></script>
  <script>
    $(document).ready(function() {
    var canvas = document.getElementById("FirstCanvas");
    var ctx = canvas.getContext("2d");
    ctx.strokeRect(10, 10, 396, 236);
    ctx.fillStyle = "red";
    ctx.fillRect(11, 11, 100, 100);
    ctx.fillStyle = "white";
    ctx.fillRect(111, 11, 34, 100);
    ctx.fillStyle = "red";
    ctx.fillRect(156, 11, 249, 100);

    ctx.fillStyle = "white";
    ctx.fillRect(11, 111, 394, 34);

    ctx.fillStyle = "red";
    ctx.fillRect(11, 145, 100, 100);
    ctx.fillStyle = "white";
    ctx.fillRect(111, 145, 34, 100);
    ctx.fillStyle = "red";
    ctx.fillRect(156, 145, 249, 100);
    });
  </script>
</head>
<body>
  <canvas id="FirstCanvas" width="416" height="256">
    <p>Flag of Denmark</p>
  </canvas>
</body>
</html>
```

What we've created resembles the flag of Denmark!

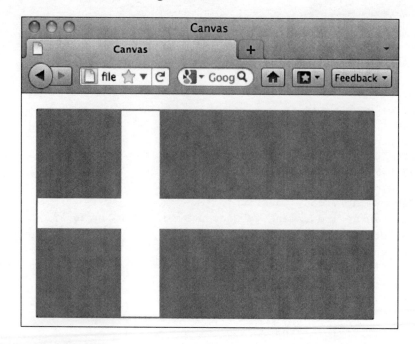

There's more...

This example may not seem overwhelming at first, but when you remember that we've created an image with hardly any HTML and no CSS whatsoever, the new `canvas` element starts to look pretty impressive.

Any way you want it

Note that while we used color names ("white" and "red") we could also use hexadecimal values or RGB or even HSL! Use whatever makes the most sense for you and your interactive project.

Similar to tables?

Think of the color and size specifications for this example almost as the old-school `tables` we used to build back in the day for layout. While certainly not the same, there are definitely similarities to that technique in this case.

Be a square first

Mastering rectangles is the first `canvas` technique that's important to have under your belt after the ability to set up the element itself. Understanding the basics of this approach will help you grasp the fundamentals of the next few recipes.

Another book weighing in at nearly 400 pages is Rob Hawkes' "*Foundation HTML5 Canvas: For Games and Entertainment*" from Friends of Ed. In it, Hawkes has created a publication for those brand new to the new `canvas` element all the way to the most seasoned expert looking to enhance skills. Sound like anyone you know? Check it out at: `http://friendsofed.com/book.html?isbn=1430232919`.

Drawing borders for images using canvas

Let's take a closer look at the super simple method of drawing borders around images using the new `canvas` element.

How to do it...

First, we'll start with our basic `canvas` code and add one new line to draw a border:

```html
<!DOCTYPE html>
<html>
<head>
  <title>Canvas</title>
  <meta charset="utf-8" />
  <script
    src="http://ajax.googleapis.com/ajax/libs/jquery/1/
    jquery.min.js"></script>
  <script>
    $(document).ready(function() {
    var canvas = document.getElementById("FirstCanvas");
    var ctx = canvas.getContext("2d");
    ctx.strokeRect(10, 20, 100, 100);
    });
  </script>
</head>
<body>
  <canvas id="FirstCanvas" width="800" height="600">
    <!-- Fallback code goes here -->
  </canvas>
</body>
</html>
```

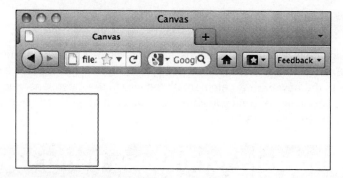

How it works...

That one line of JavaScript tells the browser to create a rectangle starting at 10 pixels from the left and 20 pixels from the top of the new `canvas` element. It draws the box 100 pixels square.

There's more...

That's nice, but if we want the border to be any other color than the default, we'll need to specify that:

```
<!DOCTYPE html>
<html>
<head>
  <title>Canvas</title>
  <meta charset="utf-8" />
  <script
    src="http://ajax.googleapis.com/ajax/libs/jquery/1/
    jquery.min.js"></script>
  <script>
    $(document).ready(function() {
    var canvas = document.getElementById("myCanvas");
    var ctx = canvas.getContext("2d");
    ctx.strokeStyle = "rgb(0, 128, 0)";
    ctx.strokeRect(10, 20, 100, 100);
    });
  </script>
</head>
<body>
  <canvas id="myCanvas" width="600" height="600">
    <!-- Fallback code goes here -->
  </canvas>
</body>
</html>
```

In this case we've used `strokeStyle` to specify an RGB color of pure green.

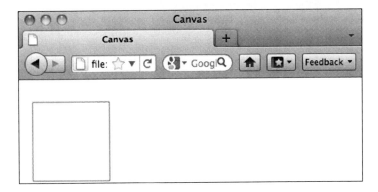

Style first

If you plan to style a border, you'll need to specify that before the border is drawn by the browser. If you specify that style afterward, the browser will simply ignore it.

Many color values work

The style attribute we just used was RGB, but the method also works with colors ("green", for example), hexadecimal values, HSL, and RGBA.

I like big borders and I cannot lie

If no border width is specified, the browser will automatically draw a one-pixel border. Here's how to change that:

```
<!DOCTYPE html>
<html>
<head>
  <title>Canvas</title>
  <meta charset="utf-8" />
  <script
    src="http://ajax.googleapis.com/ajax/libs/jquery/1/
    jquery.min.js"></script>
  <script>
    $(document).ready(function() {
    var canvas = document.getElementById("myCanvas");
    var ctx = canvas.getContext("2d");
```

```
        ctx.lineWidth = 10;
        ctx.strokeStyle = "rgb(0, 128, 0)";
        ctx.strokeRect(10, 20, 100, 100);
        });
    </script>
</head>
<body>
    <canvas id="myCanvas" width="600" height="600">
        <!-- Fallback code goes here -->
    </canvas>
</body>
</html>
```

It's just this easy:

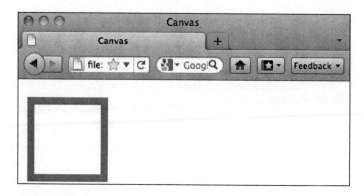

See also

`http://rgraph.net` is a graphic library specifically for the new `canvas` element. It allows you to easily create a wide variety of graph types: bar chart, bi-polar chart, donut chart, funnel chart, Gantt chart, horizontal bar chart, LED display, line chart, meter, odometer, pie chart, progress bar, rose chart, scatter graph, and traditional radar chart using HTML5, `canvas`, and JavaScript.

Rounding corners

So far we've created images and borders using square or rectangular shapes. Next we'll look at how to use the new `canvas` element to round the corners of those images and borders via JavaScript.

How to do it...

The ability to round corners is not native to `canvas` but Rob Hawkes is a super-smart guy and figured out how to make it happen. Here's what Rob did, explained at: `http://rawkes.com/blog/2010/12/11/rounded-corners-in-html5-canvas`.

```html
<!DOCTYPE html>
<html>
<head>
  <title>Canvas</title>
  <meta charset="utf-8" />
  <script
    src="http://ajax.googleapis.com/ajax/libs/jquery/1/
    jquery.min.js"></script>
  <script>
    $(document).ready(function() {
    var canvas = $("#myCanvas");
    var context = canvas.get(0).getContext("2d");

    var rectX = 10;
    var rectY = 10;
    var rectWidth = 100;
    var rectHeight = 100;
    var cornerRadius = 15;
    context.lineJoin = "round";
    context.lineWidth = cornerRadius;

    context.strokeStyle = "rgb(0, 128, 0)";
    context.strokeRect(rectX+(cornerRadius/2),
      rectY+(cornerRadius/2), rectWidth-cornerRadius,
      rectHeight-cornerRadius);
    });
  </script>
</head>
<body>
  <canvas id="myCanvas" width="600" height="600">
    <!-- Fallback code goes here -->
  </canvas>
</body>
</html>
```

How it works...

First, Rob chose a slightly different method of calling the 2d `canvas` rendering context than we did, but his method works just fine too. Check it out:

```
$(document).ready(function() {
    var canvas = $("#myCanvas");
    var context = canvas.get(0).getContext("2d");
```

The next part of Rob's code should seem quite familiar: He sets the X and Y coordinates of the image, its size, and then the border radius:

```
    var rectX = 10;
    var rectY = 10;
    var rectWidth = 100;
    var rectHeight = 100;
    var cornerRadius = 15;
```

Then Rob calls the ability to join lines and the specific border radius he wants to use. Fake it till you make it!

```
    context.lineJoin = "round";
    context.lineWidth = cornerRadius;
```

Finally there's the color of the border (still green!) and the final bit of script that ties it all together:

```
    context.strokeStyle = "rgb(0, 128, 0)";
    context.strokeRect(rectX+(cornerRadius/2), rectY+(cornerRadius/2),
        rectWidth-cornerRadius, rectHeight-cornerRadius);
```

There's more...

Now Rob—and you, if you are following along—get to be a rockstar with a beautifully rounded corner image.

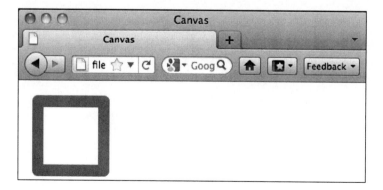

Just like the Scholastic Aptitude Tests

 Remember: `lineWidth` is to the new `canvas` element what border-radius is to CSS. The both accomplish the same thing—but by very different means.

What about IE?

It's possible to support some of the new `canvas` element's abilities in Internet Explorer 6-8 using the ExplorerCanvas library at: `http://code.google.com/p/explorercanvas`.

We're laying a foundation

For most of this chapter's group of recipes, we've only used the new `canvas` element to draw static shapes in the browser without the use of images. That may seem uneventful and perhaps even counterintuitive. The point is to give you a strong foundation with this new ability so that you can extend it to use the new `canvas` element to create games, visualize data, and allow users to draw objects dynamically.

See also

Mozilla's "People of HTML5" video series featured many of the leading voices of the HTML5 movement. John Foliot is the co-chair of the subcommittee on the accessibility of media elements in HTML5. It should come as no surprise when he laments the state of current browser support for these technologies:

> *"I think much of what HTML5 is starting to deliver will be of benefit to all users, including those using Assistive Technology. However much of what is promised is not yet supported in all browsers, and related technologies—Assistive Technologies—have a long way to come to leverage this benefit."*

Read and watch the full interview at:
`http://hacks.mozilla.org/2011/02/people-of-html5-john-foliot`.

Creating interactive visualizations

The team at Carbon Five had a daunting task: To create a physical diagram of their skills and interests. They may have started with a wall in their office, but quickly realized the new abilities the new `canvas` element brings to the table would allow interactivity and the ability to draw conclusions based on it. Here's how they did it at: `http://carbonfive.github.com/html5-playground/interest-map/interest-map.html`.

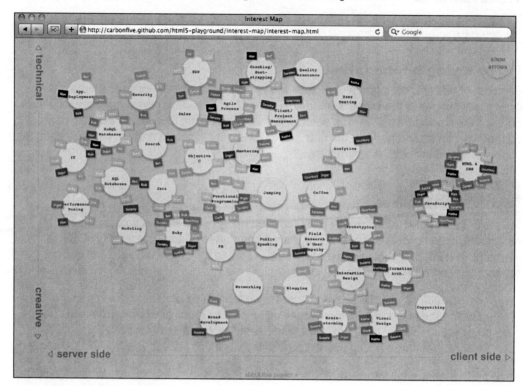

How to do it...

 It will be very helpful to view the source code at: `view-source:http://carbonfive.github.com/html5-playground/interest-map/interest-map.html` while following along with this recipe.

The Carbon Five team reminds us that canvas is not officially part of the HTML5 spec by creating this interactive visualization using an HTML4.01 Transitional DOCTYPE.

```
<!DOCTYPE html PUBLIC "-//W3C//DTD HTML 4.01 Transitional//EN"
    "http://www.w3.org/TR/html4/loose.dtd">
```

Here's a detailed look at some of what they're doing with JavaScript and the new `canvas` element. They start with some variables like the card style. Here, they do several things: set the background color, create a black border, the width of the card, and the values for a shadow around it.

```
var CARD_STYLE = {
    fill:'rgb(240,240,240)',stroke:'rgb(0,0,0)',width:.05, shadow:{x:0,
    y:4, blur:4, color:'rgba(0, 0, 0, 0.3)'} };
```

The next variable should look familiar to those who know CSS. Here, the card font weight, size, face, color, and more are set:

```
var CARD_FONT = {font:'bold 8pt Courier', color:'#555',
    yoffset:10, height:14};
```

Next, they set several more variables related to margin, width, height, scale, radius, shadow, and more.

```
var MARGIN = [75,75,75,100], WIDTH = 1000-MARGIN[1]-MARGIN[3],
    HEIGHT = 650-MARGIN[0]-MARGIN[2], CARD_SCALE=.75, CARD_RADIUS = 40,
    TAG_RADIUS = 50, CACHE_RADIUS=70, CLEAR_RADIUS = 50,
    ITERATIONS = 20, DEGREE = .5, CARD_SHADOW = 2, AXIS_ANIM=700;
```

Lastly, they set up variables for skills, people, and a people-to-skill matrix. Unfortunately, these code chunks too long for republication here.

How it works...

Variables by themselves don't do a whole lot of good unless they have functions to act upon them.

After initializing the display, the Carbon Five team uses more functions like drawing on the 2d `canvas` rendering element:

```
function draw(t) {
   var ctx = el('display').getContext('2d');
   ctx.clearRect(0,0,ctx.canvas.width,ctx.canvas.height);
   ctx.save(); ctx.globalAlpha = 1 - .75*arrow_visibility;
   each( cards, function(card) {
       var t0=card.tween(t); x = MARGIN[3] + card.lx +
          (card.x-card.lx)*t0, y = MARGIN[0] + card.ly +
          (card.y-card.ly)*t0;
      draw_card( ctx, x, y, card.index);
   });
   ctx.restore();
   if ( arrow_visibility > 0 ) {
      ctx.save(); ctx.globalAlpha = arrow_visibility;
      each( PEOPLE, function(p) { draw_interest_arrow(ctx,p,t); });
```

```
      ctx.restore();
      if (over_person) draw_over_arrow(ctx,over_person,t);
    }
    draw_axes(ctx);
  }
```

as well as creating the name tags:

```
function nametag( ctx, cardx, cardy, person, r, interest ) {
  ctx.save(); ctx.translate( cardx, cardy );
  ctx.rotate( r + .4*(Math.random()-.5) );
  ctx.translate( -TAG_RADIUS -  + 4*Math.random(), 0 );
  ctx.rotate( -r );
  draw_nametag( ctx, person, interest );
  ctx.restore();
}
```

and drawing the arrows:

```
function draw_arrow( ctx, length, head_length, head_width ) {
  var cx1 = .9*(length - head_length), cy1 = .2*head_width,
    cx2 = (length - head_length), cy2=.2*head_width;
  ctx.beginPath();
  ctx.moveTo(0,0);
  ctx.bezierCurveTo( cx1, cy1, cx2, cy2, length-head_length,
    head_width );
  ctx.lineTo( length, 0 ); ctx.lineTo( length-head_length,
    -head_width );
  ctx.bezierCurveTo( cx2, -cy2, cx1, -cy1, 0, 0 );
  ctx.closePath();
}
```

There's more...

With variables and functions already set, the last thing to do is call the canvas element itself in the HTML to give it all a space in which to run:

```
<canvas id="display" width="1000" height="650"></canvas>
```

Evil of two lessors

In the old days of the web, the Carbon Five team would have had the choice of leaving their map on a physical wall or creating a static graphic image of it for computer display. While either might render just as well as using the new canvas element, neither of them allow the team to extract valuable information the way the new canvas element does.

What about fallback content?

Interestingly, Carbon Five used no fallback content within the new `canvas` element in this instance. This is an approach you'll have to weigh carefully, as those with older browsers or who use assistive technologies will see nothing, literally nothing. Carbon Five gets away with that for this internal project. Can you?

Take him up on his offer.

When writing about the project at `http://blog.carbonfive.com/2011/02/17/visualizing-skillsets-in-html5-canvas-part-1` Carbon Five developer Alex Cruikshank went so far as to offer to create visualization maps to the first five people who wrote in with data in a reasonable format. As of publication date, it's unclear if anyone's taken him up on it.

See also

Jacob Seidelin hit another home run with his new canvas element visualization of the band Radiohead's song "Idioteque" from the album "Kid A" at: `http://nihilogic.dk/labs/canvas_music_visualization`. Jacob's pushing the limits of what can be done with the `canvas` element and JavaScript – and that's why we think he's terrific!

Bouncing a ball

We've looked at how do draw shapes using the new `canvas` element, and next we'll turn our attention to making those shapes move. Author Vinci Rufus shows us how.

How to do it...

We'll start with our usual `canvas` HTML code:

```
<!DOCTYPE html>
<html>
<head>
  <title>Canvas</title>
  <meta charset="utf-8" />
</head>
<body>
  <canvas id="FirstCanvas" width="800" height="600">
    <!-- Fallback code goes here -->
  </canvas>
</body>
</html>
```

Next up is the unique part: the JavaScript. Here, Vinci chose a slightly different method of calling the 2d `canvas` rendering context than we did, but his method works just fine too. Check it out:

```
<script>
  var context;
  function init()
  {
    context= myCanvas.getContext('2d');
    context.beginPath();
    context.fillStyle="#0000ff";
    // Draws a circle of radius 20 at the coordinates 100,
      100 on the canvas
    context.arc(100,100,20,0,Math.PI*2,true); context.closePath();
    context.fill();
  }
</script>
```

Put together, that code should look like. Note the addition of an `onLoad` function added to the `body` tag.

```
<!DOCTYPE html>
<html>
<head>
  <title>Canvas</title>
  <meta charset="utf-8" />
  <script
    src="http://ajax.googleapis.com/ajax/libs/jquery/1/
    jquery.min.js"></script>
  <script>
  var context;
  function init()
  {
    context= myCanvas.getContext('2d');
    context.beginPath();
    context.fillStyle="#0000ff";
    // Draws a circle of radius 20 at the coordinates 100,
      100 on the canvas
    context.arc(100,100,20,0,Math.PI*2,true); context.closePath();
    context.fill();
  }
</script>
</head>
<body onLoad="init();">
  <canvas id="myCanvas" width="300" height="300">
    <!-- Fallback code goes here -->
  </canvas>
</body>
</html>
```

And render this blue ball:

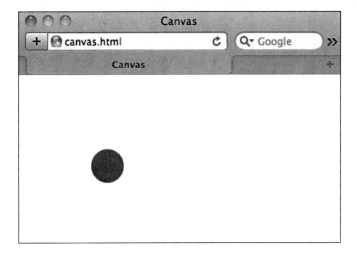

How it works...

So far Vinci's code is pretty straightforward. We saw how he called the 2d `canvas` rendering context. He sets the color of the fill next:

```
context.fillStyle="#0000ff";
```

And then draws an arc 100 pixels from the top and left and fills it with the blue he already set:

```
context.arc(100,100,20,0,Math.PI*2,true); context.closePath();
context.fill();
```

But now all we've got is a blue ball just sitting there. Next, Vinci shows us how to make it move using variables and a new function named `draw`.

There's more...

```
<!DOCTYPE html>
<html>
<head>
  <title>Canvas</title>
  <meta charset="utf-8" />
  <script
    src="http://ajax.googleapis.com/ajax/libs/jquery/1/
    jquery.min.js"></script>
  <script>
  var context;
```

```
var x=100;
var y=200;
var dx=5;
var dy=5;

function init()
{
  context= myCanvas.getContext('2d');
  setInterval(draw,10);
}
function draw()
{
  context.beginPath();
  context.fillStyle="#0000ff";
  // Draws a circle of radius 20 at the coordinates 100,
    100 on the canvas
  context.arc(x,y,20,0,Math.PI*2,true);
  context.closePath();
  context.fill();
  x+=dx;
  y+=dy;
}
</script>
</head>
<body onLoad="init();">
  <canvas id="myCanvas" width="300" height="300" >
  </canvas>
</body>
</html>
```

As you can see, the ball is in motion but has simply drawn a straight line off the edge of the `canvas`. Vinci explains why:

> *"This is because each time the* `draw()` *function is called, it draws a circle at the new coordinates without removing the old ones. That's how the* `getContext` *object works so it's not a bug; it doesn't really move the circle and, instead, it draws a circle at the new coordinates each time the function is called."*

Start again

Vinci shows us a method to erase the old circles as the new `canvas` element draws each new one:

```
<script>
  var context;
  var x=100;
  var y=200;
  var dx=5;
  var dy=5;
  function init()
  {
     context= myCanvas.getContext('2d');
     setInterval(draw,10);
  }
  function draw()
  {
     context.clearRect(0,0, 300,300);
     context.beginPath();
     context.fillStyle="#0000ff";
     // Draws a circle of radius 20 at the coordinates 100,
        100 on the canvas
     context.arc(x,y,20,0,Math.PI*2,true);
     context.closePath();
     context.fill();
     x+=dx;
     y+=dy;
  }
</script>
```

Now, the ball appears to fall down to the right outside of the `canvas` border.

Don't box me in

To ensure that the ball stays within the border of the `canvas`, Vinci wrote some logic to check if the x and y coordinates are beyond the `canvas` dimensions. If they are, he makes the ball reverse directions.

```
<script>
var context;
var x=100;
var y=200;
var dx=5;
var dy=5;
function init()
{
  context= myCanvas.getContext('2d');
  setInterval(draw,10);
}
function draw()
{
  context.clearRect(0,0, 300,300);
  context.beginPath();
  context.fillStyle="#0000ff";
  // Draws a circle of radius 20 at the coordinates 100,
     100 on the canvas
  context.arc(x,y,20,0,Math.PI*2,true);
  context.closePath();
  context.fill();
  // Boundary Logic
  if( x<0 || x>300) dx=-dx;
  if( y<0 || y>300) dy=-dy;
  x+=dx;
  y+=dy;
}
</script>
```

Now the ball should be bouncing around all four sides of the `canvas` continually.

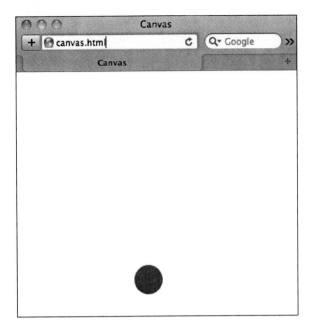

And that's one to grow on

As Vinci reminds us in his compelling tutorial at `http://sixrevisions.com/html/bouncing-a-ball-around-with-html5-and-javascript`, the bouncing ball may seem simple at first, but it's actually a key technique to understand in order to develop just about any game for the new HTML5 `canvas` element.

See also

A beautiful example of user-generated graphics can be seen at Yuri Vishnevsky's `http://weavesilk.com`. The site uses the new `canvas` element as part of an experiment in generative art. Some of the generated images are so beautiful, Yuri has made them available as stunning desktop background images. A version for iPhone and iPad is planned also.

Creating fallback content

"When authors use the `canvas` element, they must also provide content that, when presented to the user, conveys essentially the same function or purpose as the bitmap `canvas`. This content may be placed as content of the `canvas` element. The contents of the `canvas` element, if any, are the element's fallback content."
– WHATWG HTML5 Specification

What happens if someone viewing your brilliant new `canvas` application is using an older browser and is unable to recognize your coding genius? Or what happens when someone uses assistive technologies? Let's take a look.

How to do it...

If, for some reason, a user's browser won't support the new `canvas` element, it's up to us as developers to give them something valuable instead.

Here we can use an image as fallback.

```
<canvas id="clock" width="200" height="200">
  <img src="images/clock.gif" width="200" height="200" alt="clock"/>
</canvas>
```

Or text:

```
<canvas id="clock" width="200" height="200">
  <p>clock</p>
</canvas>
```

Or almost any other element.

How it works...

By now you're well versed at how `alt` tags work for image files: If an image file doesn't show up or the user relies upon assistive technologies, the `alt` tag gives them at least a valuable text label representing what they're missing. Fallback content for the new `canvas` element is a similar concept but is capable of doing and being so much more than just an `alt` tag.

There's more...

Browsers which do support the new `canvas` element will ignore the content inside the container, and just render the new `canvas` element normally.

Thanks, Mozilla

> *"If fallback content is desired, some CSS tricks must be employed to mask the fallback content from Safari (which should render just the `canvas`), and also to mask the CSS tricks themselves from IE (which should render the fallback content)." – Mozilla.org*

How will we deal with accessibility?

There is generally a consensus among specification writers and the HTML5 community at large that the new `canvas` element is only partially baked. Leaving those who use assistive technologies out in the cold just doesn't seem like the right thing to do. Watch this space.

Are we ready for <canvas>?

Many developers consider the new `canvas` element accessibility is one of the last sticking points in the new HTML5 specification. With little meaningful fallback capabilities, this new element simply feels not ready for prime time.

Interactivity using JavaScript

In this chapter, we will cover:

- ▶ Playing audio files with JavaScript
- ▶ Using the drag-and-drop API with text
- ▶ Crossbrowser video support with `vid.ly` and jQuery
- ▶ Displaying video dynamically using jQuery
- ▶ Movable video ads using jQuery
- ▶ Controlling the display of images using `Easel.js` and the `canvas` tag
- ▶ Animating a sequence of images using `Easel.js` and the `canvas` tag
- ▶ Random animation with audio using the `canvas` tag and JavaScript

Introduction

While HTML5 may put an end to the use of Flash for many rich media applications, it is causing JavaScript to become even more popular than before. There are many libraries and plugins available to enhance and extend HTML5 and CSS3 to create rich interactive experiences.

This chapter contains recipes that show how JavaScript can be used with HTML5 tags, such as audio, video, and canvas, as well as CSS3 selectors and elements.

Playing audio files with JavaScript

HTML5 introduces more flexibility in how audio files are used on the Internet. In this recipe, we will create a game to practice loading and playing sounds using the audio tag and JavaScript.

Getting ready

You will need an audio file to play, an image, and a modern browser that supports HTML5. The example files for this chapter can be downloaded from `http://www.packtpub.com/ support?nid=7940`. The Free Sound Project (`http://freesound.org`) has audio files you can use as long as credit is given to the producer, and photos can be found at `http://www.Morguefile.com` for use in your personal projects.

How to do it...

Now we are ready to create a series of buttons and a short JavaScript program that will play a random audio file when one of the buttons is pushed.

Open up your HTML editor and create the opening section of an HTML5 page.

```
<!DOCTYPE html><html lang="en"><head><meta http-equiv="Content-Type"
  content="text/html; charset=utf-8"> <title>Playing a sound file
  with JavaScript</title>
```

Because we only have a few styles, we will add them to the head area of the HTML page.

```
<style>h1{font-family:"Comic Sans MS", cursive; font-size:large;
  font-weight:bold;}
  button{ padding:5px;margin:5px; }
  button.crosshair { cursor: crosshair; }
  button.crosshairthree {margin-left:40px;
  cursor:crosshair;}
</style>
```

Three variables need to be created for the script. The opening script tag and variables should look like the following code block:

```
<script>//variables
var mySounds=new Array();
mySounds[0]="boing";
mySounds[1]="impact";
mySounds[2]="squeak";
mySounds[3]="whack";
mySounds[4]="space";
var soundElements;
var soundChoice;
```

Now that we have created the global variables for the script, we can create the functions. Type `function whackmole () {` to begin the function, then on a new line type `var i = Math.floor(Math.random() * 5);` to generate a somewhat random number using the JavaScript math library. Next, type `soundChoice = mySounds[i];` to assign the array value to `soundChoice`. Close out the function with `soundElements[soundChoice].play();}`. Your function code should currently look like the following:

```
function whackmole() {
    var i = Math.floor(Math.random() *5);
    soundChoice = mySounds[i];
    soundElements[soundChoice].play();}
```

Type `function init() {` to begin the function. On a new line, type `soundElements = document.getElementsByTagName("audio");} </script>` to complete our block of JavaScript code. It should look like the following code block:

```
function init(){
    soundElements = document.getElementsByTagName("audio");}
</script>
```

Close the head tag and type the body tag, adding an `init()` function call to it so it looks like:

```
</head><body onLoad="init();">
```

Create a heading area for the header area of the page using the `<header>` tag. Use the heading tag `<h1>` to display the title of the page:

```
<header><h1>Whack A Mole!</h1></header>
```

There are five buttons to create a balanced look, and they are all assigned a class.

```
<section> <p> <button class="crosshair" onclick="whackmole();">
    <img src="images/downmole.png" width="37" height="24"
    alt="Mole peeping out of hole"></button>
<button class="crosshair" onclick="whackmole();">
    <img src="images/downmole.png" width="37" height="24"
    alt="Mole peeping out of hole"></button></p>
```

The third button has a class name of `crosshairthree` to give us more control over positioning it on the screen.

```
<p style="padding-left:30px;"><button class="crosshair"
    onclick="whackmole();"><img src="images/downmole.png" width="37"
    height="24" alt="Mole peeping out of hole"></button></p>
    <p><button class="crosshair" onclick="whackmole();">
    <img src="images/downmole.png" width="37" height="24"
    alt="Mole peeping out of hole"></button><button class="crosshair"
    onclick="whackmole();"><img src="images/downmole.png" width="37"
    height="24" alt="Mole peeping out of hole"></button></p></section>
```

If you are using the code files from this book, the sound file tags should look similar to the code block below:

```
<section><audio id ="boing" autobuffer>
<source src="audio/cartoonboing.ogg" />
<source src="audio/cartoonboing.mp3" /></audio>
<audio id ="impact" autobuffer>
<source src="audio/cartoonimpact.ogg" />
<source src="audio/cartoonimpact.mp3" /></audio>
<audio id ="squeak" autobuffer>
<source src="audio/cartoonsqueak.ogg" />
<source src="audio/cartoonsqueak.mp3" /></audio>
<audio id ="whack" autobuffer>
<source src="audio/cartoonwhack.ogg" />
<source src="audio/cartoonwhack.mp3" /></audio>
<audio id="space" autobuffer>
<source src="audio/cartoonspaceboing.ogg" />
<source src="audio/cartoonspaceboing.mp3" /></audio>
```

Finish the page with the closing tags:

```
</section></body></html>
```

Save the file as `playing-audio-files-with-javascript.html` and view it in your browser. It should look similar to the following screenshot:

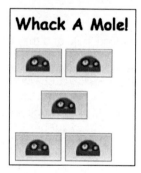

How it works...

First, we created the beginnings of a basic HTML5 page. Then, we added CSS styles to add background images to buttons and change the mouse icon to a crosshair when the mouse or pointing device moved over a button. This gave us a visual simulation of a targeting weapon and was more fun than a default mouse icon.

Three variables were created to use in the script: `mySounds`, `soundElements`, and `soundch`. The first function we created named `whackmole()` contained an internal variable `i` that held the result of a randomly generated number. `Math.random()` caused a pseudorandom number to be generated. We then multiplied it by 5, the number of our audio files, and used the result in `Math.floor()` to create a whole number with a value ranging from zero to five. This value was then assigned to the temporary variable `i` that in turn was used to populate the variable `mySounds` with a randomly generated array value. This new array value, was stored in the variable `soundChoice` with `soundChoice = mySounds[i];`. This enabled us to trigger the `play()` action of the audio tag using `soundElements[soundChoice].play();` when a button was pressed.

The second function we created was `init()`, which we later tied to the body tag using `onLoad`, so that we could grab an audio file with `getElementsByTagName` using the audio tag and its array value, as carried in the `soundElements` variable.

Next, we added the body tag `<body onLoad="init();">`, and a series of buttons containing our adorable mole image to the page. Each of the buttons contained an `onClick()` event which invoked the `whackmole()` function. Our third button had a different class than the others, `crosshairthree`, which added additional margin to the left of the button, giving it a more centered appearance.

 Firefox currently has a quirk, where if you don't list the `.ogg` audio source first, it will not find it.

Finally, we added the sound files to the page using the `<audio>` and `<source>` tags. The `ogg` and `mp3` formats for each file were listed using the source tag. Because the source tag is considered a "child" of the parent audio tag it is surrounded by, either file format would play, depending on the browser used, as different browsers currently prefer different sound file formats.

There's more...

You can see it would be very easy to create an app such as a child's read aloud page of shapes or animals by playing a different sound file for different images.

Controlling the appearance of audio clips with jQuery

The `.animate` function in jQuery opens up new ways to cause audio controls to appear, fade, and disappear when actions are taken by visitors or as part of a rich media experience. Following is an example of how you could fade and audio control away then cause it to quickly reappear:

```
<script>
  $(document).ready(function(){
```

```
    $('audio').delay(500).hide('fade', {}, 1000 ).slideDown('fast');
    });
</script>
<!- - the HTML -- ><audio id ="boing" autobuffer>
    <source src="audio/cartoonboing.ogg" />
    <source src="audio/cartoonboing.mp3" /></audio>
```

We will perform a similar trick using a video file in a recipe in this chapter.

See also

Chapter 8, Embracing Audio and Video will cover a lot more information about the audio tag and ways to use it.

Using the drag-and-drop API with text

While all browsers can natively drag images or links, dropping objects used to require complex JavaScript or third-party libraries. The drag-and-drop API is intended to provide an easier, standardized way to enable users to drop any type of object into an identified area. In reality, working with the API across browsers is a challenge. The main browsers currently supporting this API are Firefox, Chrome, and Safari.

Getting ready

Download the code for this tutorial at `http://www.packtpub.com/support?nid=7940`. The font used in the heading of this tutorial is from `http://www.fontsquirrel.com`, where you can also download a different font if you choose. This tutorial may not work with Internet Explorer. We will be creating a tic-tac-toe game that demonstrates how the drag-and-drop API works.

How to do it...

Open up your HTML editor and start by creating a basic HTML5 page. We will add two stylesheet links, one to support an `@fontface` font we will be loading for the header of the page, and our main stylesheet. Type the code as shown below, then save the file as `using-drag-drop-api.html`.

```
<!DOCTYPE html><html lang="en">
<head> <meta charset="utf-8">
<title>Using the drag-and-drop API element</title>
<link rel="stylesheet"
  href="fonts/specimen_files/specimen_stylesheet.css" type="text/css"
  charset="utf-8" /> <link rel="stylesheet" href="stylesheet.css"
  type="text/css" charset="utf-8" />
```

Let's go ahead and style the page. Create or open up a CSS file named `stylesheet.css`. Set the overall `margin` for the `body` of the page to `100px` and the default color to `#666`.

```
@charset "UTF-8";/* CSS Document */body { margin:100px; color:#666; }
```

The content tags for the page should all be set to `display:block` as shown in the following code:

```
article, aside, figure, footer, header, hgroup, menu, nav, section {
    display:block; }
```

Now, we specify the `@fontface` information. The code and font files are from a `www.fontsquirrel.com` font kit, which is included in the code files of this tutorial.

```
@font-face { /* This declaration targets Internet Explorer */ font-
    family: '3DumbRegular';src: url('3dumb-webfont.eot'); }@font-face
    {/* This declaration targets everything else */font-family:
    '3DumbRegular';src: url(//:) format('no404'), url('fonts/3dumb-
    webfont.woff') format('woff'), url('fonts/3dumb-webfont.ttf')
    format('truetype'), url('fonts/3dumb-webfont.svg#webfontlNpyKhxD')
    format('svg');font-weight: normal;font-style: normal;}
```

Add a color for the `h1` tag and set the `font-family` property to `3DumbRegular`, the name of our font.

```
h1{color:#C60;font-family: '3DumbRegular';}
```

Create a new div called `gametilebox` to hold the letters that will make up the game tiles. Set the `float` property of the box to `left` and the width and height to `280px`. Set the `padding`, `margin-right`, `border`, and `background-color` as shown in the following code snippet:

```
#gametilebox{    float:left;width:280px;    height:280px;
    padding:10px; margin-right:30px; border:1px solid #000;
    background-color:#ccc;         }
```

The game board will share many of the same properties as the tile box, so copy the styles for the `gametilebox`, paste, and name the copy "gameboard". Add a `background-image` property with a url of `images/tictactoegrid.jpg`, and set the `background-color` to `aa`.

The `gameboard div` should look like the following code:

```
#gameboard { float:left; width:280px; height:280px; padding:10px;
    margin-right:30px;border:1px solid #000;
    background-image:url(images/tictactoegrid.jpg);
    background-color:#aaa;}
```

Let's style the div blocks in which to place our letters. The float should be set to left on all of the block divs. The width should be no greater than 85px, the height no greater than 80px. They will be on a 3 by 3 grid, so the first block on the second and third rows need to have a clear:both property as well. The third block on the second and third row should have low to none padding and margin-right properties. Because there are nine of them, only a sample of the block code is shown here:

```
#blockA {float:left; width:75px; height:75px;
   padding:5px 5px 5px 2px; margin-right:10px; border:none;
   background-color:red;}
#blockB {float:left; width:75px; height:75px; padding:5px;
   margin-right:10px; border:none; background-color:blue;}
```

Now, we will set the styles for the letter game tiles. Create a new class in the stylesheet named lettertile, then set the properties for the class as shown here:

```
.lettertile {    width:60px; height:60px; padding:5px; margin:5px;
   text-align:center; font-weight:bold;font-size:36px;color:#930;
   background-color:transparent;display:inline-block;}
```

The last style we will add is for the draggable attribute. Create the style below to help with cross-browser compatibility:

```
*[draggable=true] {    -moz-user-select:none;    -khtml-user-drag:
element;
   cursor: move;}
```

The stylesheet is complete, so now we can work on the script to drag the letter tiles and drop them.

Open up the previously created html page using-drag-drop-api.html, and type the following code for IE browsers:

```
<!--[if IE]><script
   src="http://html5shiv.googlecode.com/svn/trunk/html5.js">
   </script><![endif]-->
```

Add a opening <script> tag directly below the stylesheet link, and type the first function, dragDefine(ev), which accepts an event argument, and follow it with a {. After the curly brace, type ev.dataTransfer.effectAllowed ='move'; then, on a new line, type ev.dataTransfer.setData("text/plain", ev.target.getAttribute('id')); to set the data type and the target attribute. Finally, type return true; with a closing } to complete the function.

```
function dragDefine(ev) {ev.dataTransfer.effectAllowed = 'move';
ev.dataTransfer.setData("text/plain", ev.target.getAttribute('id'));
return true;}
```

Now, we need to define the `dragOver` function. Type `dragOver(ev)` and an opening {, then invoke the `preventDefault()` function by adding `ev.preventDefault();`. The function block should look similar to the one below:

```
function dragOver(ev) {
  ev.preventDefault();}
```

The next function we need is one to indicate that the drag is complete. Type `function dragEnd(ev)`, then an opening {. Type `return true; }` to complete the function.

Type `function dragDrop(ev)` with an opening {, and go to a new line to add our first method. Type `var idDrag = ev.dataTransfer.getData("Text");` to create a drag variable that will hold the text string then type `ev.target.appendChild(document.getElementById(idDrag));`. Finish the function with `ev.preventDefault();`. The function block should look like the following code:

```
function dragDrop(ev) {
  var idDrag = ev.dataTransfer.getData("Text");
  ev.target.appendChild(document.getElementById(idDrag));
  ev.preventDefault();} </script>
```

Close the head section of the page. Type `<body><header>`, then `<h1>Drag and Drop Tic Tac Toe</h1></header>` to complete the heading of the page.

```
</head><body><header><h1>Drag and Drop Tic Tac Toe</h1></header>
```

Next, type `<section><h3>Drag the letters from the gray box to the game board (and back again!)</h3>`.

Create a div with and ID of "gametilebox" and `ondragover="dragOver(event)"` and `ondrop="dragDrop(event)"`. It should look like the following statement:

```
<div id="gametilebox" ondragover="dragOver(event)"
  ondrop="dragDrop(event)">
```

Now, we will create a `div` for each game tile. Create six "**X**" tiles and six "**O**" tiles, each with an `id` that begins with `"lettertile"` and ends in a number in value from 1-12. Each `div` will contain the class `"lettertile"` and each `draggable` attribute will contain the value `"true"`. Every tile will also contain `ondragstart="return dragDefine(event)"` and `ondragend="dragEnd(event)"`. The div block should look like the following code:

```
<div id="lettertile1" class="lettertile" draggable="true"
  ondragstart="return dragDefine(event)"
  ondragend="dragEnd(event)">X</div>
<div id="lettertile2" class="lettertile" draggable="true"
  ondragstart="return dragDefine(event)"
  ondragend="dragEnd(event)">X</div>
<div id="lettertile3" class="lettertile" draggable="true"
  ondragstart="return dragDefine(event)"
  ondragend="dragEnd(event)">X</div>
```

Now, we can create the actual `divs` for those block styles we created in **stylesheet.css**. First type `<div id= "gameboard">`. There should be a `div` for each block id, ranging from "blockA" to "blockI". Each of them will contain an `ondragover="return dragOver(event)"` and an `ondrop="dragDrop(event)"`. They should look like the following code block.

```
<div id="blockA" ondragover="return dragOver(event)"
   ondrop="dragDrop(event)"></div>

<div id="blockB" ondragover="return dragOver(event)"
   ondrop="dragDrop(event)"></div>

<div id="blockC" ondragover="return dragOver(event)"
   ondrop="dragDrop(event)"></div>
```

Close the page with the `body` and `html` closing tags, name the file "using-drag-drop-api.html", then view the results in a browser window. Drag a few letters over and the results should look similar to the following screenshot:

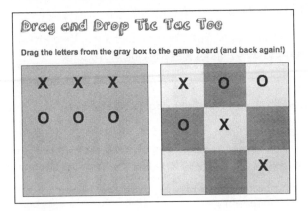

How it works...

First, we created a basic HTML5 page and added a sketchy font for the heading using `@ fontface` to give our game a fun visual look. Next, we styled the page by setting the `margin` for the `body` and all block level elements to `display:block;` to have greater control of the presentation of those elements. After styling our heading font, we define the `width` and `height` for the game tile box. This would be the container to hold the letters that make up the game tiles.

We began our script by typing an special comment tag for IE browsers to point them to an extra script file to trigger HTML5 elements: `<!--[if IE]><script src="http://html5shiv.googlecode.com/svn/trunk/html5.js"></script><![endif]-->`. It was provided under the MIT license by Remy Sharp (`http://remysharp.com/html5-enabling-script/`) to keep us all sane when working with Internet Explorer.

The function `dragDefine()` was called when a user began to drag an item. It first checked to see if an item was draggable using `dataTransfer.effectAllowed='move'`. It then set the type of data to be transferred to `text` with `dataTransfer.setData("text/plain")` and identified the target by the `id` using `target.getAttribute('id')`. The function returns true, meaning the object can be dragged.

Next, we defined the `dragOver` function, which is called when an item being dragged is over another item, and accepts an event argument shown as `ev` that is then used to invoke `preventDefault()` to allow the item to be dropped. The drag-and-drop API specification clearly states that we must cancel dragging in order to then prepare to drop.

The function `dragEnd()` was then created to return a value of true when drag is complete. It also accepted an event argument.

After completing all the dragging functions we were ready to create the code to drop the item. The `dragDrop()` function took an event argument and used that value to get the value of the text object, which it then passed to a new variable `var idDrag` to hold the text string, which in turn was used by `getElementById` to identify the correct element ID to drop. Just as with `dragEnd()`, we had to indicate it was ok to drop the object by calling the `preventDefault()` function from the drag-and-drop API.

After we closed the head area of the page, in the body we placed the content boxes to hold our letter tiles and game board. These were made up of two parent div containers which each held child divs containing letter tiles or sections of the game board grid.

The game tile box invoked the `dragOver()` function whenever a letter tile was dragged over it. The letter tile divs themselves were made draggable by `draggable="true"` and returned `dragDefine()` whenever they were dragged. When dragging stopped, they invoked the `dragEnd()` function.

Because we wanted the letter tiles to drop and stay in a specific area of the game board, we created divs for each individual block on the grid to hold our letters in place when they are dropped onto the board that would also return the `dragOver` event when an object was dragged over them, and invoke `dragDrop()` when an object was dropped on them.

Why bother with the block divs? We could have set up our game tile box on the left and the game board on the right and been done. The result would have been that when we dragged tiles from the left box to the game board, they would have dropped onto it and lined up in the order they were dropped instead of where we wanted to place them. This default behavior is fine when you want to sort a list, but not when control over precisely where an object is placed is needed.

We needed to override the default behavior that results when objects are dropped. We created nine game board blocks, all the same basic size. The main changes for each one were to the `padding` and `margin`.

Spend a few moments reading up on the drag-and-drop specification at `http://www.whatwg.org/specs/web-apps/current-work/multipage/dnd.html` and you will notice they explicitly state they are only defining a drag-and-drop mechanism, and not what operation you have to perform. Why? Users with a smart phone or other touch screen device may not have a pointing device such as a mouse.

There's more...

This demonstration of the drag–and-drop API can be built into a complete game with scoring; a game board reset button, and other interactive elements in several ways.

Create a canvas-based tic-tac-toe game

Two canvases could be used, one for the game tile box and another for the game board. The boards and game tiles could be dynamically drawn using canvas, and then scores or messages such as "you win" could be written to the screen.

Show responsive messages as the user plays

Remy Sharp has a great demo online at `http://html5demos.com/drag-anything` showing how to display messages on the screen when an object is dropped.

The source tag of the object to be dropped would be similar to:

```
<div id="draggables"><img src="../drag-drop-js/images/picean.png"
  alt="Fish" data-science-fact="Fish are aquatic vertebrates (animals
  with backbones) with fins for appendages." /> </div>
```

The "drop zone" box when the object would be dragged to might look like:

```
<div class="drop" id="dropnames" data-accept="science-fact">
  <p>Learn a science fact!</p> </div>
```

When the image was dropped into the box, instead of the image, you would see the text contained in "data-science-fact".

See also

Packt book on jQuery, other recipes in this book, an advanced HTML5 Packt book.

Crossbrowser video support with vid.ly and jQuery

Supporting most browsers requires encoding a video into multiple formats, then serving up the right one to a browser. In this recipe we will use an online video display library named vid.ly (http://www.vid.ly) to prepare and share a video on a page reliably across multiple browsers and make the background color change over time.

Getting ready

You will need a video to upload to http://www.vid.ly. Some browsers do not allow files to be served locally, so you may also want a location where you can upload your files and test pages.

How to do it...

Type `<!DOCTYPE html> <html lang="en"> <head>`, then begin adding style declarations by typing `<style type="text/css"> h2{color:#303;}`.

Style a div to contain featured content: `#featured {position:relative; padding: 40px; width: 480px; background-color:#000000; outline: #333 solid 10px; }`.

Type `video {padding: 3px;background-color:black;}` to create the style for the video tag, then add a closing `</style>` tag.

Declare the scripts used in the page. Type `<script src="http://ajax.googleapis.com/ajax/libs/jquery/1.3.2/jquery.min.js" type="text/javascript" charset="utf-8"></script>` to reference a minimized version of the main jQuery library. Then, type `<script type="text/javascript" src="http://ajax.googleapis.com/ajax/libs/jqueryui/1.7.2/jquery-ui.min.js"></script>` to reference the jQuery UI library used for the color change effect. Finally, we will reference our own script by typing `<script type="text/javascript" src="js/mycolor.js"></script>` just before the closing `</head>` tag.

Enter an opening `<body>` and `<section>` tag, then type `<header> <h2>Featured Video</h2></header>` to display the page heading.

Now, we can create the div to hold our featured content that we styled earlier. Type `<div id="featured"> <p>This video was converted to cross-browser formats by <a href="http://vid.ly">vid.ly</a></p>`.

The next step is to upload the video clips to `http://vid.ly` for conversion into multiple file formats. You will receive an e-mail when the process is complete and can then grab the code snippet for your video as seen in the following screenshot:

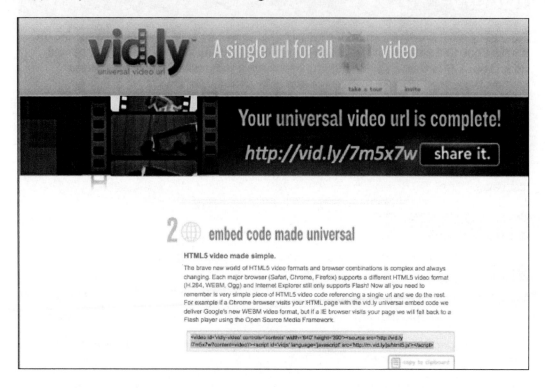

Copy the code from the site, and then paste it into your page. The `src` value in the video and script tag should be the URLs you were given by vid.ly. The code block should look like:

```
<video id= "vidly-video" controls="controls" width="480"
  height="360">
  <source src="http://vid.ly/7m5x7w?content=video"/>
  <script id="vidjs" language="javascript"
  src="http://m.vid.ly/js/html5.js"></script> </video>
```

Just to add a little extra fun, let's add another video tag to the page. Type the following code: `<p>Awwww it's a baby video!</p>`, use a different id for the video tag and resize it as shown: `<video id="tinymovie1" controls="controls" width="190" height="120">`, then use the same source tag: `<source src="http://vid.ly/7m5x7w?content=video"/><script id="vidjs" language="javascript" src="http://m.vid.ly/js/html5.js"></script></video>`, and close the page: `</div> </section></body></html>`. Save the file as `display-videos-using-videly.html`.

The last thing we are going to do is create a jQuery script to change the background color of the `#featured` div. Open up your editor and create a new file called `myColor.js`.

Type `$(document).ready(function() {` then go to a new line and type the code that will call the animate function and alter the background color: `$('#featured').animate({'backgroundColor':'#ff3333', 'color': '#ffffff'}, 6000);});` .

Load the page in your browser, and watch the colors change as the main video loads. You can see the following screenshot of how it should appear:

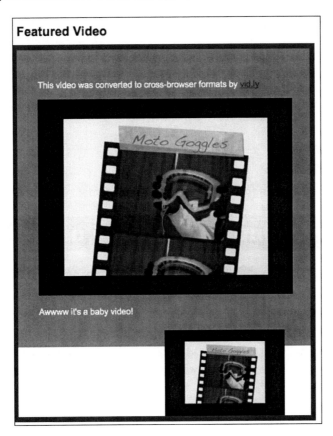

How it works...

First, we created a standard HTML5 page and began adding style declarations. We set the position of the `featured` div to relative to have more flexibility in the future in case we decided to add additional jQuery effects. A strong visual look was created by setting the `padding` to `40px` and the `outline` color to a dark gray with a weight of `10px`. The default background color was set to black (`#000000`) to give us a high contrast color to compare the ending red background against.

Next, we styled the `video` tag to give it a `background-color` of `black` while it loads. We could have also added a background image here to act as a poster.

The base jQuery script was declared next using `<script src="http://ajax.googleapis.com/ajax/libs/jquery/1.3.2/jquery.min.js" type="text/javascript" charset="utf-8"></script>`. Because it does not contain effects such as `animate()`, we needed to also reference a minimized version of the jQuery UI library used for the color change effect. We then added a reference to our own script by typing `<script type="text/javascript" src="js/mycolor.js"></script>`. An alternative way to reduce the script file size further would be to create a custom script that contained only the animate effects from the jQueryUI library.

Next, we created the main page content, including the links to the video on vid.ly. The default code vid.ly provides applies an ID of `'vidley video'` to the `video` tag, but that can be left out if you want to use your own style id or will be using a different id for each video. Another option would be to assign all videos the same class, then assigning them unique IDs as needed.

See also

Chapter 8, *Embracing Audio and Video* covers the video element in more detail.

Displaying video dynamically using jQuery

The video element gives us the power to treat videos like images and manipulate them in fun and exciting ways.

Getting ready

You will need a video available in multiple file formats (which are provided in the chapter code for this book). A server to which to upload your files is recommended, as not all browsers play files locally in a predictable way.

How to do it...

First, we have to prepare an HTML5 page in which to place it. Type the opening tags for our page: `<!DOCTYPE html> <html lang="en"> <head> <meta charset="utf-8" /> <title>Video Explosion</title>`.

Open up the `stylesheet.css` file from the downloaded code files or create a new file with the same name.

Type the following for the body `style`: body `{background: white;color:#333333; }`, then style a div tag as shown: `div {float:left; border:1px solid #444444;padding :5px;margin:5px; background:#999999;}`.

The first unique div we need to create and style is `#featured`. Type `#featured {position:relative; width: 480px; background-color:#f2f1f1;}` to create the style.

Now create a div named `details` to hold a small information box. Type `#details{ position:relative;display:block;background-color:#6CF;color:#333333; padding:10px; }` to create a div that will display next to the `featured` div.

Save the `css` file, and reference it in the head of the HTML page with the link tag by typing `<link rel="stylesheet" href="css/stylesheet.css"type="text/css" media="screen" charset="utf-8"/>`.

Type the following link to the main jQuery library below the stylesheet link: `<script src="http://jquery.com/src/jquery-latest.js" type="text/javascript" charset="utf-8"></script>`, then link to the jQuery UI library in this recipe's code file by typing `<script type="text/javascript" src="https://ajax.googleapis.com/ ajax/libs/jqueryui/1.8.10/jquery-ui.min.js"></script>`. Finally, add a link to the script we are about to create by typing `<script type="text/javascript" src="js/ explode.js"></script>` to complete the referenced scripts.

Create a new file and name it `explode.js`, and store it in a new subfolder named `js`. Type `$(document).ready(function(){}`. Between the two curly braces (`{}`) type `$('h1').effect('shake', {times:5}, 200);` Create the statement that will cause content contained in the featured div tag to explode. On a new line, type `$('#featured'). effect('shake', {times:3}, 100).delay(500).hide('explode',{}, 2000). slideDown('fast'););` to complete the script. Your block of code should look similar to the following block:

```
$(document).ready(function(){ $('h1').effect('shake',
  {times:5}, 200); $('#featured').delay(2000).hide('explode', {},
  2000 ).slideDown('fast'); });
```

Save the file and return to the HTML page.

Add a closing tag for the `</head>`, and opening `<body>`, tag to the HTML file. Next, enter an opening `<header>` tag and heading text: `<h1>Featured Moto Video</h1>` then closing the `</header>` tag to complete the header area.

Create an opening `<section>` tag then create a div by typing `<div id="featured">`, to hold our video tag and related elements. Type `<video id="movie" width="480" height="360" preload controls>`, then add a source tag for each of the three video file types: `<source src='motogoggles.ogv' type='video/ogg; codecs="theora, vorbis"'/> <source src='motogoggles.mp4' type='video/mp4; codecs="avc1.42E01E, mp4a.40.2"'/> <source src='motogoggles.webm' type='video/webm; codecs="vp8, vorbis"'/>`, then close the `</video>` tag and the featured div with `</div>`.

The final block of content is contained in the `details` div. To create it type `<div id="details">`, then add a heading tag with text `<h1>Details</h1>`, and finally a short explanatory paragraph of text: `<p>The video will explode then appear again!</p>`. Close out the `</div></section> </body></html>` tags. Save the HTML file as `exploding-video-dynamically.html`, and open it in a browser to see the results. They should look similar to the following screenshot, which shows the video breaking into sections and exploding.

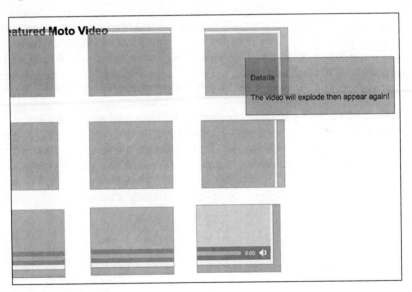

How it works...

The `stylesheet.css` file contained the styles for the featured div that determined the positioning of the video object on the page. The first important thing to notice is the `position` is set to `relative`. This makes it possible for us to move the video object and perform other actions on it using jQuery.

We created a div named `details` whose `position` was also `relative` but with the `background-color` set to `light blue (#6CF)`. The different color will help visually set it apart from the video object.

Next, we added the jQuery library scripts. The jQuery UI library is required in order for us to have access to the methods and functions contained in the `animate` class. We are referencing it locally in this example, but you could also link to it in the same way we accessed the main jQuery library.

Finally, we were able to write our own script to make elements on the page shake and explode! We created a statement to verify that the page was ready for our code by typing `$(document).ready(function(){}`. This function queries the DOM and asks if the page is loaded and ready for the script. Using this wrapper function is a best practice when creating jQuery scripts. We use the alias symbol `$` for the jQuery function to grab the `h1` selector and apply to it the action `effect` containing the `shake` parameter to make the element move sideways, which in turn contained an argument for the number of `times` to shake the element. The interval of time the shake should last was defined in milliseconds, in this case `200`. We use the selector `$('#featured')` to grab the featured div element, and just like we did with the `h1` tag, we `shake` it (only three times for variety) for a period of `100` milliseconds per shake. Now we add a few new actions. A `delay` of `500` milliseconds between the `shakes` and the explosion is appended to command using `.delay(500)`. We then append to that the `hide` action with the parameter `explode`, which will occur one time by default and will last a total of `2000 milliseconds`. After the video explodes, the `slidedown` action slides it back onto the screen with a parameter of `fast`. Note that the amount of time used in the explosion was a bit long so we could see it easily. A timing of `100-500` milliseconds would create a more realistic explosion effect. You could also have grabbed the video tag directly by using `$('video')` if you only wanted the video itself and not the background or border provided by the featured tag.

Moving back to the HTML file, we placed our video in a container div named `featured` and created a parent `video` tag that would `preload` and contain the default `controls`. Before we closed the `video` tag, we nestled a `source` tag for each of the three video file types within it so users with different browsers could watch the video: We did not provide a FLASH fallback, but we could have using a JavaScript library such as `Video.js`. We then closed the `</video>` tag and the featured div with `</div>`.

Finally we created a div to hold information about what users could expect to happen in the `details` div.

There's more...

There is so much more that can be done with the video element, JavaScript, and the canvas tag. Read on for more experiments.

More interactive explosions using video and canvas

Sean Christmann at `http://www.craftymind.com` has an amazing experiment that gives you the power to explode multiple parts of a video at once in real time while it plays using multiple canvases. You can check it out here: `http://www.craftymind.com/2010/04/20/blowing-up-html5-video-and-mapping-it-into-3d-space/` but be warned—it is very resource intensive in Firefox.

What's with all the explosions?

It doesn't seem like there is any real practical reason to break apart videos at first. However, this could be very useful for mimicking unique transition effects or responses to user actions in games.

Chroma key background replacement in real time

Firefox developers have been experimenting with manipulating the video element. They created a tutorial that explained how they performed Chroma key replacement using canvas, JavaScript, and the attributes of the video element. You can read about it and view a demo at: `https://developer.mozilla.org/En/Manipulating_video_using_canvas`.

Imagine displaying a video on a website where you displayed exotic backgrounds or created interactive mash-ups of products and people.

See also

The video element is explored in depth in *Chapter 8, Embracing Audio and Video* of this book.

Movable video ads using jQuery

We will be creating a video ad on a website that will move as the user scrolls down the page using jQuery and the video tag.

Getting ready

You will need a video file in multiple formats such as `.ogg/.ogv`, `.mp4`, and `.webm`, or use a video service such as `http://www.vid.ly.com` to serve cross-browser videos. This example was not tested in Internet Explorer, but should work fine in recent versions of Safari, Google Chrome, Opera, and Firefox.

How to do it...

We will begin by creating a typical website page. Open a new file in your editor, and save it as `movable-video-ad.html`. Type `<!DOCTYPE html> <html lang="en"><head><meta charset="utf-8" /><title>Movable Video Ad</title>` to place the first tags on the page.

Now, create a reference link for our default stylesheet `<link rel="stylesheet" href="css/main.css" type="text/css" media="screen" charset="utf-8" />` and a secondary stylesheet named `<link rel="stylesheet" href="css/scroll.css" type="text/css" media="screen" charset="utf-8" />`.

Next, create reference links for the jQuery scripts. Type `<script src="js/jquery-1.4.min.js" type="text/javascript" charset="utf-8"></script>` to reference the core jQuery code. Add the link statement `<script type="text/javascript" src="js/jquery-ui-1.7.2.custom.min.js"></script>`. The final script to which we will link is our own script that we will create for the recipe named `myAd.js`, which will be stored in a subfolder we create named "js". Type `<script type="text/javascript" src="js/myAd.js"></script>` to link to the file.

Type `</head><body><div id="container">`to begin the content area of the page. Display a page heading by typing `<header> <h1>Motocross Mania</h1></header>`.

Begin adding page content by typing `<div id="content"> <h2>No dirt = no fun</h2>`. The div that will contain the ad can now be added to the page by entering the text `<div id="motoad"><h3>Buy this movie!</h3>`, and then a movie title enclosed in paragraph element tags `<p><strong>MotoHelmet</strong></p>`.

A video tag `<video width="190" height="143" preload controls>` should then be added. Type source tags containing each video format as shown in the following code block:

```
<source src='video/motohelmet.ogv' type='video/ogg; codecs="theora,
   vorbis"'/> <source src='video/motohelmet.mp4' type='video/mp4;
   codecs="avc1.42E01E, mp4a.40.2"'/>
   <source src='video/motohelmet.webm' type='video/webm; codecs="vp8,
   vorbis"'/></video>
```

Close the `</div>` tag and save progress so far.

Create a paragraph with an id of intro `<p id="intro">` to contain the text `We review the best motorcross gear ever!!!`. Follow the paragraph tag and text with a list of dummy links: `<ul><li><a href="#">Helmets</a></li> <li><a href="#">Gloves</a></li><li><a href="#">Goggles</a></li></ul>`, close the paragraph with `</p>`, then create a new div to contain a dummy news content block followed by two more dummy div blocks , a footer tag, and the closing page elements, as shown in the code block below:

```
<div id="news"><h2>Latest News</h2>
   <p>Trip Ousplat admits he doesn't do his own stunts! "My mom makes
```

```
me use a stunt double sometimes," The shy trick-riding sensation
explains.</p>
<p>Gloria Camshaft smokes the competition for a suprise win at the
Hidden Beverage Playoffs</p>
<p>Supercross competitors report more injuries; jumps more extreme
than ever</p><p>James Steward still polite, reporters bored</p>
</div><div id="filler"><h2>On Location</h2>
<p>Grass is not greener as there is no grass on most motorcross
trails experts claim </p></div> <p id="disclaimer">Disclaimer!
Anything you choose to do is at your own risk. Got it?
Good.</p><footer><p>&copy; Copyright 2011 Motocross Extreme
Publications, Inc.</p></footer></div></body></html>
```

Now, we will style the page elements in the `main.css` file. The first crucial style is the `#container` div. It should have a margin of `0 auto` and a width of `650px`. Next the `#motoad` div should be styled to `float right` and contain a `width` of `200px` to hold the video element. Finally, the `#intro` div should contain a shorter width of `450px`. The three styles should look similar to the code block shown here:

```
#container{ margin:0 auto;text-align:left; width: 650px;}
#motoad{ float:right;width:200px;}
#intro{width:450px;}
```

The rest of the styles are minor adjustments to padding and color or other standard declarations.

Now, open the `scroll.css` file to define the styles to help our ad scroll. We will cascade the attributes of `#motoad` to form a div block that can then be moved. Next, define the `height` of the `#content` attribute, and the width of the paragraph and h2 elements. The styles in `scroll.css` should now look like:

```
#motoad {display:block;position: relative; background-color:#FC0;width
:200px;padding:10px;}
#content { height:1000px;}
p {width:450px;}h2 {width:460px;}
```

Save the file, and get ready to create our jQuery script.

Open or create `myAd.js` and begin by typing the document ready function `$(document).ready(function(){}` and curly braces. Click enter between the curly braces and type the scroll function `$(window).scroll(function() {`. After the opening curly brace of that function type the command: `$('#motoad').stop().animate({top: $(document).scrollTop()}, 'slow', 'easeOutBack');`. Close the script with "`});});`" as well. Our jQuery script should now look like the following code block:

```
$(document).ready(function(){  $(window).scroll(function() {
$('#motoad').stop().animate({top: $(document).scrollTop()},'slow','eas
eOutBack'); });  });
```

Save all the files and load the HTML page in a browser window. The page should look like the following screenshot before you begin scrolling the page.

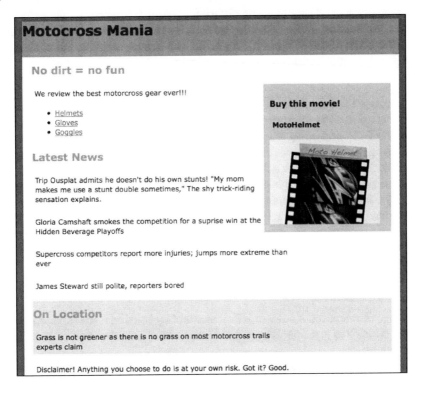

Try scrolling up and down the page. The ad should move up and down the page as well. The result should look similar to the following screenshot:

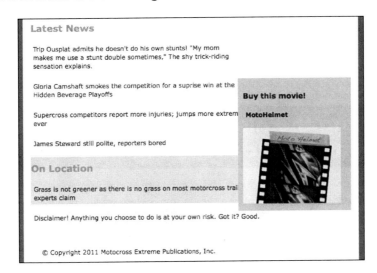

How it works...

After to creating a typical HTML page with different content elements, we were ready to style the CSS pages. We separated the CSS into two files, `main.css` and `scroll.css`, so that when we call the scroll function in our jQuery script and actively apply it, the content elements on the page shrink so that our ad can easily move without blocking any information on the page.

We wanted to cause the `#motoad` div tag to move whenever the window scroll event was called. To do this we use the alias symbol `$` for the jQuery function to grab the `window` selector from the DOM and apply to it the action `scroll` containing the default scroll action parameters. Using this function, we then created our command to control the behavior of our `#motoad` div block. We gave it the action of `stop`, so it would then be ready to animate. The `animate` action was chained to the `stop` command. The first parameter of `animate` that we applied to the `#motoad` div caused the div to move when the scroll bar was moved in the document window. The parameter `slow` controlled the speed at which the ad would move up and down and the parameter `easeOutBack` referenced an easing command to create a fluid animation movement instead of an abrupt start or stop.

There's more...

In this recipe, we've animated a custom HTML element by causing it to respond to user actions on the page. This just one way we can subtly add effects that can be used for real-world solutions.

Have HTML element, will travel

Explore the jQuery UI library and you will be inspired by the many ways you can manipulate and style any HTML element. Visit `http://jqueryui.com` for demos and documentation.

See also

Learning jQuery: Better Interaction Design and Web Development with Simple JavaScript Techniques, available from Packt Publishing.

Controlling the display of images using Easel.js and the canvas tag

The JavaScript library `Easel.js` reduces the complexity of creating animations and rich interactive environments with the `canvas` tag. In this recipe, we will use a series of images in a single file named "`sprites`" to show how to use `Easel.js` to control which graphic image in the sprite is selectively displayed.

Getting ready

You will need to download the `Easel.js` library or use the copy in the code files for this recipe.

How to do it...

Create the opening tags for an HTML5 file. Your code should look similar to the following code block:

```
<!DOCTYPE HTML><html><head><meta http-equiv="Content-Type"
    content="text/html; charset=UTF-8"><title> Animating images using
    BitmapSequence and SpriteSheet</title>
```

Next, link to the main stylesheet `styles.css` used in this recipe: `<link href="styles. css" rel="stylesheet" type="text/css" />`.

Next, we will import the `Easel.js` Framework library by inserting links to the following script files: `UID.js`, `SpriteSheetUtils.js`, `SpriteSheet.js`, `DisplayObject.js`, `Container.js`, `Stage.js`, `BitmapSequence.js`, and `Ticks.js`. You can see the path and link for each script file here:

```
<script src="easeljs/utils/UID.js"></script><script
    src="easeljs/utils/SpriteSheetUtils.js"></script><script
    src="easeljs/display/SpriteSheet.js"></script><script
    src="easeljs/display/DisplayObject.js"></script><script
    src="easeljs/display/Container.js"></script><script
    src="easeljs/display/Stage.js"></script><script
    src="easeljs/display/BitmapSequence.js"></script><script
    src="easeljs/utils/Tick.js"></script>
```

Next, create and opening `<script>`tag and declare the following three variables: `var canvas;var stage;var critterSheet = new Image();` for our script.

Type `function init() {` to begin the function, and follow it with `canvas = document. getElementById("testCanvas");` to tie the canvas in the body of the page to the canvas variable. Prepare to load a new `spriteSheet` by typing `critterSheet.onload = handleImageLoad;`. The `critterSheet` variable stores the source of the sprite images. Type `critterSheet.src = "images/moles.png";` to load our own series of mole images. The function block should look like the code block below:

```
function init() {
    canvas = document.getElementById("testCanvas");
    critterSheet.onload = handleImageLoad;
    critterSheet.src = "images/moles.png"; }
```

The second function we will create is `handleImageLoad()`. Type function `handleImageLoad() {` then `stage = new Stage(canvas);` to create a new instance of the stage. Type `var spriteSheet = new SpriteSheet(critterSheet, 76, 80);` to create a new `spriteSheet`. Create a new bitmap sequence variable called `critter1` to live on it and define its position on the stage using x and y coordinates by typing: `var critter1 = new BitmapSequence(spriteSheet); critter1.y = 85; critter1.x = 85;`. Add a critter from the second image on our sprite sheet `moles.png` by typing `critter1.gotoAndStop(1);`. Next, add it to the stage using the command `stage.addChild(critter1);`.

Clone the first `critter1` variable we created, and pass its value to a new critter variable by typing `var critter2 = critter1.clone();`. Position the new variable to the right of the first critter by adding to its current location value using `critter2.x += 120;`.

Type `critter2.gotoAndStop(0)` to assign a value to the `critter2` variable. The code block for cloning critter 1 and critter 2 should look like the following code block:

```
var critter2 = critter1.clone();
critter2.x += 120;
critter2.gotoAndStop(0);
stage.addChild(critter2);
```

The Tick interval `Tick.setInterval(300);` and listener `Tick.addListener(stage);` are the last two statements we will add to the script. Close the brace (`}`) for the `handleImageLoad()` function, and type a closing script tag.

Close the `</head>` tag, then enter the opening body tag with an `onload` attribute that calls the `init()` function. Create a div named `"description"` for content. Add a div named `canvasHolder` to contain the canvas element. Display the image file `moles.png` at the bottom of the page.

```
<body onload="init();">
  <div class="description">Using <strong>BitmapSequence</strong> to
    animate images from a <strong>SpriteSheet</strong>.
  </div>
  <div class="canvasHolder">
    <canvas id="testCanvas" width="980" height="280"
      style="background-color:#096"></canvas>
  </div>
  </p><p>The original moles.png spritesheet file with all
    the images:<br/><img src="images/moles.png"/></p>
</body></html>
```

Save the files as `whack-mole-easel-test-single.html`. The result can be seen in the following screenshot:

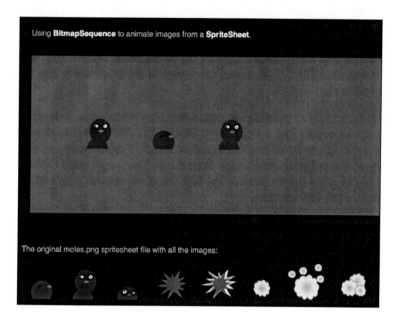

How it works...

After we took care of setting up the beginnings of an HTML5 page we were ready to import the `Easel.js` framework and create our main script.

We created an opening `<script>`tag and declared the following global variables: `var canvas;var stage;var critterSheet = new Image();` for our script.

The function `init()` which was created would be invoked when the page is loaded. It contained the `canvas` variable in the process of being assigned the selector `testCanvas` using `document.getElementById("testCanvas");` to tie the canvas in the body of the page to the canvas variable. Next, we prepare to load a new `spriteSheet` by typing `critterSheet.onload = handleImageLoad;`. The `critterSheet` variable stores the source of the sprite images. Typing `critterSheet.src = "images/moles.png";` gave us access to our own series of mole images.

The second function we created was `handleImageLoad()`. In this function, we did most of our work, starting with creating a new instance of the stage using `stage = new Stage(canvas);`. Next, we created a new `spriteSheet` using `var spriteSheet = new SpriteSheet(critterSheet, 76, 80);` to create a new `spriteSheet`.

Now that we had a sprite sheet instance, we could create a new bitmap sequence variable called `critter1` to live on it and define its position on the stage using x and y coordinates by typing: `var critter1 = new BitmapSequence(spriteSheet);critter1.y = 85;critter1.x = 85;`. Next, we referenced the frames we wanted to add by number so that we applied the correct action first to the critter and then to the stage. We linked the `critter1` variable to the second image on our sprite sheet `moles.png` by typing `critter1.gotoAndStop(1);`. We added the image to the stage using the command `stage.addChild(critter1);`.

We cloned the first `critter1` variable we crated and passed its value to a new critter variable by typing `var critter2 = critter1.clone();`. We positioned the new variable to the right of the first critter by adding to its current location value using `critter2.x += 120;`. We assigned the critter its own image from the `moles.png` image file by commanding the `BitSequence` to `goto` the location of the first image on `moles.png` and `stop` there and assign that to the `critter2` variable.

We added `Tick.setInterval(300);`, which applied a time period of `300` milliseconds between `Ticks`. The Tick interface acts as a global timing device, giving us the ability to return frame rates per second (FPS) if needed. We added a listener to the stage `Tick.addListener(stage);` which behaves like other types of listeners in that it listens for ticks. This can be used to help redraw the stage at a specified time, or perform other timing related actions.

We used the `onload` attribute to call the `init()` function in the `body` tag. This causes the `init()` function to be invoked on page load.

See also

Animating a sequence recipe.

Animating a sequence of images using Easel.js and the canvas tag

We can animate image strips called sprites by creating arrays and functions using the `Easel.js` JavaScript library and then manipulating them with the `canvas` element. In this recipe, we will animate the same strip but display two differently timed sequences.

Getting ready

Download the code files for this recipe to use the `Easel.js` framework library as well as supporting files. You will need a recent browser that will display HTML5 elements to view properly and test the code used in this recipe.

How to do it...

Create the opening tags for an HTML5 file. Your code should look similar to the following code block:

```
<!DOCTYPE HTML><html><head><meta http-equiv="Content-Type"
    content="text/html; charset=UTF-8"><title> Animating images using
    BitmapSequence and SpriteSheet</title>
```

Link to the main stylesheet `styles.css` used in this recipe: `<link href="styles.css" rel="stylesheet" type="text/css" />`.

Import the `Easel.js` Framework library by inserting links to the following script files: `UID.js`, `SpriteSheetUtils.js`, `SpriteSheet.js`, `DisplayObject.js`, `Container.js`, `Stage.js`, `BitmapSequence.js`, and `Ticks.js`. Refer to the previous example for how the framework block should look.

Create an opening `<script>` tag and declare the following three variables: `var canvas;var stage;var critterSheet = new Image();` for our script.

Type `function init(){` to begin the function and follow it with `canvas = document.getElementById("testCanvas");`.

Prepare to load a new `spriteSheet` by typing `critterSheet.onload = handleImageLoad;`. Type `critterSheet.src = "images/moles.png";` to load our own series of mole images. The function block should look like the following code block:

```
function init() {
    canvas = document.getElementById("testCanvas");
    critterSheet.onload = handleImageLoad;
    critterSheet.src = "images/moles.png";}
```

The second function we will create is `handleImageLoad()`. Type function `handleImageLoad() {` then `stage = new Stage(canvas);` to create a new instance of the stage. Type `var spriteSheet = new SpriteSheet(critterSheet, 80, 80);` to create a new `spriteSheet`. Now that we have a sprite sheet, create a new bitmap sequence variable named `critter1` to live on it and define its position on the stage using x and y coordinates by typing: `var critter1 = new BitmapSequence(spriteSheet);` and then `critter1.y = 100;critter1.x = 90;`. Next, we will create an array to map to each image on the original `spritesheet` file by entering `var frameData = {shymole:0, upmole:1, downmole:2, whacked:3, whackedow:4, clouds:5,tinycloud:6, cloudgroup:7};` so that we have eight name values, each of which is tied to an array id.

The code block we have so far for `handleImageLoad()` should look like the following:

```
function handleImageLoad() {
    stage = new Stage(canvas);
    var spriteSheet = new SpriteSheet(critterSheet, 80, 80);
    var critter1 = new BitmapSequence(spriteSheet);
    critter1.y = 100;
    critter1.x = 90;
    var frameData = {shymole:0, upmole:1, downmole:2, whacked:3,
        whackedow:4, clouds:5,tinycloud:6, cloudgroup:7};
```

Create a new `spriteSheet` using it as a parameter by typing: `spriteSheet = new Sprite Sheet(critterSheet, 80, 80, frameData);`.

Create a new bitmap sequence variable named `critter1` and apply the image sprite by typing: `critter1gotoAndStop(0);`. Add `critter1` to the `stage` using `stage.addchild(critter1);`.

Clone the first `critter1` variable, and pass its value to a new critter variable by typing `var critter2 = critter1.clone();`. Define the x value of the new variable using `critter2.x += 120;`. Assign the critter its own image from the `moles.png` image file by typing `critter2.gotoAndStop(5);` The code block for adding a new `spriteSheet`, creating critter 1 and cloning `critter 2` should look like the following code block:

```
spriteSheet = new SpriteSheet(critterSheet, 80, 80, frameData);
critter1.gotoAndStop(0);
stage.addChild(critter1);
var critter2 = critter1.clone();
critter2.x += 120;critter2.gotoAndStop(5);
```

Type: `var critter3 = critter2.clone(); critter3.spriteSheet = spriteSheet;`. Just like with the other critter variables we created earlier, redefine the x value of `critter3` by adding 10 to its current value: `critter3.x += 10;`. The following code block shows what we have done:

```
var critter3 = critter2.clone();
critter3.spriteSheet = spriteSheet;
critter3.x += 10;
```

Reference the image `frames` in `moles.png` by name by typing `critter3.gotoAndStop("upmole");`. Swap the current `upmole` frame image for a different frame by cloning a new variable and referencing a new frame: `var critter4 = critter3.clone(); critter4.gotoAndStop("downmole");`. Move that frame over 10 pixels by typing: `critter4.x += 10;`.

Swap the frames out one more time and move our new frame over 10 pixels to the right: `var critter5 = critter4.clone(); critter5.gotoAndStop("shymole"); critter5.x += 10;`. Let's take a look at the block of code we should have so far:

```
critter3.gotoAndStop("upmole");
var critter4 = critter3.clone();
critter4.gotoAndStop("downmole");
critter4.x += 10;
var critter5 = critter4.clone();
critter5.gotoAndStop("shymole");
critter5.x += 10;
```

Cycle through the frames in our `moles.png` file by typing:

`var critter6 = critter1.clone(); critter6.x = critter5.x + 100; critter6.gotoAndPlay(3); stage.addChild(critter6);`.

Add a second animation sequence to the stage, changing the timing of the animation by referencing a different starting frame when the new critter sprite is added to the stage: `var critter7 = critter1.clone(); critter7.x = critter6.x + 100; critter7.gotoAndPlay(1); stage.addChild(critter7);`.

Our two animation sequences should now contain the following code:

```
var critter6 = critter1.clone();
critter6.x = critter5.x + 100;
critter6.gotoAndPlay(3);
stage.addChild(critter6);
var critter7 = critter1.clone();
critter7.x = critter6.x + 100;
critter7.gotoAndPlay(1);
stage.addChild(critter7);
```

The Tick interval `Tick.setInterval(200);` and listener `Tick.addListener(stage);` are the last two statements we will add to the script. Close the brace (`}`) for the `handleImageLoad()` function and type a closing script tag.

Type `</head>`, then `<body onload="init()">`. Create a div named "description" to hold content. The last div is `canvasHolder`, containing the canvas element. Set the width to `600`, the height to `280`, and the background color to a light gray (`#ccc`). A link to the image file `moles.png` is added so users can see the image sprites referenced in `moles.png`.

Save the file, and open it in a browser window. You should see a still frame on the left side (the image of the mole head with eyes closed) and two animation sequences cycling on the right side of the screen. The following screenshot shows how the two sequences are loading the same frames but with different timing.

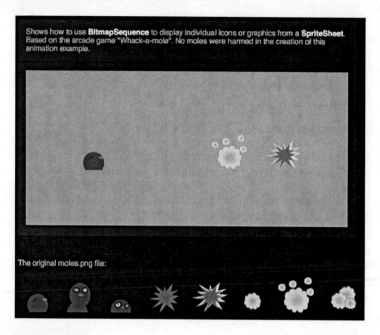

How it works...

The first steps in the recipe of creating the HTML page and referencing the canvas are the same as in the previous recipe.

After creating the `spriteSheet`, we created a new variable to hold our sprite frames called `critter1` and defined the `x` and `y` coordinates for the frame location by typing: `var critter1 = new BitmapSequence(spriteSheet);` `critter1.y = 100;critter1.x = 90;`.

We created the array `var frameData` to declare eight key/value pairs. We were then able to create a new `spriteSheet` that took the parameters for a `spriteSheet` name, a default height and width for each frame, and loaded all the frames from `moles.png` at once into the `spriteSheet` using `frameData`.

Next, we experimented with using `frameData` to reference frames by number value and name key, creating a series of bitmap sequences, then replacing them with their clones.

We animated sequences and placed them on the stage. They both followed the same format but started their animation sequences on different frames by changing the number argument in the `gotoAndPlay` action.

Finally, we added `Tick.setInterval(200);`, which applied a time period of 200 milliseconds between Ticks. The Tick interface acts as a global timing device which gives us the ability to return frame rates per second (FPS) if needed. We added a listener to the stage `Tick.addListener(stage);` which behaves like other types of listeners in that it listens for ticks. This can be used to help redraw the stage at a specified time, or perform other timing related actions. We used the `onload` attribute to call the `init()` function in the `body` tag. This causes the `init()` function to be invoked on page load.

There's more...

`Easel.js` and other similar libraries to make controlling HTML5 elements easier are cropping up everywhere. Take caution on how you use them though as some may not be stable enough for use in production environments.

Pirates Love Daisies and so should you

The creator of `Easel.js` was asked by Microsoft to create a proof of concept web game named Pirates love daisies (`http://www.pirateslovedaisies.com`) made entirely using HTML5 and JavaScript with heavy reliance on the `Easel.js` library to manipulate the `canvas` element. You can play the game in any web browser and in what may be an ironic twist; it contains special features for visitors using the Internet Explorer 9 browser.

The return of old school computer animation techniques

When I first began playing games on a computer, it was a big deal for a game to have 256 colors on the screen and 8-bit animations. Computer animators used a lot of tricks to replicate effects such as water moving. Revisit those days (or discover them for the first time with this demo from effect games: `http://www.effectgames.com/demos/canvascycle/`.

See also

There is a whole chapter in this book full of canvas recipes. Go devour them now if you skipped them.

Random animation with audio using the canvas tag and JavaScript

In this recipe we will use the canvas tag to draw and animate a series of shapes. We will also loop an audio file using the audio tag to play while the animation displays. We are adapting an original animation created by Michael Nutt. We will be creating a slower, more relaxing animation that looks like waving grass.

Getting ready

You will need a recently updated browser, such as Firefox 3.6 or Google Chrome, and an audio file in multiple formats. It does display at a different (smaller) size in Opera browsers 9 and 10. The audio will also not play in those versions of Opera.

How to do it...

First, open a new HTML5 page and name it `random-animation-with-audio.html`. Enter the beginnings of an HTML5 page including the page title:

```
<!DOCTYPE html> <html lang="en"> <head><meta charset="utf-8" />
<title>Canvas Reggae</title>.
```

Then, add links to the JavaScript and CSS files that will be imported when the page loads: `<script type="text/javascript" src="js/animatedlines.js"></script><link rel="stylesheet" href="css/stylesheet.css" type="text/css" media="screen" charset="utf-8" />`, and close the head tag with `</head>`.

Enter `<body onLoad="init();">` to activate the `init()` function when the page loads.

Next we create the header for the page `<header><h1>CANVAS Reggae</h1></header>`, and then add the canvas element by typing `<canvas id="tutorial" width="480" height="360"></canvas>`.

Create a new div with an of `id` credits to hold a link to Michael's site: `<div id="credits">Based on Canvas Party by <a href="http://nuttnet.net/">Michael Nutt</a>  `. Then add a link to the div to grab the audio element and apply the `pause()` function to the music when the link is clicked. `<a href="#" onClick="document.getElementsByTagName('audio')[0].pause();">[OFF]</a></div>`.

Now, enter the audio tag, and set autoplay to true and loop to loop: `<audio autoplay="true" loop="loop">` Create two source tags to contain the audio formats: `<source type="audio/ogg" src="audio/randomreggae.ogg" /><source type="audio/mpeg" src="audio/randomreggae.mp3" />`.

Before closing the audio tag, we will add a string of text that will appear if the audio tag is not supported: `Your browser doesn't recognize the HTML5 audio tag`.

Close the audio, body, and html tags, and save the page.

Before we create our script, open the `stylesheet.css` page, and type the following:

```
body { margin: 0; background-color: #000; color: #FFF; font-family:
   Helvetica, sans-serif; }
a { color: #FFF; }
h1 { position: absolute; top: 0; margin: auto; z-index: 50; padding:
   10px; background-color: #000; color: #FFF; }
div#credits { position: absolute; bottom: 0; right: 0;
   padding: 10px; }
audio { position: absolute; visibility: hidden; }
```

Now that the HTML and CSS pages are built, we will tackle the animation script. Create a new JavaScript file and name it `animatedLines.js`. We will place it in a new subfolder named `js`.

First, we will declare the flatten variable and create a new array function: `var flatten = function(array) { var r = [] ;`. Next, within the function, we will create a `for` statement to declare an array beginning with one object (`var i = 0`) and then increment the size of the array while the length of the array is greater than i. `for(var i = 0; i < array.length; i++) {`. Using the `push` function we will add new values to the array by typing: `r.push.apply(r, array[i]);}` then finally we end the function by returning the array: `return r; }`.

Our script so far should look like the following code block:

```
var flatten = function(array) {
   var r = [];
   for(var i = 0; i < array.length; i++) {
      r.push.apply(r, array[i]);     }
   return r; }
```

Next, we will create a function named shuffle that accepts an array as an argument. Type `function shuffle(array) { var tmp, current, top = array.length;`. Inside the function, we have an if/while loop to move through the values in the array. Add it to the script by entering: `var tmp, current, top = array.length; if(top) while(--top) { current = Math.floor(Math.random() * (top + 1)); tmp = array[current]; array[current] = array[top]; array[top] = tmp; }`. Return the array value at the end of the function. Our function to shuffle array values randomly should now look like the following code block:

```
function shuffle(array) {
   var tmp, current, top = array.length;
   if(top) while(--top) {
      current = Math.floor(Math.random() * (top + 1));
```

```
        tmp = array[current];
        array[current] = array[top];
        array[top] = tmp; }
    return array; }
```

Now, we are ready to create a global `canvas` variable and a `context` variable by typing: `var canvas;` and `var ctx;` respectively.

With those variables created, we can add the `init()` function to the script, where all the action starts. Type `function init() {` then enter the statement to associate our canvas variable with the canvas element: `canvas = document.getElementById('tutorial');`.

Now, we will create an `if` statement to set the width and height attributes of our canvas variable: `if (canvas.getContext) {canvas.width = window.innerWidth; canvas.height = window.innerHeight - 100; ctx = canvas.getContext('2d'); ctx.lineJoin = "round"; setInterval("draw()", 300); }`. This completes the `init()` function.

Next, we add a listener for our browser window to detect when it is being resized: `window.addEventListener('resize', function() {canvas.width = window.innerWidth; canvas.height = window.innerHeight - 100; }); }`.

The most recent additions to our script should now look like:

```
function init() {
  canvas = document.getElementById('tutorial');
  if (canvas.getContext) {
    canvas.width = window.innerWidth;
    canvas.height = window.innerHeight - 100;
    ctx = canvas.getContext('2d');
    ctx.lineJoin = "round";
    setInterval("draw()", 300); }
    window.addEventListener('resize', function() {
      canvas.width = window.innerWidth;
      canvas.height = window.innerHeight - 100;  }); }
```

We are finally ready to create a function to draw shapes onto the canvas. This function will contain most of the script that powers the animation of the shapes. Type `function draw() {ctx.globalCompositeOperation = "darker"; ctx.fillStyle = '#000'; ctx.fillRect(0, 0, canvas.width, canvas.height); ctx.globalCompositeOperation = "lighter";` to set the look of the canvas background.

Now, we will enter the colors to use in the animation. We will create an array of arrays containing rgba values. Type: var colors = ["rgba(134, 154, 67, 0.8)", "rgba(196, 187, 72, 0.8)", "rgba(247, 210, 82, 1)", "rgba(225, 124, 20, 0.8)"];. Our colors are defined, so now we will set the width and height of the shapes using an array containing individual arrays of width and height values: var data = [[[5, 20], [15, 2]], [[50, 12], [10, 14], [3, 21]], [[60, 8]], [[30, 24], [15, 4], [10, 17]], [[5, 10]], [[60, 5], [10, 6], [3, 26]], [[20, 18]], [[90, 11], [40, 13], [15, 10]], [[70, 19]],].

Now we can animate the shapes by changing their width and height using data = shuffle(data);.

To animate the shapes up and down as well as side to side, we need to "flatten" or squish their height. Create a new variable to contain the var flatData = flatten(data);

Now we will be contorting the lines so they appear to wave by pulling them in different directions and using bezierCurve. This is a large function block contained within the draw() function we created earlier, so enter the link() function as shown here:

```
link(topPos, bottomPos, width) {
  var padding = 100;
  ctx.lineWidth = width;
  ctx.beginPath();
  var height = parseInt(canvas.height - padding);
  var pull = 100;
  var topLeft = topPos + (width / 2) + padding;
  var bottomLeft = bottomPos + (width / 2) + padding;
  ctx.moveTo(topLeft, padding);
  ctx.bezierCurveTo(topLeft, pull, bottomLeft, height - pull,
    bottomLeft, height);
  ctx.stroke(); }
```

Now while we are still in the draw() function let's add a new variable to represent the starting point for a shape, and then add a for loop to create a new variable that can hold an array of data value sets. Below is the variable and loop code: Var topStartingPoint = 0; for(var i in data) { var group = data[i]; var color = colors[i % colors. length]; ctx.strokeStyle = color;.

Take it further by creating a nested for loop that passes a group of data values to a new variable named line: for(var j in group) { var line = group[j]; which we can then manipulate after creating a bottomStartingPoint variable with an initial value of zero: var bottomStartingPoint = 0;.

A third nested for loop will allow us to control the positioning and movement of the shapes further: for(var k in flatData) { if(flatData[k][1] < line[1]) { bottomStartingPoint += flatData[k][0] + 11; } }.

Finally, we use link to set the top and bottom starting points for a line, `link(topStartingPoint, bottomStartingPoint, line[0]);`, then assign the `topStartingPoint` the value of its current value plus the line array. The final statement sets the `topStartingPoint` value to its current value plus five: `topStartingPoint += line[0]; } topStartingPoint += 5; }}`. Save the script file.

Open the file `random-animation-with-audio.html` in a browser, and you should see the lines sway back and forth similar to what is shown in the following screenshot:

How it works...

First, we created our HTML5 page with links to the JavaScript and CSS files that would be imported when the page loaded: `<script type="text/javascript" src="js/animatedlines.js"></script><link rel="stylesheet" href="css/stylesheet.css" type="text/css" media="screen" charset="utf-8" />`. To activate our animation sequence, we placed the `init()` function in the body tag of the HTML page. The `init()` function in the `animatedLines.js` JavaScript file will be initialized by `<body onLoad="init();">` when the page loads.

We used the body style to set a global default margin of 0, a background-color, font color, and font-family for the page. We styled a basic link color, then styled the h1 heading tag so it would display at the top with position: absolute; top: 0; and always appear above most other content blocks by setting the z-index to 50. The #credits div was positioned to appear at the bottom-right corner of the page and the audio tag was hidden using visibility: hidden.

We created a new script named animatedLines.js and first defined a series of variables and functions to control the behavior of the shapes.

We set up an array named flatten that would add new values to itself. We next needed a function to rotate randomly through array values. We used the Math.floor(Math.random() statement to calculate a random number, and multiply the result by the sum of the current value of the variable top + 1. We then returned a whole number value to the variable current.

We defined the dimensional values of the canvas variable by grabbing the ID of the canvas element on page load using document.getElementById. We set the width and height attributes of our canvas variable with some help from the DOM: canvas.height = window.innerHeight - 100; ctx = canvas.getContext('2d'); then created a statement to apply a lineJoin to the 2d context of the canvas with a parameter of round. We set the speed the lines were drawn on the canvas to 300 milliseconds using the setInterval() function. The higher the number, the slower the animation looks. We added a listener for our browser window to detect when it is being resized using window.addEventListener, which contained parameters for the size of the browser window and the canvas.

The shapes were then drawn onto the canvas using the draw() function. The globalCompositeOperation = "darker"; was used to darken lines as they moved across each other. Areas of the lines brightened as they overlapped in the front area of the canvas stage using globalCompositeOperation = "lighter"; to set the look of the canvas background.

The colors used to decorate the lines need to be in rgba format. The 'a' in rgba refers to the alpha value, which controls the visibility of each color. Each rgba value set was contained in an array, which in turn became a list of arrays. We needed a matching number of width and height value sets for the lines. These were stored in the array var data.

We next assigned the data array the value returned from our shuffle() function so we could randomize the appearance of the lines on the screen. Then, we assigned to the variable flatData the value returned from the flatten() function. Assigning a pull value to each line enabled us to move it over a set number of pixels. We combined this with bezierCurve to cause the lines to bend.

There's more...

Combining the audio tag, canvas animations, and JavaScript sounds like a fun way to create cool visualization effects. These are heavily dependent upon browser support though, so many web browser users won't be able to view them properly at this time. By which I mean most standard browsers won't be able to play them as far off as a year or two.

Visualizing your audio with cutting edge browsers

If you have downloaded the beta Firefox 4, you have access to the Firefox Audio and Video API. You will be able to view and create your own audio visualizations using tools like the Spectrum Visualizer:

```
http://www.storiesinflight.com/jsfft/visualizer/index.html
```

Pushing the implementation of audio in HTML5

Alexander Chen has been experimenting with audio and canvas by porting Flash-based app. He has run into some issues with using multiple audio files that are detailed here on his blog:

```
http://blog.chenalexander.com/2011/limitations-of-layering-html5-
audio/
```

See also

The canvas and audio/video chapters in this book.

8
Embracing Audio and Video

In this chapter, we will cover:

- ▸ Saying no to Flash
- ▸ Understanding `audio` and `video` file formats
- ▸ Displaying `video` for everybody
- ▸ Creating accessible `audio` and `video`
- ▸ Crafting a slick `audio` player
- ▸ Embedding `audio` and `video` for mobile devices

Introduction

"Flash was created during the PC era – for PCs and mice. Flash is a successful business for Adobe, and we can understand why they want to push it beyond PCs. But the mobile era is about low power devices, touch interfaces and open web standards – all areas where Flash falls short. The avalanche of media outlets offering their content for Apple's mobile devices demonstrates that Flash is no longer necessary to watch video or consume any kind of web content." - Steve Jobs

Like many of the other new technologies we've looked at already, in the open source HTML5 standard, the new `audio` and `video` elements are more mature and usable than ever before. That's a good thing, because users' expectations for multimedia are much higher than ever before. Back in the day we used 300-baud modems that took 10 minutes to download one photo. Later, we used Napster to illegally download MP3 `audio` files. Now, we stream television and pornography on our mobile devices. Since the bandwidth pipe has gotten fatter and fatter, our demand for interactive entertainment has become virtually insatiable. It's time for the money shot.

For years the battle was between QuickTime, RealPlayer, and Flash for video playback dominance on the web. These browser plugins were easy to install and *usually* produced expected results.

Over time, QuickTime and RealPlayer continued as playback platforms but the makers of the proprietary Flash tool also created a robust development environment, allowing not just designers but also developers to see it as a viable platform.

While QuickTime and RealPlayer still exist, Flash has won the war. For animations and cartoons, Flash is the ideal tool. But is it the best to serve up `audio` and `video` anymore? Steve Jobs sure didn't think so.

In 2010, Jobs, head of Apple Computer, drew a line in the sand and said Flash would never appear on his best selling iPhones and iPads. Instead, he came out strongly in favor of the open HTML5 standard and ignited an online holy war.

Soon, pronouncements of "The Death of Flash" made headlines in the media and throughout the blogosphere. Some wrote with such bile it was as if a dam had burst and all the accumulated filth and scum was allowed to flood our collective multimedia conversations.

Quickly, even non-web designers and developers took notice, like when C.C. Chapman, noted author of the book "*Content Rules*" expressed his dissatisfaction with The Today Show not being available on his iPad:

@cc_chapman
C.C. Chapman

Bummer! Wanted to watch The Today Show web stream, but it is flash so no iPad watching.

11 hours ago via Twitter for iPad   ☆ Favorite ↻ Retweet ↩ Reply

The issue has quickly permeated our online entertainment discussions. You no longer have to be a web designer or developer to know there's a real issue here.

C.C. spoke simply and to the point, but the author knows he's managed to put his foot in his mouth when talking about the Flash/HTML5 `video` war that Steve created. Sometimes he's argued his point with too much gusto and bravado, but the truth is those with clearer heads like web designer Jessica Bonn are right when they remind us that Flash and HTML5 `video` can peacefully coexist.

In less than a year since Steve made his pronouncement, sites like ABC, CBS, CNN, ESPN, Facebook, Fox News, MSNBC, National Geographic, Netflix, The New York Times, NPR, People, Sports Illustrated, Time, Vimeo, The Wall Street Journal, YouTube, and more have adopted the new HTML5 `audio` and `video` elements. As of this writing, more than 60 percent of all web `video` is now HTML5 ready. It's safe to say that the new HTML5 `audio` and `video` capabilities are some of the most exciting and anticipated new developments!

Browsers that support the new HTML5 `audio` and `video` elements include:

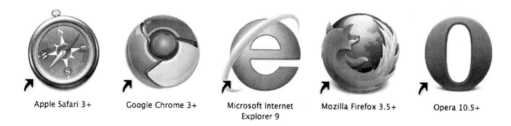

Apple Safari 3+   Google Chrome 3+   Microsoft Internet Explorer 9   Mozilla Firefox 3.5+   Opera 10.5+

In this chapter, we'll look at real-life examples of saying no to Flash, understanding the new `video` and `audio` file formats, displaying `video` for everybody, creating accessible `audio` and `video`, crafting a slick `audio` player, and embedding `audio` and `video` for mobile devices.

Now, let's get cooking!

Saying no to Flash

The author's mom used to say there's a time and place for everything, and we believe there's a time and place for Flash. It's just that now with more mature technology, there's less time and less place for Flash in this author's opinion.

In the bad old days, if we wanted to use a YouTube video like "Neutraface", the typography world's answer to Lady Gaga's "Pokerface", in a web page, we'd have to work with some ugly code like this:

```
<object width="640" height="390">
  <param name="movie"
  value="http://www.youtube.com/v/xHCu28bfxSI?fs=1&amp;hl=en_US">
  </param>
  <param name="allowFullScreen" value="true"></param>
  <param name="allowscriptaccess" value="always"></param>
  <embed
    src="http://www.youtube.com/v/xHCu28bfxSI?fs=1&amp;hl=en_US"
    type="application/x-shockwave-flash" allowscriptaccess="always"
    allowfullscreen="true" width="640" height="390"></embed>
</object>
```

That's long, ugly, convoluted, and won't pass a validation test. It also relies on a third-party plugin. Ugh.

For years, we suffered with that junk, but no more. Now we can rebuild it—we have the technology.

How to do it...

Instead of that bloated `object` code, now we can use something much more elegant:

```
<video src="videosource.ogv"></video>
```

That's all that's required. It's short, pretty, and it validates. And best of all, it doesn't require a plugin. Tell me again why we thought Flash was a good idea.

To add a bit more style and functionality, let's include just a little more code.

```
<video src="videosource.ogv" controls height="390"
   width="640"></video>
```

How it works...

That code should be pretty straightforward. As you might guess, `src` refers to the source `video` file, `controls` indicate the `video` should play with standard playback and volume controls, and `height` and `width` are self explanatory.

Modern browsers now have their own native HTML5 `audio` and `video` playback controls. Let's take a look at each one, starting with Apple Safari:

This is how Google Chrome displays the playback controls:

Microsoft Internet Explorer 9 displays it differently:

Then, Mozilla Firefox does it differently still:

It should come as no surprise that Opera displays the playback controls in yet another way:

Every single one of those looks different. If each of those different appearances are sufficient for your needs, great! If not, that will definitely require more work to get those to act and appear similar.

There's more...

There are a few optional attributes we could include, too. They are:

- `autobuffer` – This Boolean attribute tells the browser to start downloading the song or movie even before the user clicks the play button.
- `autoplay` – As you might guess, this tells the browser to start playing the HTML5 `audio` or `video` automatically.
- `loop` – Also a Boolean attribute, it plays the HTML5 `audio` or `video` file over and over.
- `preload` – The preload attribute starts loading the file before it's even played.
- `poster` – The `poster` attribute is a static placeholder image displayed while the new HTML5 `video` loads. This attribute wouldn't apply to an HTML5 `audio` file, obviously.

Whether you add none or all of these optional attributes, you'll still end up with a prettier, more semantic, more accessible method of displaying `audio` and `video` than relying upon Flash to serve it up for you.

Some good news

Unlike the `canvas` chapter, the good news about the new HTML5 `audio` and `video` elements is that they are accessible. Right out of the box, the new HTML5 `audio` and `video` elements feature keyboard accessibility. Since the browser now handles the new HTML5 `audio` and `video` elements natively, it can support your keyboard just as if it had buttons instead of keys. This alone could go a long way toward acceptance of this new technology.

Video with style

The new HTML5 `audio` and `video` elements are visually stylable with CSS. We can use CSS to not only control the size of the player but also add `:hover` and `:transform` effects. In addition, we can use JavaScript to control the new HTML5 `audio` and `video` behavior. Cool!

Cover your assets

One area where Flash does provide an advantage is in protecting your `audio` and `video` content. Remember that by nature, the new HTML5 `audio` and `video` elements are open source and feature no digital rights management. If protecting your `audio` or `video` file from being downloaded is a deal breaker for you, the new HTML5 `audio` and `video` elements are not the tools for you—Flash probably still is. That's not to say that Flash offers ultimate protection against thievery—it's simply to say that out of the box, Flash obscures the ability to find the media track, where the new HTML5 `<audio>` and `<video>` elements by default leave those files right out in the open to anyone. Flash Media Server, however, does allow you to completely protect your assets.

Still not sure whether to choose HTML5 audio and video or Flash? Try this list of handy tips.

The benefits of HTML5 include:

- **Accessibility:** If accessibility matters to you (and it should) then the new HTML5 `audio` and `video` elements are your best options.
- **iOS:** If you want your `audio` and `video` to display on the iPhone or iPad, HTML5 is your only choice.
- **Mobile:** Mobile devices other than Apple's have great support for the new HTML5 `audio` and `video` elements.
- Video/Audio **Streaming:** If the content you're streaming isn't proprietary and doesn't require rights management, HTML5 is the perfect option for you.

The benefits of Flash include:

- **Accessibility:** If you don't care about the blind or deaf, don't support them. Who cares if you get sued, right?

- **Animation:** Without a doubt, the best reason to use Flash is if you have intensive animation on your site. Sites like `http://jibjab.com` couldn't exist without it.

- **Desktop-only development:** If you don't need to support mobile users. That's just a fad anyway.

- Video/Audio **Streaming:** If you don't like to share and must lock your `audio` or `video` down so it's not easy for people to download, stick with Flash.

- **Webcams:** If you use webcams (and other than `http://chatroulette.com`, who does that anymore?), then Flash is the way to go.

Is this *really* the most compelling reason to use Flash?

See also

Want to be able to play the new HTML5 `audio` and `video` elements in all major browsers, including all the way back to Internet Explorer 6? Who doesn't? If that's the case, check out the free, open-source Projekktor project at `http://projekktor.com`. The brain child of Sascha Kluger, Projekktor uses JavaScript to ensure the various supported browsers each see the specific HTML5 `video` file format they can correctly interpret and display.

Understanding audio and video file formats

There are plenty of different `audio` and `video` file formats. These files may include not just `video` but also `audio` and metadata—all in one file. These file types include:

- `.avi` – A blast from the past, the Audio Video Interleave file format was invented by Microsoft. Does not support most modern `audio` and `video` codecs in use today.

- `.flv` – Flash `video`. This used to be the only `video` file format Flash fully supported. Now it also includes support for `.mp4`.

- `.mp4` or `.mpv` – MPEG4 is based on Apple's QuickTime player and requires that software for playback.

How it works...

Each of the previously mentioned `video` file formats require a browser plugin or some sort of standalone software for playback. Next, we'll look at new open-source `audio` and `video` file formats that don't require plugins or special software and the browsers that support them.

- **H.264** has become of the most commonly used high definition `video` formats. Used on Blu-ray Discs as well as many Internet `video` streaming sites including Flash, iTunes Music Store, Silverlight, Vimeo, YouTube, cable television broadcasts, and real-time videoconferencing. In addition, there is a patent on H.264 is therefore, by definition, not open source. Browsers that support H.264 `video` file format include:

Apple Safari 3.1+   Google Chrome 3+   Microsoft Internet
                                                    Explorer 9

 Google has now partially rejected the H.264 format and is leaning more toward its support of the new WebM `video` file format instead.

- **Ogg** might be a funny sounding name, but its potential is very serious, I assure you. Ogg is really two things: Ogg Theora, which is a `video` file format; and Ogg Vorbis, which is an `audio` file format. Theora is really much more of a `video` file compression format than it is a playback file format, though it can be used that way also. It has no patents and is therefore considered open source. We'll discuss Ogg Vorbis in the next section.

Fun fact: According to Wikipedia, "Theora is named after Theora Jones, Edison Carter's controller on the Max Headroom television program."

Browsers that support the Ogg `video` file format include:

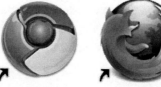

Google Chrome 3+   Mozilla Firefox 3.5+   Opera 10.5+

> ▸ **WebM** is the newest entrant in the online `video` file format race. This open source `audio/video` file format development is sponsored by Google. A WebM file contains both an Ogg Vorbis `audio` stream as well as a VP8 `video` stream. It is fairly well supported by media players including Miro, Moovidia, VLC, Winamp, and more, including preliminary support by YouTube. The makers of Flash say it will support WebM in the future, as will Internet Explorer 9. Browsers that currently support WebM include:

Google Chrome 6+   Mozilla Firefox 4+   Opera 10.6+

There's more...

So far this may seem like a laundry list of `audio` and `video` file formats with spotty browser support at best. If you're starting to feel that way, you'd be right.

The truth is no one `audio` or `video` file format has emerged as the one true format to rule them all. Instead, we developers will often have to serve up the new `audio` and `video` files in multiple formats while letting the browser decide whichever one it's most comfortable and able to play. That's a drag for now but here's hoping in the future we settle on fewer formats with more consistent results.

Audio file formats

There are a number of `audio` file formats as well. Let's take a look at those.

- **AAC** – Advanced Audio Coding files are better known as AACs. This `audio` file format was created by design to sound better than MP3s using the same bitrate. Apple uses this `audio` file format for its iTunes Music Store. Since the AAC `audio` file format supports DRM, Apple offers files in both protected and unprotected formats. There is an AAC patent, so by definition we can't exactly call this `audio` file format open source. All Apple hardware products, including their mobile iPhone and iPad devices as well as Flash, support the AAC `audio` file format. Browsers that support AAC include:

Apple Safari 3+   Microsoft Internet Explorer 9

- **MP3** – MPEG-1 Audio Layer 3 files are better known as MP3s. Unless you've been hiding under a rock, you know MP3s are the most ubiquitous `audio` file format in use today. Capable of playing two channels of sound, these files can be encoded using a variety of bitrates up to 320. Generally, the higher the bitrate, the better the `audio` file sounds. That also means larger file sizes and therefore slower downloads. There is an MP3 patent, so by definition we can't exactly call this `audio` file format open source either. Browsers that support MP3 include:

Apple Safari 3+   Microsoft Internet Explorer 9

- **Ogg** – We previously discussed the Ogg Theora `video` file format. Now, let's take a look at the Ogg Vorbis `audio` format. As mentioned before, there is no patent on Ogg files and are therefore considered open source.

Another fun fact: According to Wikipedia, "Vorbis is named after a *Discworld* character, Exquisitor Vorbis in *Small Gods* by *Terry Pratchett*."

Google Chrome 3+   Mozilla Firefox 3.5+   Opera 10.5+

File format agnosticism

We've spent a lot of time examining these various `video` and `audio` file formats. Each has its own plusses and minuses and are supported (or not) by various browsers. Some work better than others, some sound and look better than others. But here's the good news: The new HTML5 `<video>` and `<audio>` elements themselves are file-format agnostic! Those new elements don't care what kind of `video` or `audio` file you're referencing. Instead, they serve up whatever you specify and let each browser do whatever it's most comfortable doing.

Can we stop the madness one day?

The bottom line is that until one new HTML5 `audio` and one new HTML5 `video` file format emerges as the clear choice for all browsers and devices, `audio` and `video` files are going to have to be encoded more than once for playback. Don't hold your breath for this to change any time soon.

Displaying video for everybody

According to author Mark Pilgrim, your HTML5 web `video` work flow will look something like this:

- Make one version that uses WebM (VP8 and Vorbis).
- Make another version that uses H.264 baseline `video` and AAC "low complexity" `audio` in an MP4 container.
- Make another version that uses Theora `video` and Vorbis `audio` in an Ogg container.
- Link to all three `video` files from a single `<video>` element, and fall back to a Flash-based `video` player.

Kroc Camen did exactly that when he created "Video for Everybody", a chunk of HTML code that displays the new HTML5 `video` element if the user's browser can handle it and a Flash movie if it can't—all without JavaScript. Let's look at how Kroc did it at `http://camendesign.com/code/video_for_everybody`.

How to do it...

```
<video controls height="360" width="640">
  <source src="__VIDEO__.MP4" type="video/mp4" />
  <source src="__VIDEO__.OGV" type="video/ogg" />
  <object width="640" height="360" type="application/
    x-shockwave-flash" data="__FLASH__.SWF">
    <param name="movie" value="__FLASH__.SWF" />
    <param name="flashvars" value="controlbar=over&amp;
      image=__POSTER__.JPG&amp;file=__VIDEO__.MP4" />
    <img src="__VIDEO__.JPG" width="640" height="360" alt="__TITLE__"
      title="No video playback capabilities, please download the
      video below" />
  </object>
</video>
```

```
<p><strong>Download Video:</strong>
  Closed Format: <a href="__VIDEO__.MP4">"MP4"</a>
  Open Format: <a href="__VIDEO__.OGV">"Ogg"</a>
</p>
```

Looking closely, it's easy to see what Kroc did. First, he called the browser-native playback controls, as well as the new HTML5 `video` element's associated `height` and `width`.

```
<video controls height="360" width="640">
```

Next, one by one, Kroc calls each of the new HTML5 `video` sources in order, beginning with an MP4 file. Desktop browsers won't care much which order the HTML5 `video` files are included in, but the iPad is picky about wanting an MP4 file specified first, so fine. You win again, Steve Jobs.

```
<source src="__VIDEO__.MP4" type="video/mp4" />
<source src="__VIDEO__.OGV" type="video/ogg" />
```

Kroc then hedges his bets by calling a Flash `video` version of the same file for wimpy browsers that can't handle the new HTML5 `video` element.

```
<object width="640" height="360" type="application/x-shockwave-flash"
  data="__FLASH__.SWF">
  <param name="movie" value="__FLASH__.SWF" />
  <param name="flashvars" value="controlbar=over&amp;
    image=__POSTER__.JPG&amp;file=__VIDEO__.MP4" />
  <img src="__VIDEO__.JPG" width="640" height="360" alt="__TITLE__"
    title="No video playback capabilities, please download the
    video below" />
</object>
```

Finally, Kroc adds a nice extra touch by prompting the user to optionally download the new HTML5 `video` file itself in both closed (MP4) as well as open (Ogg) formats. Sharing is caring.

```
<p><strong>Download Video:</strong>
  Closed Format: <a href="__VIDEO__.MP4">"MP4"</a>
  Open Format: <a href="__VIDEO__.OGV">"Ogg"</a>
</p>
```

 Of course you'd replace things like "_VIDEO_.MP4" with the path to your own files.

This approach is so full of win because no matter what web browser you use, you get to see *something*—all without requiring JavaScript or downloading Flash.

How it works...

The concept is really quite simple: If your browser is capable of playing a new HTML5 `video` element file, that's exactly what you'll see. If it's not capable of that, a Flash movie is also included in the code stack, so you should see that instead. If, for some reason, your browser won't natively support the new HTML5 `video` element and the Flash player crashes or isn't available, you'll see a static image in its place. Everybody's covered.

Browsers that will display the new HTML5 `video` element using this approach include:

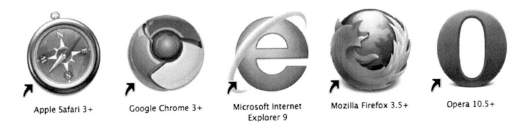

| Apple Safari 3+ | Google Chrome 3+ | Microsoft Internet Explorer 9 | Mozilla Firefox 3.5+ | Opera 10.5+ |

Browsers that will display Flash `video` using this approach include:

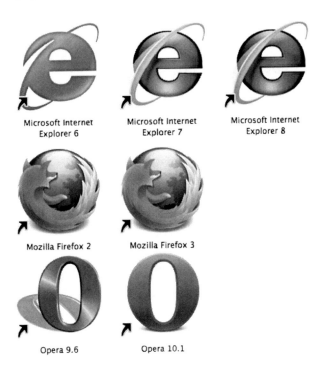

Microsoft Internet Explorer 6

Microsoft Internet Explorer 7

Microsoft Internet Explorer 8

Mozilla Firefox 2

Mozilla Firefox 3

Opera 9.6

Opera 10.1

There's more...

All other Flash `video` embedding methods prompt the user to download Flash if it isn't already installed. "Video for Everybody" is unique in that it doesn't do that. Author Kroc Camen did that by design, saying:

> *"Users have enough problems with security already without random websites prompting them to install things—and it's even more annoying for people who don't want or cannot use Flash anyway."*

A mime is a terrible thing to waste

Kroc reminds us to ensure our servers are using the correct `mime-types` and suggests placing these lines in your `.htaccess` file:

```
AddType video/ogg    .ogv
AddType video/mp4    .mp4
AddType video/webm   .webm
```

External "Video for Everybody"

There's now a "Video for Everybody" plugin for WordPress at `http://wordpress.org/extend/plugins/external-video-for-everybody`. Now you can easily use Kroc's approach on your blog too.

Be flexible with your approach

Later we'll look at an approach that accomplishes much the same thing as Kroc's approach does, but this time with JavaScript. Remember: Do what makes the most sense for you, your project, and most importantly, your customers.

See also

Humanstxt.org is a project to make the developers behind websites more known. The site encourages developers to include a small text file that contains information about each of the team members that contributed to creating and building the site. Check it out at: `http://humanstxt.org`.

Creating accessible audio and video

We've looked quite extensively at how to serve online HTML5 `video` to people regardless of their browser but haven't paid much attention to those who rely on assistive technologies. That ends now.

How to do it...

First, we'll start with Kroc Camen's "Video for Everybody" code chunk and examine how to make it accessibility friendly to ultimately look like this:

```
<div id="videowrapper">
  <video controls height="360" width="640">
    <source src="__VIDEO__.MP4" type="video/mp4" />
    <source src="__VIDEO__.OGV" type="video/ogg" />
    <object width="640" height="360" type="application/
      x-shockwave-flash" data="__FLASH__.SWF">
      <param name="movie" value="__FLASH__.SWF" />
      <param name="flashvars" value="controlbar=over&amp;
        image=__POSTER__.JPG&amp;file=__VIDEO__.MP4" />
      <img src="__VIDEO__.JPG" width="640" height="360"
        alt="__TITLE__" title="No video playback capabilities,
        please download the video below" />
    </object>
    <track kind="captions" src="videocaptions.srt" srclang="en" />
    <p>Final fallback content</p>
  </video>
  <div id="captions"></div>
  <p><strong>Download Video:</strong>
    Closed Format: <a href="__VIDEO__.MP4">"MP4"</a>
    Open Format: <a href="__VIDEO__.OGV">"Ogg"</a>
  </p>
</div>
```

How it works...

The first thing you'll notice is we've wrapped the new HTML5 `video` element in a wrapper `div`. While this is not strictly necessary semantically, it will give a nice "hook" to tie our CSS into.

```
<div id="videowrapper">
```

Much of the next chunk should be recognizable from the previous section. Nothing has changed here:

```
<video controls height="360" width="640">
  <source src="__VIDEO__.MP4" type="video/mp4" />
  <source src="__VIDEO__.OGV" type="video/ogg" />
  <object width="640" height="360" type="application/
    x-shockwave-flash" data="__FLASH__.SWF">
    <param name="movie" value="__FLASH__.SWF" />
    <param name="flashvars" value="controlbar=over&amp;
```

```
    image=__POSTER__.JPG&amp;file=__VIDEO__.MP4" />
  <img src="__VIDEO__.JPG" width="640" height="360" alt="__TITLE__"
    title="No video playback capabilities, please download the
    video below" />
</object>
```

So far, we're still using the approach of serving the new HTML5 `video` element to those browsers capable of handling it and using Flash as our first fallback option. But what happens next if Flash isn't an option gets interesting:

```
<track kind="captions" src="videocaptions.srt" srclang="en" />
```

What the heck is that, you might be wondering.

> *"The `track` element allows authors to specify explicit external timed text tracks for media elements. It does not represent anything on its own." - W3C HTML5 specification*

Here's our chance to use another new part of the HTML5 spec: the new `<track>` element. Now, we can reference the type of external file specified in the `kind="captions"`. As you can guess, `kind="captions"` is for a caption file, whereas `kind="descriptions"` is for an `audio` description. Of course the `src` calls the specific file and `srclang` sets the source language for the new HTML5 `track` element. In this case, en represents English. Unfortunately, no browsers currently support the new `track` element.

Lastly, we allow one last bit of fallback content in case the user can't use the new HTML5 `video` element or Flash when we give them something purely text based.

```
<p>Final fallback content</p>
```

Now, even if the user can't see an image, they'll at least have some descriptive content served to them.

Next, we'll create a container `div` to house our text-based captions. So no browser currently supports closed captioning for the new HTML5 `audio` or `video` element, we'll have to leave room to include our own:

```
<div id="captions"></div>
```

Lastly, we'll include Kroc's text prompts to download the HTML5 `video` in closed or open file formats:

```
<p><strong>Download Video:</strong>
  Closed Format: <a href="__VIDEO__.MP4">"MP4"</a>
  Open Format: <a href="__VIDEO__.OGV">"Ogg"</a>
</p>
```

There's more...

In addition to the optional `controls` attribute for the new HTML5 `audio` and `video` elements, there's also the optional `loop` attribute. As you might guess, this example would allow the HTML5 `video` to keep playing over and over:

```
<video controls height="360" loop width="640">
```

Always consider accessibility

That final descriptive content we're defaulting to could be an alternate place to serve downloadable links to those using accessibility technologies. It would obfuscate the download ability from those who can see or hear, so you should determine if that approach works for you.

Browser support

The web browsers that have the best accessibility support for the new HTML5 `audio` and `video` elements include:

Microsoft Internet   Mozilla Firefox 4+   Opera 11+
Explorer 9

See more

You can keep track of HTML5 accessibility at `http://html5accessibility.com`. The site tracks what new HTML5 features like `audio` and `video` are available and in which browsers. You might be surprised to discover that as of this writing, Opera is the least accessibility friendly web browser, rating even below Microsoft Internet Explorer 9. Surprise, surprise.

See also

Video.Js is another free, open-source HTML5 video player. It's lightweight, using no images, but remains fully skinnable via CSS. It looks great and supports Apple Safari, Google Chrome, Microsoft Internet Explorer 9, Mozilla Firefox, and Opera with fallback support for IE 6-8. It even works for mobile devices like the iPhone, iPad, and Android. Check it out at `http://videojs.com`.

Crafting a slick audio player

Neutron Creations Principal and Co-Founder and front-end developer Ben Bodien created a customized HTML5 `audio` player for Tim Van Damme's The Box podcast at `http://thebox.maxvoltar.com`. Ben's creation is fast, intuitive, and slick. Let's take a deeper look at how he did it.

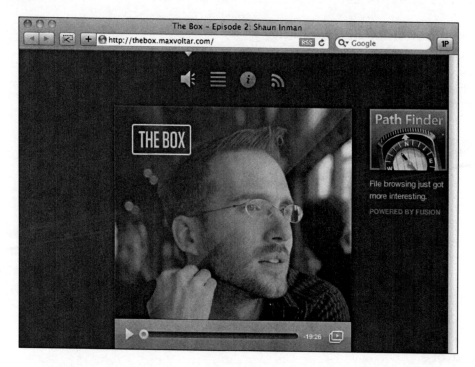

Ben's custom HTML5 `audio` player features an attractive photo of the person being interviewed (Shaun Inman, in this case), a play/pause button, a track indicating playback progress, and the ability to pop the HTML5 `audio` player itself out into a separate window if you so choose. That's it. Nothing more is needed. As an added touch, notice the detail of the slight transparency of the HTML5 `audio` player bar. Smooooth.

How to do it...

At first, Ben's markup seems deceptively simple:

```
<p class="player">
  <span id="playtoggle" />
  <span id="gutter">
    <span id="loading" />
    <span id="handle" class="ui-slider-handle" />
```

```
      </span>
      <span id="timeleft" />
   </p>
```

Wait a minute, I hear you thinking, "Where's the HTML5 audio tag?!" Never fear. Ben's a clever guy and has a plan for this. But first let's examine what he's done so far.

```
   <p class="player">
```

This one's simple so far. Ben creates a wrapping element (a `<p>` in this case) to put his player in. Could he have used a `<div>` instead? Perhaps. Do what makes the most sense for you and your project.

```
   <span id="playtoggle" />
```

Ben then uses this self-closing (notice the trailing slash at the end) span for the play/pause toggle button.

```
   <span id="gutter">
      <span id="loading" />
      <span id="handle" class="ui-slider-handle" />
   </span>
```

Now, it gets interesting. Ben's "gutter" span houses the timeline track with a bar indicating the loading or buffering progress of the HTML5 audio file and the circular element indicating the playback head, which you can "scrub" back and forth if you choose.

```
   <span id="timeleft" />
```

Finally, Ben uses another self-closing span to display the remaining time, in minutes and seconds.

> The `<span>` element does the job, but it isn't very semantic, is it? Patrick H. Lauke was quick to point out that using focusable elements would go a long way toward making this approach accessible to those who rely on assistive technologies.

How it works...

Ben uses jQuery to detect support for HTML5 audio.

```
if(!!document.createElement('audio').canPlayType) {
   var player = '<p class="player"> ... </p>\
      <audio>\
         <source src="/path/to/episode1.ogg" type="audio/ogg"></source>\
         <source src="/path/to/episode1.mp3"
```

```
        type="audio/mpeg"></source>\
      <source src="/path/to/episode1.wav" type="audio/
        x-wav"></source>\
    </audio>';
  $(player).insertAfter("#listen .photo");
}
```

In that chunk of code, we can see how if the browser supports HTML5 `audio`, it gets served the full HTML5 `<audio>` tag, complete with fallbacks to `.ogg`, `.mp3`, and `.wav`, a file format we haven't worked with yet. Since the new HTML5 `<audio>` and `<video>` elements are file format agnostic, a `.wav` file should work just fine too.

Ben has created a simple bit of JavaScript to allow browsers to do what they feel most comfortable doing. Consider this approach if it makes sense for you and your project, but remember that you're relying on JavaScript to do the heavy lifting, as opposed to other approaches we've looked at that don't rely on it.

 Note that if you use a `<div>` to contain the HTML5 `video` player, that JavaScript would have to be adjusted as well. Simply put, the `<p class="player">` ... `</p>` would be changed to `<div class="player">` ... `</div>`.

There's more...

So far, we've set the markup for the player and "sniffed" to see which file format any particular browser wants. Now, we need to add some functionality.

```
audio = $('.player audio').get(0);
loadingIndicator = $('.player #loading');
positionIndicator = $('.player #handle');
timeleft = $('.player #timeleft');
if ((audio.buffered != undefined) && (audio.buffered.length != 0)) {
  $(audio).bind('progress', function() {
    var loaded = parseInt(((audio.buffered.end(0) / audio.duration)
      * 100), 10);
    loadingIndicator.css({width: loaded + '%'});
  });
}
else {
  loadingIndicator.remove();
}
```

And then add a function to calculate the position of the playback head to determine the time remaining, being careful to include a leading zero if the time remaining calls for it.

```
$(audio).bind('timeupdate', function() {
    var rem = parseInt(audio.duration - audio.currentTime, 10),
    pos = (audio.currentTime / audio.duration) * 100,
    mins = Math.floor(rem/60,10),
    secs = rem - mins*60;
    timeleft.text('-' + mins + ':' + (secs > 9 ? secs : '0' + secs));
    if (!manualSeek) { positionIndicator.css({left: pos + '%'}); }
    if (!loaded) {
        loaded = true;
        $('.player #gutter').slider({
            value: 0,
            step: 0.01,
            orientation: "horizontal",
            range: "min",
            max: audio.duration,
            animate: true,
            slide: function() {
                manualSeek = true;
            },
            stop:function(e,ui) {
                manualSeek = false;
                audio.currentTime = ui.value;
            }
        });
    }
});
```

The only thing left to invoke is the play/pause button functionality.

```
$(audio).bind('play',function() {
    $("#playtoggle").addClass('playing');
}).bind('pause ended', function() {
    $("#playtoggle").removeClass('playing');
});
$("#playtoggle").click(function() {
    if (audio.paused) { audio.play(); }
    else { audio.pause(); }
});
```

Style and substance

After the simple markup and detailed JavaScript to create Ben's customized HTML5 `audio` player, the only thing left is to style it:

```css
.player {
  display: block;
  height: 48px;
  width: 400px;
  position: absolute;
  top: 349px;
  left: -1px;
  -webkit-box-shadow: 0 -1px 0 rgba(20, 30, 40, .75);
  -moz-box-shadow: 0 -1px 0 rgba(20, 30, 40, .75);
  -o-box-shadow: 0 -1px 0 rgba(20, 30, 40, .75);
  box-shadow: 0 -1px 0 rgba(20, 30, 40, .75);
  border-top: 1px solid #c2cbd4;
  border-bottom: 1px solid #283541;
  background: #939eaa;
  background: -webkit-gradient(linear, 0% 0%, 0% 100%,
    from(rgba(174, 185, 196, .9)), to(rgba(110, 124, 140, .9)),
    color-stop(.5, rgba(152, 164, 176, .9)),
    color-stop(.501, rgba(132, 145, 159, .9)));
  background: -moz-linear-gradient(top, rgba(174, 185, 196, .9),
    rgba(152, 164, 176, .9) 50%, rgba(132, 145, 159, .9) 50.1%,
    rgba(110, 124, 140, .9));
  background: linear-gradient(top, rgba(174, 185, 196, .9),
    rgba(152, 164, 176, .9) 50%,
    rgba(132, 145, 159, .9) 50.1%, rgba(110, 124, 140, .9));
  cursor: default;
}
#playtoggle {
  position: absolute;
  top: 9px;
  left: 10px;
  width: 30px;
  height: 30px;
  background: url(../img/player.png) no-repeat -30px 0;
  cursor: pointer;
}
#playtoggle.playing {background-position: 0 0;}
#playtoggle:active {top: 10px;}
#timeleft {
  line-height: 48px;
  position: absolute;
  top: 0;
  right: 0;
  width: 50px;
  text-align: center;
  font-size: 11px;
```

```
    font-weight: bold;
    color: #fff;
    text-shadow: 0 1px 0 #546374;
}
#wrapper #timeleft {right: 40px;}
#gutter {
    position: absolute;
    top: 19px;
    left: 50px;
    right: 50px;
    height: 6px;
    padding: 2px;
    -webkit-border-radius: 5px;
    -moz-border-radius: 5px;
    -o-border-radius: 5px;
    border-radius: 5px;
    background: #546374;
    background: -webkit-gradient(linear, 0% 0%, 0% 100%, from(#242f3b),
        to(#516070));
    background: -moz-linear-gradient(top, #242f3b, #516070);
    background: linear-gradient(top, #242f3b, #516070);
    -webkit-box-shadow: 0 1px 4px rgba(20, 30, 40, .75) inset,
        0 1px 0 rgba(176, 187, 198, .5);
    -moz-box-shadow: 0 1px 4px rgba(20, 30, 40, .75) inset,
        0 1px 0 rgba(176, 187, 198, .5);
    -o-box-shadow: 0 1px 4px rgba(20, 30, 40, .75) inset,
        0 1px 0 rgba(176, 187, 198, .5);
    box-shadow: 0 1px 4px rgba(20, 30, 40, .75) inset,
        0 1px 0 rgba(176, 187, 198, .5);
}
#wrapper #gutter {right: 90px;}
#loading {
    background: #fff;
    background: #939eaa;
    background: -webkit-gradient(linear, 0% 0%, 0% 100%,
        from(#eaeef1), to(#c7cfd8));
    background: -moz-linear-gradient(top, #eaeef1, #c7cfd8);
    background: linear-gradient(top, #eaeef1, #c7cfd8);
    -webkit-box-shadow: 0 1px 0 #fff inset, 0 1px 0 #141e28;
    -moz-box-shadow: 0 1px 0 #fff inset, 0 1px 0 #141e28;
    -o-box-shadow: 0 1px 0 #fff inset, 0 1px 0 #141e28;
    box-shadow: 0 1px 0 #fff inset, 0 1px 0 #141e28;
    -webkit-border-radius: 3px;
    -moz-border-radius: 3px;
    -o-border-radius: 3px;
    border-radius: 3px;
    display: block;
    float: left;
    min-width: 6px;
    height: 6px;
```

```
    }
    #handle {
      position: absolute;
      top: -5px;
      left: 0;
      width: 20px;
      height: 20px;
      margin-left: -10px;
      background: url(../img/player.png) no-repeat -65px -5px;
      cursor: pointer;
    }
    .player a.popup {
      position: absolute;
      top: 9px;
      right: 8px;
      width: 32px;
      height: 30px;
      overflow: hidden;
      text-indent: -999px;
      background: url(../img/player.png) no-repeat -90px 0;
    }
.player a.popup:active {background-position: -90px 1px;}Content matters
```

It's a lot easier and more rewarding to spend the time to create something interesting when the content it's wrapping is compelling. The Box audio interviews are always a good listen—it's just too bad the author Tim Van Damme doesn't publish them more often. Here's hoping that changes in the future. Check it out at `http://thebox.maxvoltar.com`.

Being careful with details

This approach works beautifully when there's one new HTML5 `audio` or `video` element on a page at a time to deliver. If you require more than one, you're going to have to modify the JavaScript to tie into multiple "hooks" in the markup.

See also

SublimeVideo takes a different approach to HTML5 online `video` playback: In this case, the player is not created or hosted by you, but by the makers of the player itself in the cloud. The benefit is that you always have the latest, freshest version of the player possible. That way when new features are available or bugs are fixed, there's nothing for you to do. You automatically have the freshest features. Check it out at `http://sublimevideo.net`.

Embedding audio and video for mobile devices

We've really only touched on the mobile experience thus far but as development increases for ever-smarter mobile units, we need to turn our attention to getting our new HTML5 `audio` and `video` to display on those devices. Here's how.

How to do it...

Now that we know how to choose a HTML5 `audio` or `video` file format for our intended audience, we can now turn our attention to making sure they can hear or view it not just on their desktop computers and laptops, but also on their mobile devices.

We'll start by creating a free account with `http://vimeo.com`. Once your registration is complete, choose the Upload | Video ability in the main menu. You'll choose the file you want to upload, add optional metadata, and let the Vimeo servers do their work setting up your file. Next is when the real excitement begins: Embedding the `video`. Choose **Tools | Embed This Video** from the Vimeo main menu.

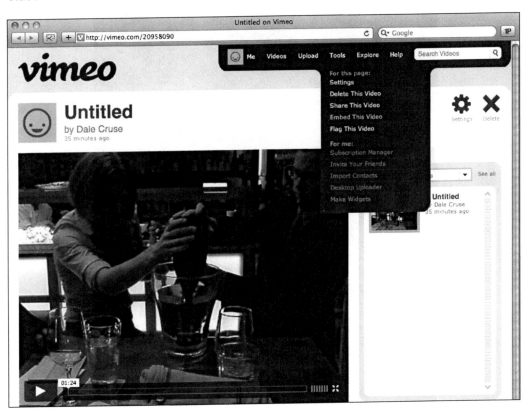

How it works...

Vimeo used to use the now old-fashioned Flash embedding method we looked at earlier. Now it uses an iFrame-based method that will allow the HTML5 `video` to be played on the iPhone, iPad, and other mobile devices. Here's a sample, based on a `video` the author uploaded:

```
<iframe src="http://player.vimeo.com/video/20958090" width="400"
   height="300" frameborder="0"></iframe><p><a
   href="http://vimeo.com/20958090">Untitled</a> from <a
   href="http://vimeo.com/user6281288">Dale Cruse</a> on <a
   href="http://vimeo.com">Vimeo</a>.</p>
```

There's more...

Once you copy and paste that iFrame-based code snippet onto a web page and view it on an iPhone or iPad, you should have a mobile-friendly HTML5 `video` that you can make full size just like this one:

Vimeo offers much more

Vimeo also allows you to add friends from your e-mail contact list, create `video` subscriptions, make widgets, and much more. They now even offer Video School to help educate users on the most effective ways of capturing, editing, and sharing your `videos`.

Coming full circle

YouTube, the world's most popular online `video`-viewing site, also now uses an iFrame-based approach to embedding `videos` now too. We can take the same "Neutraface" `video` we started with at the beginning of this chapter, use the new iFrame-based embedding approach, and end up with something much more semantic and friendly. It also passes validation!

```
<iframe title="YouTube video player" width="1280" height="750"
    src="http://www.youtube.com/embed/xHCu28bfxSI?rel=0&amp;hd=1"
    frameborder="0" allowfullscreen></iframe>
```

Look at how much prettier that is!

We've come full circle and fully transformed our `video` capturing, editing, and playback abilities to work in modern browsers while supporting both those who rely on assistive technologies and those on mobile devices. And that's one to grow on.

See also

Is Adobe cutting its own throat? Hardly. In early 2011, Adobe introduced a free Flash-to-HTML5 converter, codenamed "Wallaby". Unfortunately, many designers and developers felt Adobe over-promised when it claimed Wallaby could export Flash to HTML5 using web standards. The truth is all it does is convert the simplest animation created in Flash CS5 or later to simple markup and style. There's no ability to convert ActionScript to JavaScript, an ability that would truly make the tool valuable. Check out the Wallaby announcement over at John Nack's blog at `http://blogs.adobe.com/jnack/2011/03/wallaby-flash-to-html5-conversion-tool-now-available.html`.

9
Data Storage

In this chapter, we will cover:

- ▶ Testing browsers for data storage support
- ▶ Using browser developer tools to monitor web storage
- ▶ Setting and getting session storage variables
- ▶ Setting and getting a local storage variable
- ▶ Converting local storage strings to numbers using `parseInt`
- ▶ Creating a web SQL database
- ▶ Using a web SQL database
- ▶ Creating a cache manifest and using sites offline
- ▶ Displaying the current location using the Geolocation API and `geo.js`

Introduction

HTML5 introduces a new way to store information without using cookies. This gives designers and developers more flexibility in how dynamic content is processed and displayed. We will begin with testing browsers for support of the three main data storage methods, and end by creating an HTML5 page that uses local storage to store and access a video. Although each of these recipes build on each other, you do not have to complete them in the order they are presented. The example files from this chapter are available for download at `http://www.packtpub.com/support?nid=7940`.

Testing browsers for data storage support

Knowing how to test quickly whether a browser supports a data storage method you want to use will make developing pages and applications easier. In this recipe, we will create a script that queries a browser's DOM to test for support of different data storage methods.

Getting ready

You will need access to a modern browser such as Firefox 3.6, or the latest versions of a popular browser such as Google Chrome, Opera, Safari, or Internet Explorer.

How to do it...

First, we are going to create a simple html page. Open an HTML editing program or a text editor, and enter the starting code for a basic HTML5 page:

```
<!doctype html><html lang="en"><head><title>Client-side Storage Test
  for HTML5</title>
<meta charset="utf-8">
```

The look of the test page now needs to be styled. We will use `<style>` tags within the `<head>` tags HTML page, but you could also place them in a separate CSS file.

```
<style>
#results { background-color: #ffcc99; border: 1px #ff6600 solid;
  color: #ff6600; padding: 5px 20px; margin-bottom: 10px; }
#results .value { font-weight: bold; }
#results h3 { color: #333333; }
</style>
```

Type a closing `head` tag, then create a `body` tag as shown below. Notice the big difference is we are calling a `RunTest()` function to activate when the page loads.

```
</head><body onload="RunTest();">
```

Create a paragraph tag with descriptive text similar to what is show below. Close the tag, and create an `<h3>` header tag to contain the result heading.

```
<p>Does your browser support all storage methods?</p>
<div id="results"><h3>Browser Data Storage Support Results</h3>
```

Now, type each storage method followed by a span tag that is styled by the class value. Type the ID of the storage method and the text "not supported". Close the span tag and add a break tag to separate the results onto individual lines in the browser window. The results' display area should look like the following code block:

```
Session Storage: <span class="value" id="session">not supported</
span><br/>
Local Storage: <span class="value" id="local">not supported</span>
  <br />
Database Storage: <span class="value" id="db">not supported</span>
  <br /></div>
```

We are almost done creating our test page. Create a paragraph explaining the purpose of the test. Finish the content area off with a `<footer>` tag to contain the script block we will be adding next. The descriptive text should look like the following code:

```
<p>The test above shows whether the browser you are currently using
  supports a data storage method.</p>
<footer>
```

Now, we will add `script` tags so that the browser will process a small test program:

```
<script language="javascript">
function RunTest() {

for (var mydata in window)
{
```

Next, we will create a case statement that includes a block of code for each data storage method we are going to test:

```
switch (mydata) {
case "sessionStorage":
  document.getElementById("session").innerHTML = "supported";
break;
case "localStorage":
  document.getElementById("local").innerHTML = "supported";
break;
case "openDatabase":
  document.getElementById("db").innerHTML = "supported";
break;
} }} </script> </footer> </body> </html>
```

Save the file as `data-storage-support-test.html`, and open it in your browser window. You should see a result similar to the following screenshot:

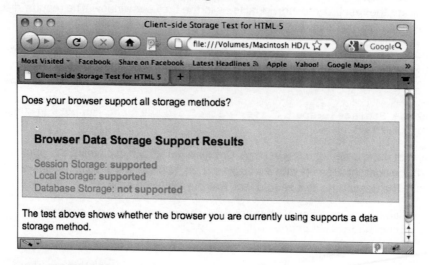

How it works...

The HTML5 test page we created used a small snippet of JavaScript code to query the browser to see if it supported specific storage methods. We began by writing a standard HTML5 page with the appropriate `<html>`, `<head>`, and other document tags. If you need a refresher on them, they are covered in the earlier chapters of this book. Next, we set up the opening block of a JavaScript code snippet using the simplified `<script>` tag. The HTML5 JavaScript API is covered in more detail elsewhere in this book. We created a function named `RunTest()` to contain the variables and code. Two variables were then created. The variable supp was given the value of an empty string. This would contain the final support result for each storage method. We're looping through the properties of the window object. During each iteration the current property is temporarily stored in the `mydata` variable. This allows us to test the property against the three cases.

Next, we use a switch statement to test the `mydata` variable against the particular properties in which we are interested. Because we are only testing a single value at a time, and the list is short, this is a good way to test for support of each storage method. The body of the `switch` statement contained three cases, one for each storage method. Each case contains an expression that must be evaluated. If the storage method is supported, the final action of each case is to change the value of the result text in the main body of the document from "not supported" to "supported" if the expression evaluates as true. If the case does not evaluate as true, then the text displayed in the result section of the page will remain unchanged.

After creating the code we controlled the presentation of the results using CSS styles. A container to display the box was created using a div tag named results, and a background color, font colors, and weight were specified. This was the last block of code for the head section of the html page.

The body section of the page was then created. The test was set to activate when page loaded in the browser using the `onload` command. The opening text and title for the result box were written, and the display text for each result was tied to a unique ID. The closing tags were then entered to complete the page. After saving the page, the results were then displayed on the screen when the test page was viewed in the browser window. The browser used in the screenshot was Firefox 3.6.13. The results we saw mirrored the current support Firefox offers in versions 3.6 and 4.0.3 for storage methods. This helped us determine that we could expect Firefox visitors to view and use any features easily on a web page that depended on local storage and session storage methods. They would be unable to take advantage of any features dependent upon WebSQL.

There's more...

Testing sites and online applications has never been easier. There are many tools and services available that can be used to test on different platforms and across browsers.

Mobile testing

You can download multiple browsers on smart devices, such as the iPod Touch or iPad, enabling you to test the responsiveness of your rich media content on mobile devices and different browsers.

Adobe browser lab

Adobe CS5 is not required to try Adobe BrowserLab, an online cross-browser testing tool that is integrated with Adobe CS5 products. Visit `https://browserlab.adobe.com` to learn more.

Free cross-browser and OS testing with BrowserShots

An alternative for those on a budget and with time to spare is `BrowserShots.org`. This site enables visitors to enter the URL of their website and then select from an enormous list of browsers and operating systems. It can take a few minutes for the results to appear using the free version of the service.

Using browser developer tools to monitor web storage

Web storage can be challenging to test. Using developer tools in browsers, such as Safari or Firefox addons such as Firebug, make it easier to diagnose issues and track the values of variables. In this recipe, we will use the native developer tools in the Google Chrome browser to explore the key/value pairs stored in the local storage area of a browser.

Getting ready

You will need a recent version of the Google Chrome browser and one of the local storage code files for this chapter.

How to do it...

Open one of the local storage exercise files from this chapter in a Google Chrome browser window.

Click **View**, select **Developer** from the **View** menu, and then choose **Developer tools** from the **Developer** fly-out menu.

When the **Developer** window appears over the current page, select the **Resources** tab, click **Local Storage** in the navigation area of the Google Chrome Developer Tools window, and then the submenu within it. You should see a result similar to the following screenshot:

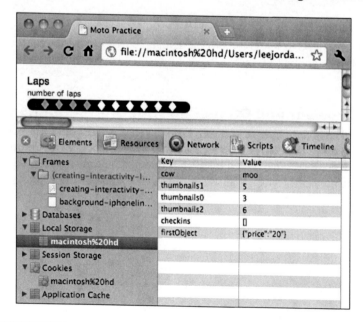

The Local Storage section under the Resources tab of the Google Developer tools window gives us access to local storage areas for each page. It displays keys and their corresponding values on the right side of the screen. If you right-click on an object you will have the option to delete it.

How it works...

We loaded a page that we knew used local storage to test how the Google Developer tools window available in the Google Chrome browser would display key/value pairs.

When we navigated down the left menu of the developer tools we could choose from different web storage methods and other resources.

There's more...

There are many free plugins and native browser tools of which developers can take advantage.

Use a Firebug addon even if you don't use Firefox

Firefox users have long enjoyed debugging and browsing websites and other online applications using the Firebug addon (`http://getfirebug.com/downloads`). Users of Opera, Google Chrome, Safari, and IE 6+ can use Firebug Lite (`http://getfirebug.com/firebuglite`) and experience similar functionality with a lightweight bookmarklet they can easily add to their browser.

Safari developer tools are native to the Safari browser

With the Safari browser open, click **Safari**, select **Preferences**, and click on the **Advanced** tab. Click the checkbox next to "**Show develop menu in menu bar**" to begin using the native developer tools.

Setting and getting a session storage variable

Session storage and local storage both share the web storage API. In this recipe, we will define two session storage variables, and then display them on the screen.

Getting ready

You will need an up-to-date browser that supports session storage. Safari and Google Chrome respond best if you are testing your files locally on your computer.

How to do it...

First, we will create the head area of an HTML5 page and an opening body tag:

```
<!DOCTYPE HTML><html><head><meta http-equiv="Content-Type"
    content="text/html; charset=UTF-8"><title>Show me the session
    storage</title></head><body>
```

Add a `section` and an `article` tag. Give the article tag an ID of "aboutyou".

```
<section><article id="aboutyou"><p></p></section>
```

Next, we will create two session storage variables using the `setItem` method as show in the following code block:

```
<footer><script>sessionStorage.setItem('nickname', 'Jumpin Joseph');
    sessionStorage.setItem('interest', 'bike ramps and bmx racing');
```

Now we will display the session storage variables we just set on the screen using the `getElementByID` and `getItem` methods:

```
document.getElementById('aboutyou').innerHTML = ("Your nickname is: "
    + sessionStorage.getItem('nickname') + "." + " You are interested
    in: " + sessionStorage.getItem('interest') + ".");
</script></footer></body></html>
```

The results should display on the HTML page in the browser similarly to how they are shown in the following screenshot:

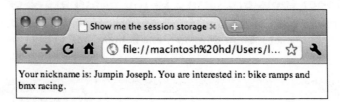

How it works...

We set two session variables to unique values in this example. Session storage uses key/value pairs, so each variable must be set with a value when created. By default, these values are strings.

We defined a session variable for the person's nickname by typing `sessionStorage.setItem('` then added a name for our variable.

We named the variable "nickname" and gave it the value of "Jumpin Joseph": `'nickname', 'Jumpin Joseph');`.

When we created a second session variable to contain the variable named "interest" and its value, we used the same syntax format as we did when setting the first session variable.

Although normally these variables would be populated with values from a form, we focused on using the correct syntax in the example. The sessionStorage keyword identified the type of storage method. We followed that with a period which attached the action setItem to the keyword. The variable nickname was then declared and given a value of Jumpin Joseph. What this will tell the browser when it is used is to create a new session storage variable named "nickname" and store the value of "Jumpin Joseph" inside it. We then created a second session storage variable just because we could. We will use a form to pull variable values in the local storage example in this chapter to give a full lifecycle view of storage method creation, usage, and destruction.

There's more...

Session storage gives us a more powerful way to provide short-term client side storage.

One browser, one session

Session storage is best used for situations that do not benefit from visitors using multiple tabs of their browser to navigate a site, and where the need for storage is temporary. While the data storage area of the HTML5 specification is still evolving, and the security does not have a long track record for use by financial institutions or other websites where information must be highly secure, there are still many useful ways to take advantage of session storage.

See also

Setting and getting a local storage variable recipe.

Setting and getting a local storage variable

Although session storage is temporary, and lasts only as long as a browser session is active. Local storage persists even after a browser is closed. In this recipe, we will create a story-writing application using the HTML5 contenteditable attribute and local storage.

Getting ready

You should be using a recently updated browser. This recipe works best in Google Chrome and Safari but also functions fine in Firefox.

How to do it...

First create a basic HTML5 page, and then add a script tag between the opening and closing head tags. The script should link to the 1.5.2 minimized jQuery library at `http://ajax.googleapis.com/ajax/libs/jquery/1.5.2/jquery.min.js`. Your code should now look similar to the following block:

```
<!DOCTYPE html><html lang="en"><head><script
  src="http://ajax.googleapis.com/ajax/libs/jquery/1.5.2/
  jquery.min.js"></script>  <meta http-equiv="Content-Type"
  content="text/html; charset=utf-8">
  <title>Local Storage: Storywriter</title>
```

Next, we will add CSS styles to set the `background-color` and text `color` of the article tag as well as the `font-family`.

```
<style>  article{background-color: #9F6;color:#333;
  font-family:Verdana, Geneva, sans-serif}  p{}  </style>
```

Close the head tag and create opening tags for the `body` and `header` elements. Add an h1 tag to display `Storywriter` as the page title, and close the `header` tag.

```
</head><body>  <header>    <h1>Storywriter</h1>  </header>
```

Create opening tags for the `section` and `article` elements. Add an id of "mypage" to the `article` element, and set the `contenteditable` attribute to "`true`".

```
<section><article id="mypage" contenteditable="true">
```

Next, create a paragraph tag which contains the placeholder text `type something`, and then close the paragraph, `article`, and `section` tags. Add descriptive instructional text between two em tags. What you just entered should look like the following code:

```
<p>type something</p>    </article>  </section><em>And then what
  happened? I'll remember next time you open this browser. </em>
```

Create a `script` tag, and then declare the jQuery function by typing `$(function(){`.

Invoke the `document.getElementById` method with an argument string of "`mypage`", assigning it to the variable '`edit`'.

Next, we need to add an event handler triggered by the blur event on the '`edit`' element. Type `$(edit).blur(function(){`, and then type `localStorage.setItem('storyData", this.innerHTML);});` to complete the function.

Now that local storage can store strings with `setItem`, we can use `getItem` to push the stored string content back onto the page by typing `if ( localStorage.getItem('storyData') ) { edit.innerHTML = localStorage.getItem('storyData'); } });`

The script code block should now look like the following code block:

```
<script>$(function() {  var edit = document.getElementById('mypage');
  $(edit).blur(function() {    localStorage.setItem('storyData',
  this.innerHTML);  });  if ( localStorage.getItem('storyData') ) {
  edit.innerHTML = localStorage.getItem('storyData'); } });</script>
```

Close the body and HTML tags, and save the file. Open it in a browser window. You should now be able to begin typing your own story and see the entered text display on the page, even if you close the browser and reopen it again later. It should look similar to the following screenshot:

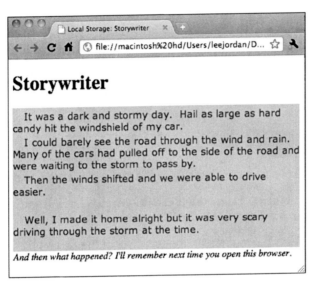

How it works...

When we set the `article` tag's `contenteditable` attribute to `true`, we told the browser to allow users to enter text. Most HTML5 elements can have a `contenteditable` attribute declared and then set to `true` or `false`. We then captured the content as it was entered using `document.getElementById` using the id `mypage`. The `getElementById` jQuery method searches the document for a specific ID name listed in its argument. We then added an event handler on the `blur` event to smooth the look of the text being entered. We also stored the text at the same time using the local storage method `setItem` and the variable `storyData`. Finally, we used the `getItem` local storage method to check if `storyData` existed, and if it did, to load it into an editable HTML element with `edit.innerHTML` and `getItem`.

Earlier chapters in this book on HTML5 elements, and PACKT jQuery books.

Converting local storage strings to numbers using parseInt

In this recipe, we will take a string value from local storage and convert it into an integer so we can perform a mathematic operation on it by using `parseInt`.

Getting ready

We will be using Modernizr (`http://www.modernizr.com`) to detect if local storage is available, hosting it locally in a subfolder named "`js`". You will also need at least one recently updated browser.

How to do it...

Create the beginnings of a new html page up to the title tag as shown in the code block below:

```
<!DOCTYPE html><html lang="en"><head><meta charset="utf-8">
  <title>Using numbers with local storage</title>
```

Next, add styles to specify the font-family, the text color of the h1 and h2 tag, and a background-color and height for the h2 tag.

```
<style>body{font-family:Verdana, Geneva, sans-serif;}
  h1{color:#333; }h2{color:#C30;background-color:#6CF;
  height:30px;}</style>
```

Add an IE HTML5 shiv, hosted by Google, and a link to a local Modernizr JavaScript file:

```
<!--[if IE]><script
  src="http://html5shiv.googlecode.com/svn/trunk/html5.js"></script>
  <![endif]--><script type="text/javascript" src="js/
  modernizr-1.7.min.js"></script>
```

Perform a check to see if local storage is supported by the browser with some help from the Modernizr script:

```
<script>if (Modernizr.localstorage) {
// window.localStorage is available!}
  else {// the browser has no native support for HTML5 storage
    document.getElementByID('yayanswer').innerHTML = "Local Storage
    is not supported by your browser. Maybe it's time for
    an update?";}
```

Create a function named `storemyradius()`, declare a variable named `myradiusToSave`, and assign it `document.getElementById('myradius').value;` to pass the value entered by the visitor into the text field when they click save.

```
function storemyradius() {var myradiusToSave =
    document.getElementById('myradius').value;
```

Add an `if` statement to check if `myradiusToSave` is null. Below that, create a local storage `setItem` method with a key of "myradius" and a value of "myradiusToSave". Place a function call to `displaymyradius();` before the closing bracket of the `if` statement and the `storemyradius` function as shown in the following code block:

```
if (myradiusToSave != null) {
    localStorage.setItem('myradius',
    myradiusToSave);displaymyradius();}}
```

Create a function named `displaymyradius`, which accepts no arguments, and then add a variable named `myradius`. Assign to it the JavaScript function `parseInt` containing a local storage `getItem` method with an argument of "myradius" and a radix of 10. The function should look like the following code block so far:

```
function displaymyradius() {  var myradius =
    parseInt(localStorage.getItem('myradius'),10);
```

In the same function, create an if statement that will check to see that the `myradius` variable is not null and is greater than zero. Create the variable `diameter`, and assign as its value the result of multiplying 2 times the value in `myradius`. Use `document.getElementById` and `innerHTML` to display the value of the diameter variable along with the message "The diameter of the circle is" between the h2 tags in the body of the HTML page.

```
if (myradius != null && myradius > 0) {var diameter = 2 *
    myradius;document.getElementById('yayanswer').innerHTML = "The
    diameter of the circle is: " + diameter + "!";}}
```

Create a function named `clearmyradius` that accepts no arguments, and then create an `if` statement that checks if the local storage `getItem` method contains a value that is not null. Between the `if` statement brackets, place the local storage `removeItem` method with an argument string of "myradius" and a call to the local storage `clear` method. Close the script and head tags. The code we just wrote should look similar to the following code block:

```
function clearmyradius() {if (localStorage.getItem('myradius') !=
    null) {localStorage.removeItem('myradius');
    window.localStorage.clear();}}</script></head>
```

Create opening body, section, hgroup and h1 tags, and type "localStorage Number Conversion" before the closing h1 tag. Create an h2 tag and assign it an ID of "yayanswer". Close the hgroup tag, and then add a label tag for the myradius text field. Type "Enter the radius of the circle:" as the label text. Create an input form field tag with an ID of "myradius" and a maxlength of "4". Create two input buttons, one with an onclick value that calls the function storemyradius(); and another with an onclick value that calls the function clearmyradius();. Close the section, body, and html tags, and save the page. The final block of code should look like the following one:

```
<body ><section><hgroup><h1>localStorage Number Conversion</h1>
  <h2 id="yayanswer"></h2></hgroup><label for="myradius">Enter the
  radius of the circle:</label><input id="myradius" maxlength="4" />
  <input onclick="storemyradius();" name="save" type="button"
  value="save"><input onclick="clearmyradius();" name="clear"
  type="button" value="clear"></section></body></html>
```

Here is how the finished HTML page should look in a Google Chrome browser window:

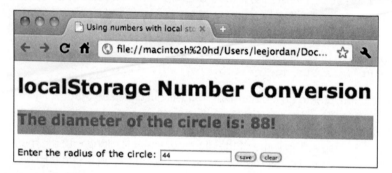

How it works...

The text field displayed in the HTML page accepts what the visitor types and passes it as a value to the storemyradius() function. We declared a variable named myradiusToSave and assigned it document.getElementById('myradius').value; which stored the value contained in myradius. It in turn will pass the value entered in the text field "myradius" to the setItem method of local storage. Before the value can be passed to local storage we needed to verify that myradiusToSave actually contained a value that was not null. If it is not null, then there is data to save to local storage. The value was then saved to local storage, using setItem as a part of a key/value pair. To use the myradius value as a number, we needed to convert it back from a string to an integer. This was done by calling the parseInt JavaScript function. Next, we created a variable named diameter to hold the result of our diameter formula, which is 2 multiplied by the value of the radius. Finally, we returned the result to the screen using the getElementbyId method.

The other option we had on the page was to clear the value of the local storage variable. While we could have just used the `removeItem` method, using the clear method as well insured that there were no other local storage variables lurking around. A refresh of the page with Google Developer Tools open verified that the local storage area was empty.

There's more...

Currently by default `localStorage` stores all data as strings. We just practiced converting `localStorage` variables into integers, but they can also be converted into objects such as arrays.

Storing and retrieving arrays in localStorage

There will be many times when you will want to use arrays with `localStorage` to save progress in a game or retain user data or messages. You can use the JSON library by Douglas Crockford to streamline the storing and retrieving of arrays. Visit `https://github.com/douglascrockford/JSON-js` to download code and learn more about JSON.

Create a new HTML5 page, and add script tags between two footer tags. Declare a new variable array named "horsedef", and assign it the following key/value pairs as shown here:

```
var horsedef = {"species":"equine","legs":4,"ears":2,
    "purposes":{"front":"neigh","behind":"flick"}};
```

Now, set a new item named "describehorse" in local storage, while also using `JSON` to turn our array `horsedef` into a string as shown here:

```
window.localStorage.setItem('describehorse',
    JSON.stringify(horsedef));
```

Retrieve the values from local storage using JSON parse:

```
console.log( alert('A horse is a horse of course! ' + JSON.parse
    (localStorage.getItem('describehorse')) ); // => Object {
    species="equine", more...} </script>
```

Save the page, and open a browser window. You should see an alert box showing the key/value pairs in the `horsedef` array that were passed to `describehorse` as shown in the following screenshot:

The page at file://macintosh%20hd/ says:

A horse is a horse of course!
{"species":"equine","legs":4,"ears":2,"purposes":
{"front":"neigh","behind":"flick"}}

OK

Beware of cross-site callbacks when using JSON. It is usually best to download and use a file off your own server. Always download your copy of JSON directly from the source. Don't fall for imitations like JSONP.

Creating a Web SQL Database

In this recipe we will create a web SQL database and give it attributes that define its version, name, size, and description.

Getting ready

You will need to be using a current browser that supports web SQL databases.

How to do it...

Create a new HTML5 file, and place opening and closing script tags between two footer tags. Declare a variable named db, then assign openDatabase() to it. Give openDatabase the following arguments: 'mymotodb', '1.0', 'Motocross Rider List DB', 2 * 1024 * 1024, and then close the declaration. The code should look like the following snippet:

```
<script>var db = openDatabase('mymotodb', '1.0',
  'Motocross Rider List DB', 2 * 1024 * 1024);</script>
```

Save the file.

How it works...

All web SQL databases use the openDatabase method to assign values to a database. The first argument "mymotodb" was the name of the database. The next and required argument was the version number. The number here must match whenever the user attempts to use the web SQL database. Next, we defined the description of the database, then the estimated size. Once all the arguments are defined for the requested openDatabase method, the database is created and a first (and invisible) transaction takes place—the creation of the database itself.

There's more...

Browser implementation of specifications such as Web SQL databases has been very unpredictable and so has the support of such specifications themselves within the web development community.

Web SQL may be replaced by SQLite

The Web SQL database specification itself is no longer being maintained by the W3C, but it works reasonably well in most browsers. It is possible within the next year or so that enough major stakeholders will agree on how to implement a different client-side database solution such as SQLite, but such things can be difficult to predict. Keep an eye on the specification at `http://www.w3.org/TR/webdatabase/` for updates on current options for using client-side databases.

Using a Web SQL database

In this recipe, we will take the database we created in the previous recipe and add tables and data to it then display the results on an HTML page.

Getting ready

You will need a current browser and an HTML5 page with basic tags for the head area and body area.

How to do it...

On a basic HTML5 page, add an `h1` tag to display a page heading, and then create a `div` tag with an ID of `"status"` to hold our results as shown in the following code block:

```
<!DOCTYPE HTML><html><head><meta http-equiv="Content-Type"
content="text/html; charset=UTF-8"><title>Using WEB SQL
Databases</title></head><body><article><section><header><h1>Today's
Riders</h1></header><div id="status" name="status"></div>
</section></article><footer>
```

Begin the script as shown in the previous recipe to create the database if you have not already. Create a new variable named info, and then create a new transaction that contains a function that accepts an argument. Using the passed argument, create a table named RIDERS with a unique id and a row named `ridername`. The code should look similar to the following block:

```
var info;db.transaction(function (tx) {   tx.executeSql('CREATE TABLE
IF NOT EXISTS RIDERS (id unique, ridername)');
```

Add data into the table rows, with a number for the unique id and a text string for each name:

```
tx.executeSql('INSERT INTO RIDERS (id, ridername)
VALUES (1, "Joe Fly")');   tx.executeSql('INSERT INTO RIDERS (id,
ridername) VALUES (2, "Gira Ettolofal")');   });
```

Perform a query to pull data from the database:

```
db.transaction(function (tx) {   tx.executeSql('SELECT * FROM RIDERS',
    [], function (tx, results) {
```

Create a new variable and `for` loop to cycle through results and print them to the screen:

```
var len = results.rows.length, i;    for (i = 0; i < len; i++){
    info = "<p><b>" + results.rows.item(i).ridername + "</b></p>";
    document.querySelector('#status').innerHTML +=  info;    } },
    null);});
```

Close the script and the HTML page.

```
</script></footer></body></html>
```

How it works...

When we open the page we just created in a browser, we'll see the information we used the database to display. This is because the query and loop work together to look through the database and display the appropriate information.

Today's Riders

Joe Fly

Gira Ettolofal

There's more...

Security and database transactions in HTML5 can be poorly executed. Care should be taken to safeguard any pages that accept SQL queries in a production environment.

Save script code in a separate file

To keep things simple in this recipe, we did not stash the SQL query code and JavaScript in a separate file. This could be done by saving the code in a subfolder such as `../js/myCode.js`. Beware using web SQL, Indexed DB or any other type of browser-based query APIs for secure information.

Guard against SQL injection on production servers

Anytime there is an editable field, some bot is likely going to come along and try to perform a SQL Injection attack. Basic precautions can be taken by using "?" within transaction requests. The following code shows an example.

```
store.db.transaction(function(tx) {   tx.executeSql( "insert into
    bmxtricks " + "(time, latitude, longitude, trick) values
    (?,?,?,?);",    [bmxtricks.time, bmxtricks.latitude,
    bmxtricks.longitude, bmxtricks.trick], handler, store.onError );});
```

See also

Packt books on SQL, any Packt HTML5 books that also cover client-side databases.

Creating a cache manifest for offline storage

In this recipe we will create a cache manifest file to enable us to store an HTML5 page offline and still view the images and video displayed on the page.

Getting ready

You will need an HTML5 page, such as the one provided in the code files of this recipe, and access to upload files to a server, and then view them on a computer, smart phone, or other web-enabled device with a browser.

How to do it...

First, we will create the Cache Manifest file. This should be created in a simple text editor. It should contain all the files and supporting code a user will need to access while offline. The first thing listed is the current file type (CACHE MANIFEST). The version number of the manifest should also be included. Notice we add paths to all the files we want the users to have access to in the following block of code:

```
CACHE MANIFEST
# version 0.1

itsallgooed.html
css/Brian Kent Font License.txt
css/exact-css-from-tutorial.css
css/font-stylesheet.css
css/plasdrip-webfont.eot
css/plasdrip-webfont.svg
css/plasdrip-webfont.ttf
css/plasdrip-webfont.woff
css/plasdrpe-webfont.eot
css/plasdrpe-webfont.svg
css/plasdrpe-webfont.ttf
css/plasdrpe-webfont.woff
css/style.css
images/gooed-science-logo.jpg
images/promo-bg.jpg
images/gakposter.png
movie/GakHowTo.mp4
movie/GakHowTo.ogv
movie/GakHowTo.webm
```

Add a manifest attribute to the `index.html` page between the opening `DOCTYPE` tag and `head` tags as shown:

```
<!DOCTYPE html> <html lang="en" manifest="gooed.manifest"> <head>
```

Finally, create a `.htaccess` file to create the correct mime type:

```
AddType text/cache-manifest .manifest
```

The page should display similar to the following:

How it works...

Creating a cache manifest gives a browser a checklist to use when loading a page offline. While the idea behind storing a page offline is that it should not need to update frequently, using a version number allows the author to push updates to the user the next time they connect to the Internet.

Not all browsers or systems can properly interpret the manifest file type, so including an `.htaccess` file ensures that the cache manifest is recognized correctly.

You can exclude files that you feel are not crucial to lower the size of the offline page and reduce load time.

Displaying the current location using geolocation and geo.js

In this recipe, we will use the geolocation specification and `geo.js` to display the current location of an active user on a map, and show their current latitude and longitude.

Getting ready

Visit `http://code.google.com/p/geo-location-javascript/` to download the latest version of `geo.js`, or grab the link URL from the wiki (`http://code.google.com/p/geo-location-javascript/wiki/JavaScriptAPI`) to link to it directly online.

How to do it...

First, we will create HTML5 opening page tags: `<head></head>`.

Then, in the meta tag, we will set the name attribute to `"viewport"`, and define the following values for the content attribute: `width = device-width; initial-scale=1.0; maximum-scale=1.0; user-scalable=no;`

Now, declare a script tag with the src attribute of: `http://code.google.com/apis/gears/gears_init.js`

Then, call the `geo.js` script: `src="js/geo.js"`.

The code block should look like the following so far:

```
<html><head><meta name = "viewport" content = "width = device-width;
  initial-scale=1.0; maximum-scale=1.0; user-scalable=no;"> <script
  src="http://code.google.com/apis/gears/gears_init.js"
  type="text/javascript" charset="utf-8"></script><script
  src="js/geo.js" type="text/javascript" charset="utf-8"></script>
```

Add a script tag for the Google Maps API: `<script type="text/javascript" src="http://maps.google.com/maps/api/js?sensor=false"></script>`.

Now, we will create a function to initialize the map named `initialize_map()`, and then create an array named `myOptions` to store the map attributes. The attributes are based on the Google Maps API. They should look similar to the following code block:

```
<script>function initialize_map(){ var myOptions = { zoom: 4,
    mapTypeControl: true, mapTypeControlOptions: {style:
    google.maps.MapTypeControlStyle.DROPDOWN_MENU}, navigationControl:
    true, navigationControlOptions: {style:
    google.maps.NavigationControlStyle.SMALL},
    mapTypeId: google.maps.MapTypeId.ROADMAP }
```

Add a new map to the page named map using the method `google.maps.Map()`, which takes the `document.getElementById` element as an argument, which in turn is being passed the id `"map_canvas"`. The other method accepted by `google.maps.Map` is `myOptions`.

```
map = new google.maps.Map(document.getElementById("map_canvas"),
    myOptions); }
```

Create the `initialize()` function, and add an `if` statement to check if the `geo_position_js.init()` function is active. Enter a new status for the div with the id of `"current"` using `document.getElementById` and `innerHTML`. Type `"Receiving..."` for the status text.

```
function initialize(){ if(geo_position_js.init()){
    document.getElementById('current').innerHTML="Receiving...";
```

Add helper message text to display if we are not able to fetch the location or if for whatever reason the browser does not support fetching the current position, as shown in the following code block:

```
geo_position_js.getCurrentPosition(show_position,function(){document.
    getElementById('current').innerHTML="Couldn't get location"},
    {enableHighAccuracy:true}); }
    else{document.getElementById('current').innerHTML="Functionality
      not available"; }}
function show_position(p){
    document.getElementById('current').innerHTML=
    "latitude="+p.coords.latitude.toFixed(2)+"
    longitude="+p.coords.longitude.toFixed(2);
    var pos=new google.maps.LatLng(
    p.coords.latitude,p.coords.longitude);
    map.setCenter(pos); map.setZoom(14);
```

Create a new variable named `infowindow` to display the `google.maps InfoWindow`, a bubble that will display when a marker is clicked. Give it a text string of "yes" to display. Create a new marker tied to the current position of the user, along with title text for the marker that will display on mouse or pointer hover. Add an event listener to detect when the marker is clicked.

```
var infowindow = new google.maps.InfoWindow({ content:
    "<strong>yes</strong>"}); var marker = new google.maps.Marker({
    position: pos, map: map, title:"Here I am!"       });
    google.maps.event.addListener(marker, 'click', function() {
    infowindow.open(map,marker);});});}</script >
```

Style the page to control the font-family, padding, and the look of the title and current divs.

```
<style>body {font-family: Helvetica;font-size:11pt;
    padding:0px;margin:0px} #title {background-color:#0C3;padding:5px;}
    #current {font-size:10pt;padding:5px;}</style></head>
```

Create an `onLoad` command in the body tag that initializes both `initialize_map();` and the `initialize();` function on page load. Create a new `div` to display the page title and a second `div` with an id of "current" to display the current status of the location fetching process. Finally, create a `div` with an id of `map_canvas` to contain the map once it displays, and set the width and height of the `div` using an inline style. Close the tags and save the page.

```
<body onLoad="initialize_map();initialize()"><div id="title">Where am
    I now?</div> <div id="current">Initializing...</div>
    <div id="map_canvas" style="width:320px;
    height:350px"></div></body></html>
```

Open up the page in a browser window, and you should see a result similar to the following screenshot:

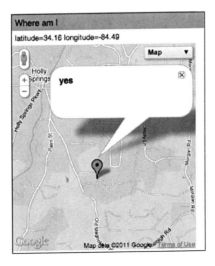

How it works...

Using `geo.js` simplifies using geolocation for multiple devices. It provides prepared error messages and follows the W3C implementation standards, as well as the ability to "fall back" to tools such as Google Gears. First, we had to create a script with variables to contain arrays of map display and processing options, instantiate a new map object, and draw a marker to pin the current location of the user onto the screen. Hovering over the pin displayed a bubble window with title text. This same text could contain a link to pull and show driving directions, reviews, or notes. When the page was loaded, the map options creation function `map_initialize()`, and the main action triggering function `initialize()` was called. A temporary status message was displayed while the current location of the user was determined with the help of `geo.js`, and the map was drawn.

Index

working 192

Mozilla Firefox
People of HTML5, video series 155
URL 8

MP3 219

multiple background images
about 79, 81
multiple empty divs, content search 82, 83
utilizing 80
working 81

Multiple backgrounds 92

multiple sidebars
displaying, <aside> tag used 22, 23

mydata variable 242

N

non-supported browsers
alternate content, displaying 109-11

numbers
converting to numbers, parseInt 250-252

number tag
browser support 135
JavaScript 135
using 134

O

object code 213

Ogg 217-219

onClick() event 173

onclick event handler 118

onload attribute 201

onload command
working 243

onLoad function 160

opacity 92

openDatabase method 254

Opera 10

outline algorithm
accessibility 29
applying 28
exception 29
working 29

P

parseInt
using, for local storage strings to number
conversion 250-252

picker
browser support 140
creating, to display date 138-140
creating, to display time 138-140

placeholder attribute 118, 119

placeholder text
displaying 116-119
onclick event handler 118
placeholder attribute 118, 119
placeholder attribute, using 118
placeholder text 119
value attribute 118

poster attribute 214

preload attribute 214

preventDefault() function 179

Priceline.com 42

progressive enhancement 10

promo page, HTML5
creating 29-32

pubdate attribute
about 46
browsers 48
specifying 46, 47
working 48

R

random audio animations
audio implementation, in HTML5 208
audio visualization, cutting edge browsers
used 208
canvas tag, using 202
working 206, 207

range tag
browser support 136
JavaScript 136
using 135, 136

Thank you for buying
HTML5 Multimedia Development Cookbook

About Packt Publishing

Packt, pronounced 'packed', published its first book "*Mastering phpMyAdmin for Effective MySQL Management*" in April 2004 and subsequently continued to specialize in publishing highly focused books on specific technologies and solutions.

Our books and publications share the experiences of your fellow IT professionals in adapting and customizing today's systems, applications, and frameworks. Our solution based books give you the knowledge and power to customize the software and technologies you're using to get the job done. Packt books are more specific and less general than the IT books you have seen in the past. Our unique business model allows us to bring you more focused information, giving you more of what you need to know, and less of what you don't.

Packt is a modern, yet unique publishing company, which focuses on producing quality, cutting-edge books for communities of developers, administrators, and newbies alike. For more information, please visit our website: www.packtpub.com.

Writing for Packt

We welcome all inquiries from people who are interested in authoring. Book proposals should be sent to author@packtpub.com. If your book idea is still at an early stage and you would like to discuss it first before writing a formal book proposal, contact us; one of our commissioning editors will get in touch with you.

We're not just looking for published authors; if you have strong technical skills but no writing experience, our experienced editors can help you develop a writing career, or simply get some additional reward for your expertise.

JSF 2.0 Cookbook

ISBN: 978-1-847199-52-2   Paperback: 396 pages

Over 100 simple but incredibly effective recipes for taking control of your JSF applications

1. Discover JSF 2.0 features through complete examples

2. Put in action important JSF frameworks, such as Apache MyFaces Core, Trinidad, Tomahawk, RichFaces Core, Sandbox and so on

3. Develop JSF projects under NetBeans/Glassfish v3 Prelude and Eclipse/JBoss AS

4. Part of Packt's Cookbook series: Each recipe is a carefully organized sequence of instructions to complete the task as efficiently as possible

Core Data iOS Essentials

ISBN: 978-1-849690-94-2   Paperback: 340 pages

A fast-paced, example-driven guide guide to data-drive iPhone, iPad, and iPod Touch applications

1. Covers the essential skills you need for working with Core Data in your applications

2. Particularly focused on developing fast, light weight data-driven iOS applications

3. Builds a complete example application. Every technique is shown in context

4. Completely practical with clear, step-by-step instructions.

Please check **www.PacktPub.com** for information on our titles

iPhone Applications Tune-Up

ISBN: 978-1-849690-34-8   Paperback: 321 pages

High performance tuning guide for real-world iOS projects

1. Tune up every aspect of your iOS application for greater levels of stability and performance

2. Improve the users' experience by boosting the performance of your app

3. Learn to use Xcode's powerful native features to increase productivity

4. Profile and measure every operation of your application for performance

Flex 3 with Java

ISBN: 978-1-847195-34-0   Paperback: 304 pages

Develop rich internet applications quickly and easily using Adobe Flex 3, ActionScript 3.0 and integrate with a Java backend using BlazeDS 3.2

1. A step-by-step tutorial for developing web applications using Flex 3, ActionScript 3.0, BlazeDS 3.2, and Java

2. Build efficient and seamless data-rich interactive applications in Flex using a combination of MXML and ActionScript 3.0

3. Create custom UIs, Components, Events, and Item Renders to develop user friendly application

Please check **www.PacktPub.com** for information on our titles

Lightning Source UK Ltd.
Milton Keynes UK
UKOW040920151211

183841UK00001B/67/P